FREE PEOPLE,
FREE MARKETS

FREE PEOPLE, FREE MARKETS

HOW THE WALL STREET JOURNAL OPINION PAGES SHAPED AMERICA

* * * *

George Melloan

ENCOUNTER BOOKS  NEW YORK ∗ LONDON

First American edition published in 2017 by Encounter Books, an activity of Encounter for Culture and Education, Inc., a nonprofit, tax exempt corporation. Encounter Books website address: www.encounterbooks.com

Manufactured in the United States and printed on acid-free paper. The paper used in this publication meets the minimum requirements of ANSI/NISO Z39.48—1992 (R 1997) (*Permanence of Paper*).

FIRST AMERICAN EDITION

LIBRARY OF CONGRESS CATALOGING-IN-PUBLICATION DATA

Names: Melloan, George, 1927– author.
Title: Free people, free markets: how the Wall Street Journal opinion pages shaped America / by George Melloan.
Description: New York : Encounter Books, 2017. | Includes bibliographical references and index.
Identifiers: LCCN 2016048072 (print) | LCCN 2017010311 (ebook)
ISBN 9781594039317 (hardback) | ISBN 9781594039324 (ebook)
Subjects: LCSH: Wall Street Journal. | Op-ed pages—United States—History. Press and politics—United States—History. | Dow Jones & Co.—History.
Classification: LCC PN4899.N42 W335 2017 (print) | LCC PN4899.N42 (ebook)
DDC 071/.471—dc23
LC record available at https://lccn.loc.gov/2016048072

TABLE OF CONTENTS

Preface .... *vii*

1   *Dow and the Coal Miners* 1

2   *Barron Foresees a Fragile Peace* 11

3   *Hamilton Hates Prohibition* 29

4   *Kilgore Dissects the New Deal* 37

5   *Pearl Harbor's 'Stark Reality'* 59

6   *Royster Counsels JFK* 77

7   *Forecasting a Vietnam Defeat* 103

8   *Joining the Fray* 115

9   *Kissinger Scolds Bartley* 123

10   *The Supply-Side Revolution* 139

11   *We Tangle with the Times* 163

12   *The Rise of the Naderites* 173

13   *Maggie and Deng* 187

14   *On the Road Again* 195

15   *Portents in Prague* 209

16   *'On to Baghdad,' We Urge* 217

17   *Celebrating a Collapse* 221

18   *Bob and 'Arkansas Mores'* 233

19   *'We've Won!'* 243

20   *The Horror of 9/11* 259

21   *Cancer Claims Bob* 273

22   *Two Wars, On Iraq and Drugs* 283

23   *Murdoch Keeps the Faith* 301

24   *Modern Times* 321

25   *The Trump Shock* 333

26   *Dow's Legacy* 345

PREFACE

Amidst the wreckage Google and its peers have made of traditional newspapering, one notable survivor stands out: The Wall Street Journal. The Journal has taken its lumps as mass-market advertising has shifted heavily toward electronic media that can deliver text, sound and video to many millions of viewers at a fraction of the cost of the capital and labor-intensive process of inking miles of newsprint on expensive printing presses and delivering the finished product, a newspaper, to the subscriber's door. Printed media have thus been starved of their traditional source of revenue, the advertisers who bought space on printed pages to present their wares.

But the Journal is still robust, thanks in part to the foresight of its management decades ago in making an early entrance of its own into electronic journalism. The online Journal today is comparable in readership to the newsprint edition. At a time when most newspapers are losing readers, Journal circulation continues to rise.

The Journal also benefits from something less tangible, the force of its distinctive personality. Personality might seem like a strange word to apply to an inanimate object. But newspapers down through the years have all possessed traits of personality, attracting sufficient loyalty among readers to be welcomed into homes in much the same manner as a helpful friend with ideas and information to impart. It's not unusual to hear someone refer to a newspaper or magazine as his "Bible."

Not surprisingly, the part of a newspaper that elevates it to the level of a friend, or perhaps an enemy, is the opinion section. All great newspapers make opinions available to their readers. If they offered only straight news, they would be at a competitive disadvantage to faster ways to deliver information, like radio and TV, not to mention smartphones. As the late Journal editor Robert L. Bartley once wrote, editorial pages deliver the news of ideas, whereas other departments of newspapers deliver the news of events. Without an opinion section, newspapers would be far blander, and in today's highly competitive, high-tech media, would have little to offer the reader in terms of added value.

The Wall Street Journal is America's most widely circulated newspaper. As of the last quarter of 2016, global sales, six days a week, of its print and digital editions averaged nearly 2.4 million copies. Of that number, the Asian edition accounted for 101,000 and the European edition 111,000. The Journal's 2,000 journalists operate from 85 news bureaus in 51 countries throughout the world. Printed Journals flow from 26 plants strategically located in the United States and other countries to ensure timely delivery to subscribers. Reporters are equipped with the latest communications technology to beam their reports and images to editors, who then edit the copy and make up the separate editions electronically. WSJ.com processes the copy, and some unique offerings, for online readers.

* * * *

Journal editorial pages have become one of the world's most important centers for discussion and debate of public policy issues, particularly policies that have a bearing on the economic health of important nation-states, America foremost among them. Monetary, fiscal, regulatory, income transfer and national security issues are debated daily. Critiques of the decisions of public officials and legislators uphold the responsibility that was thrust on the fourth estate by America's founders when they enshrined press freedom in the First Amendment of the Constitution. Increasingly, policy makers themselves, not least the president, ask for space in the Journal's letters or opinion columns to explain themselves or promote ideas. Journal readers, a large cohort of whom are themselves policy makers, get a lot of thoughtful argumentation and analysis for their money.

At the center of the Journal's forum for debate is the Review & Outlook column, written by members of the Journal's editorial board and edited by Paul Gigot, editor of the opinion pages. Paul and his fellow writers carry on a tradition dating back almost to the founding of The Wall Street Journal in 1889. Charles Dow, the cofounder of the Journal, created Review & Outlook primarily to present his views on stock market developments. But late in his career, he broadened his field of interest. Thomas Woodlock, one of the early editors, once wrote that the first of what could be reasonably called an "editorial" was written by Dow in 1902, just months before he died, a defense of the right of labor unions to bargain freely with employers for contracts setting levels of compensation and terms of employment. He stipulated, however, that if unions entered into contracts, they must abide by them because contracts are sacrosanct.

Thus began the Journal's daily commentary on the often dramatic news events of a century unlike any that had gone before in the rapidity of technological advancement, sharp gains in living standards for the masses, and human destruction by war on a scale never before seen or imagined. Amazingly, the liberal (in the 19th-century sense) attitudes of the founding intellectual, Charles Dow, have continued to guide that commentary up to the present day. These views were summed up by a latter-day Journal editor in four words, "free people, free markets." Amazingly also, those words are today controversial, assailed by a sizable crowd of intellectuals and politicians who, despite American accomplishments, doubt the efficacy of market capitalism. This book is a history detailing the turmoil that free-market capitalism and its Journal editorial page defenders have survived down through the ages.

CHAPTER 1

Dow and the Coal Miners

The year 1889 was a time of vigor and excitement in the American economy. Risk-takers with capital were building railroad lines, long and short, creating an intricate network of rails, siding and switches that was opening up more and more of the continent to travel and shipping. Canning factories were springing up alongside the railroads, giving farmers and food processors greater access to the national market for cash crops like grains, fruit and vegetables and thereby offering households an expanding selection of affordable groceries. The steel and coal industries were thriving because railroads needed steel, and train engines needed coal and also because railroad development meant that producers could ship steel, coal and other commodities to a broadening range of buyers in the towns and cities that had sprung up throughout the great North American continent. Even Alaska was not out of reach to adventurers attracted to that vast and remote region by the discovery of gold in the Klondike.

New York's Wall Street reflected the excitement because that was the principal trading center for the shares in new joint-stock companies that were being formed to build railroads and factories. It was in that year that The Wall Street Journal was born in a barren basement room down some steps to the rear of a soda fountain at 15 Broad Street, just a few yards from where Broad intersected Wall and where the New York Stock Exchange now stands. The printed newspaper was born when Charles Dow, Edward Jones and Charles Bergstresser, who had been circulating handwritten financial and business news bulletins to traders and investors, acquired a small hand-operated printing press.

Thomas Woodlock, an Irish immigrant who joined the firm not long after its inception, later provided a colorful description of the three partners. The Woodlock sketches, recorded in a 1982 Journal history written by Lloyd Wendt, described Dow, the prime mover, as a tall, slightly stooped, black-bearded, dark-eyed Connecticut Yankee with a "grave air and the measured speech of a college professor." His resume included reporting stints on the Springfield (Massachusetts) Republican and the Providence (Rhode Island) Journal. He had sought, but failed to find, a mining fortune in Leadville, Colorado, but had learned a lot about mining stocks in the process. He had then come to New York and a job with Wall Street's Kiernan News Agency.

Not long afterward, in November 1882, he teamed up with two other Kiernan employees, Jones and Bergstresser, to start their own news agency, Dow Jones & Co. Bergstresser supplied much of the capital but somehow never attached his name to the partnership. It was he who would later supply the name for their newspaper.

The redheaded Jones was born in Worcester, Massachusetts, and first met Dow when they worked on the Providence Journal. He was, according to a later description by Woodlock, "tall and ruddy, swift in his motions, as high-strung as a race horse, tempestuous in manner and speech, with a mind quick as lightning and a nose for news."

Bergstresser was a short and stocky "Pennsylvania Dutchman" with a black beard who wore thick glasses that enlarged his eyes and gave him a pugnacious look. Woodlock wrote that "he had a fine memory, a capacity for penetrating recesses where no other reporter could gain access." He also took shorthand and, according to Woodlock, was never accused of misquoting anyone.

News agencies in those days created bulletins on flimsy sheets of paper interleaved with carbon paper, writing the news with a stylus on the top sheet and making as many as 24 copies at a time. Boy runners would distribute the flimsies to clients. The Dow Jones runners must have resembled Fagin's boys in "Oliver Twist" as they dodged among the carriages and beer wagons and jostled men in top hats, except that they were engaged in an honest business, not picking pockets. The partnership thrived, and after seven years the three bought their old-fashioned printing press and started a more practical way of serving their growing list of clients, a printed newspaper, although meanwhile keeping their news bulletin service up and running.

Today, what was then a little four-page newspaper has become the largest-circulation newspaper in America, delivered both on newsprint and the World Wide Web to readers not only in the United States but throughout the planet. It is said to be one of the nation's most influential publications, not only because it still digs hard for news, in the manner of Dow, Jones and Bergstresser, but because its editorial pages provide a daily diet of vigorous commentary.

Jones specialized in collecting news while sharing in the conviviality of stock traders, bankers and hangers-on in the barroom of the Windsor Hotel at Fifth Avenue and 46th Street, a place sometimes referred to as the "all-night Wall Street." He also kept the dozen or so boy runners in line with a strict disciplinary code and the force of his personality. Bergstresser did his digging in the daytime, successfully mining the money houses on Wall and Broad streets for news.

An account of late 19th-century Wall Street reporting was given much later by Oliver Gingold, an Englishman who joined Dow Jones in 1900 and played a key role in stock market coverage for a further 60-plus years. Journal reporter Cynthia Crossen quoted him in an article about the Journal's history on the occasion of the sale of Dow Jones & Co. to Rupert Murdoch's News Corp. in 2007.

Said Gingold: "In those days, a financial journalist was a combination private detective, stenographer and gossip columnist. Gathering news was a bare-knuckle business. Many companies refused to issue annual reports even to their own stockholders. Reporters spent long hours waiting outside directors' rooms or corporate offices for a chance at buttonholing an insider. Messengers shadowing the reporters ran the news back to the office where scribes made carbon copies—as many as 24 at a time—that were hand delivered to subscribers.

"What soon distinguished Dow Jones from its competitors was its revolutionary approach to financial journalism: Instead of collaborating with companies and investors to manipulate the financial markets—and taking a piece of the action—they would try to impartially distinguish fact from rumor. From the beginning, they forbade their employees from investing in companies they were covering (a rule sometimes observed in the breach). An early Wall Street Journal motto was succinct but audacious: 'The truth in its proper use.'"

All three of the founders were talented, but it was Dow, quiet and studious, who was the philosophical and ethical pillar of the operation. He insisted that his team remain aloof from the constant offers of bribes from brokers and investors to reporters willing to promote their stocks. He kept a check on Eddie Jones, whose evenings at the Windsor sometimes brought him into contact with ambitious speculators.

And thus it was he who was most responsible for earning Dow Jones a reputation for probity, which served them well in a place and era where well-founded, honest reporting was of great value to subscribers who were in the business of betting large sums on the stock of this or that railroad or bank. Aside from the moral and ethical dimensions, Dow, a student of markets, would demonstrate that integrity had market value, a lesson that would not be lost on future editors of the Journal.

It was also Dow who ultimately began to offer opinions on subjects broader than the trading of stocks and bonds, venturing into questions of corporate management or public policy. It was he who early on started the Review & Outlook column, which still carries the institutional opinions, or editorials, of the Wall Street Journal.

Those editorials today, more than a century later, still in some sense reflect the personality of Charles Dow. For example, the Journal editorial writers sail under the pennant, "Free People, Free Markets," which is very much in keeping with what we know of the philosophy of Charles Dow. They defend the sanctity of contracts, holding that, when legally and voluntarily made between private individuals, they should be upheld not only by the parties but by the law. Dow argued that markets could not exist without mutual trust, and that was true of the rambunctious Wall Street of the Gay Nineties just as it is today.

Yet another parallel with today was the founders' belief in sound money. They argued strongly against the Sherman Silver Purchase Act of July 14, 1890, which required the U.S. Treasury to buy 4,500,000 ounces of silver a month. Since the Treasury issued newly printed paper dollars for the silver, this was simply a way of engaging in the politically tempting practice of inflating the currency, something the Journal has been wary of throughout its history because it has been a tempting way for politicians to repay public debts with cheaper dollars while at the same time falsely blaming the rising cost of living and erosion of public savings on producers and merchants.

The act was popular with silver miners, of course, but also the powerful farm lobby, because it enabled farmers to more easily pay off their land purchase debts. A downside, in addition to higher living costs, was its effects on the working of the then-existent gold standard, which had provided sufficient monetary soundness to facilitate rapid U.S. and European economic growth in years previous. Foreigners grew suspicious of the dollar and began to demand physical gold, which resulted in a gold outflow, sending U.S. supplies of physical gold down to a dangerous level.

The Journal at that time was just an upstart, but it had influence with Wall Street and New York banks. It helped win repeal of the silver act in January 1893. Journal opinion editors today would be overjoyed if they could achieve a monetary victory of that importance. Despite sharp criticism from the Journal, the modern Federal Reserve Board has persisted in its dubious faith in the economic efficacy of its artificial suppression of interest rates, thus encouraging excessive borrowing, particularly by the government, and costing savers and pension funds many billions of dollars in lost earnings.

When Dow expanded his oeuvre from market commentary to a broader range of editorial topics as the turn of the 19th century approached, one of the subjects that engaged him was the rising militancy and influence of organized labor. By one count, there were 37,000 strikes between 1881 and 1905, some of them violent. One of the most dramatic was the 1894 Pullman Strike, an attempt to shut down the railroads led by Socialist Eugene V. Debs. President Grover Cleveland was only able to end the strike by calling out the army to enforce a court order.

One of Dow's most interesting editorials addressed the issues raised by the strike of anthracite miners in eastern Pennsylvania in May 1902. John Mitchell, leader of the United Mine Workers of America, had taken some 100,000 miners off the job to back his demands for union recognition, a shorter working day and more pay. The 163-day strike was a major issue because it threatened to reduce the winter fuel supply for a nation then wedded to coal for most of its energy, including home heating. As compared to "soft" or bituminous coal, anthracite "hard" coal has a high carbon content. It was a vital ingredient for high-quality carbon steel production. Many railroad locomotives of the era were designed to use it because it was relatively smokeless, and its high heat and slow burning gave trains a longer range before refueling.

In addition to the economic threat, there was a sociological element as well. Many of the miners were recent immigrants from middle Europe trying to gain an economic foothold in a new land. Some of these Poles, Hungarians and the like spoke very little English and were vulnerable to exploitation by the mining companies in the absence of union representation.

Since the steel, railroad and mining stocks were affected, a Wall Street editor might have been expected to take the side of management. But, partly because of industry leaders' arrogance in the face of union demands, Dow took an evenhanded approach instead. He defended collective bargaining, writing that "a combination of labor is just as legal, just and moral as a combination of capital."

However, he was opposed to "union shops" agreements that required union membership as a condition of employment, regarding them as infringements on the rights of workers. He also wrote eloquently cautioning labor unions that once they had signed a contract with management, they should adhere to it. Contracts freely arrived at were a moral obligation for both parties.

In his usual analytical style, Dow argued that the ability to enter into a contract was a mark of freedom. A slave couldn't make a contract because he was not free to uphold its terms, being subject to the wishes of his master. Only a free man could enter into a contract; hence, private contracts were artifacts of freedom and thus sacrosanct, he wrote.

The strike was ultimately settled by the hyperactive Theodore Roosevelt by means of a federally backed Anthracite Coal Strike Commission. The miners got a 10% pay raise and a one-hour reduction, to eight hours, in the working day. It was said to be the first presidential intervention in a major strike, setting a precedent that, in some future cases where political partisanship was involved, would not win favor from Journal editorialists.

The Dow commentary shows that the youthful Wall Street newspaper was already broadening its participation in the national debate beyond the realm of stocks and markets. But it was with regard to markets that Dow would make a lasting name for himself. In those early days, he originated a means for taking the minute-to-minute temperature of the stocks listed on the New York Stock Exchange by inventing the Dow Jones averages. The first average, compiled in 1884 when Dow Jones was still only a news service, consisted of nine railroad and two industrial stocks, chosen because they were actively traded. Dow simply divided the closing prices of his chosen stocks each day by 11 to get an average.

Out of that primitive beginning, which Dow himself improved by adding more stocks, would grow the carefully managed market samples that comprise the averages of today. It's interesting how closely the Dow readings have paralleled those of newer and broader samples, such as the S&P 500, suggesting that Dow's original design, as modified to reflect stock splits and the emergence of important new industries, was fundamentally sound.

Since Dow was primarily a market analyst, there is not a sufficient record from those early days to offer an account of what he thought about a broad range of issues. He was no doubt less skeptical of federal regulation than the editors of today. A hint of that comes from the writing of Woodlock, who became editor of the Wall Street Journal on Dow's death in 1902 (Jones had already departed to join a stock brokerage, and Bergstresser had become less active) and whose 50th-anniversary recollections provide some of the best records of those early days.

Woodlock suggests that Dow looked with favor on the Interstate Commerce Act of 1887, which was enacted under pressure of shippers to bring the rates and service terms of the railroads under federal regulatory control. If true, that would have been counter to free-market principles. A free marketer would have answered the complaints of the shippers that, even though they were captive to the railroads that served them, the combinations of shippers and railroads serving separate regions were in competition with each other in urban markets where the lines terminated and thus had an interest in keeping the costs of the shipped products competitive. Moreover, the railroads, built at great expense, had to charge rates sufficient to amortize their debts and meet operating costs. Dow would have known all this.

Woodlock's later recollection may have been colored by his own attitude toward regulation. After leaving the Journal in 1905, he became a Wall Street railroad analyst. In 1926, Calvin Coolidge appointed him a commissioner of the Interstate Commerce Commission (ICC). He spent four years as a regulator before returning to the Journal as a columnist.

But even if it is correct that Dow favored the ICC, it should be remembered that federal regulation of commerce and industry was far more limited in the 1880s than today. The federal government was small and in good favor with much of the industrialized North, because Abraham Lincoln had recently won a war to preserve the union. There can be little doubt that the tycoons of the 19th century invited political interventions with their sometimes high-handed business practices.

The arguments for federal regulation were based on far different circumstances at the turn of the century than now. Western grain shippers in particular argued that the railroads were in a position to take unfair advantage because shippers had no alternative way to get their products to market. Motor vehicles and trunk roads were still in the future, so there were no trucks to compete with the railroads. The farmers wanted lower shipping costs, and it seems that in the case of the ICC, farmers had more muscle in Congress than the railroads.

Dow's own writings, including his stand on free collective bargaining and his interest in measuring market trends, support the conclusion that he was very much in the "free people, free markets" camp. Even today's editors don't oppose all forms of market regulation, for example, Securities and Exchange Commission rules that require corporations to promptly inform the public of any decisions that materially affect the value of their securities. Dow Jones built a business, the Dow Jones Newswires, on providing corporations with a medium for doing just that, and every reporter and editor quickly learned the importance of getting information that might move the market onto the wire as quickly as possible.

A skeptic might say that it's far-fetched to suggest that the founders of Dow Jones in their cellar print shop set the tone and standards of the modern Journal, with its printing presses and electronic network serving just about every populated area of the world. But it is not so implausible, really. Customs and mores are handed down from generation to generation, and if that is true in a social sense, why can't it be true of a long-lived business organization, particularly one that puts its institutional opinions on public view every day? Americans still hark back to the writings of Founding Fathers like James Madison and Thomas Jefferson for political guidance, and the

Constitution those founders so carefully designed still is the basis for decisions by America's highest court.

Editorial writing bears a certain resemblance to jurisprudence. A well-run editorial page adheres to precedents, fundamental principles established by core editorials of the past. Journal editors have by and large adhered to the principle that when an editor decides to depart from a precedent, he must let his readers know that he is doing so and explain why. An editorial page that merely reflects the daily changing whims of the editor is not likely to acquire the confidence and loyalty of readers.

Charles Dow could see the importance of establishing a reputation for integrity. When that reputation for integrity was put to the test 60 years later in a tussle with General Motors, its largest advertiser, the Journal scored high, and that may have been the event that set it on the growth path that has allowed it to reach its present level of size and influence. More about that later.

CHAPTER 2

Barron Foresees a Fragile Peace

D ow died in late 1902, but before his death he had arranged to sell Dow Jones & Co. to his longtime friend and associate, Clarence Walker Barron. Barron, who lived in Boston, had developed a news agency similar to Dow Jones called the Boston News Bureau at roughly the same time Dow Jones was building clientele in New York. Early on, when both were using flimsies and runners, he and Dow struck a deal wherein they would share news from their two financial centers, giving both a greater scope of coverage. So it was natural then when Dow was in bad health and looking for a buyer, he would turn to Barron.

Barron handled the deal, but it was actually his wife, Jessie Waldron Barron, who came up with most of the cash in support of Barron's promissory notes, and she became the sole proprietor of Dow Jones. She first relied on Tom Woodlock to edit the Journal, but in 1905 Woodlock had a quarrel with the remaining founder, Bergstresser, and offered his resignation. Jessie Barron accepted it.

She turned to his second-in-command, British-born William Peter Hamilton, a skillful writer and editorialist, to lead the Journal. He would continue to write editorials until 1929. Dow had put the Review & Outlook column on the front page, a placement he thought appropriate for what he regarded as the voice of the newspaper. Hamilton, a former war correspondent for British newspapers who had covered the 1893–94 Matabele uprising against the British South Africa Company in what is now Zimbabwe, had a forthright style equal to that of Woodlock. He once famously said: "You can't write a 50-50 editorial. Don't believe the man who tells you there are two sides to every question. There is only one side, the truth."

That, of course, assumed that the editorial writer would actually know and be able to utter the truth, which is always a bit problematical. But Hamilton was counseling editorial writers not to shrink from expressing what they believed to be the truth out of fear of criticism, disfavor or punishment. The principle he expressed—be bold, take a position and don't equivocate—would become a hallmark of Journal editorials for many years thereafter and is still observed today.

Editor Hamilton on May 11, 1911, had some doubts about the "muckrakers," writers who were gaining public notice with their attacks on the industrial tycoons who had built large national business organizations, at that time called "trusts." Ida Tarbell and Lincoln Steffens, who both wrote for McClure's Magazine, were among the most prominent, Tarbell for her assaults on Standard Oil's John D. Rockefeller. She had a special grudge against Rockefeller because he had put her father, an oil tank manufacturer, out of business.

The Journal itself was already known for its investigative journalism, but Hamilton thought the muckrakers went too far. He wrote that one consequence, surely unforeseen by the proprietors of the magazines that carried their articles, was that they conveyed the impression that great wealth could only be acquired by dishonesty, which he argued was patently untrue. He added that "there is no place which has less use for a liar and a cheat than Wall Street," observing that market transactions require a high degree of trust. He added: "We prefer not to extend the comparison to politics. The returns from Ohio are not all in."

A few days later, he argued that most laymen have "no objection to the accumulation of large individual wealth if the public is better served thereby." But he added that "our natural distrust of corporations is doubtless well founded. The Standard Oil Company is sentenced to be hanged for crimes almost outside the statute of limitations. Probably nothing would have happened to it if it could have confined the record to the past ten years and lived down the admitted atrocities of the previous thirty." The 10 years of good behavior he was referring to was a period when Standard Oil had served the public interest rather well by using its economies of scale to push the price of kerosene, a fuel almost everyone used at that time, by something like 70%. It was broken up anyway into separate companies by Teddy Roosevelt under terms of the Sherman Anti-Trust Act.

Hamilton had a gift for cutting satire. A brief item appended to a May 22, 1912, editorial noted, "[A] new farmers organization of 150,000 farmers [has been formed] to 'influence' legislation—and any other combination with the same end would be denounced by every farmer in the land." Hamilton's sarcasm was prophetic. The farm lobby in the early 20th century, when over half the U.S. population was agrarian, had a powerful influence on federal legislation. The farm lobby's success in getting subsidies and protections from Congress would cause the country—and farmers themselves in the end—a lot of grief over the next two decades. Federal "aid" to farmers led to overproduction and low commodity prices, and ultimately, to the Hawley-Smoot tariffs that virtually shut down global trade and prolonged the Great Depression.

In March 1912, the Journal quoted an article by former president Theodore Roosevelt, making his unsuccessful bid for a return to the White House, in which he explained his views on "trust-busting," which had won him lasting fame when he was president from 1901 to 1909. He argued that "the people have a right to govern themselves, that they have a right to rule and that we must obtain social and industrial justice through genuine popular government."

But he cautioned "that our aim must be to control business not to strangle it...What our people want is that the evils of big business be eradicated and the advantages, the benefits preserved." Teddy himself was not enamored of the muckrakers, at one point charging that they were simply antibusiness, not instruments for reform.

Hamilton and his predecessor Thomas Woodlock were less circumspect about political partisanship than Dow had been. Woodlock was caught up in the excitement generated by the charismatic Republican Teddy Roosevelt in the presidential election of 1904. So were a lot of other people. Roosevelt, who as vice president had succeeded to the presidency on the assassination of President William McKinley in Buffalo on September 14, 1901, defeated Democrat Alton B. Parker in a landslide with 56% of the popular vote.

Although Teddy had been founder of the Progressive movement, which was antagonistic toward big corporations, he was not antibusiness. He simply felt that government should hold the trump cards, so he used the new antitrust laws to assert government power over the private sector. He railed against "malefactors of great wealth."

Whatever Teddy was, he was certainly not content to let competition take its natural course, as it often does, toward survival of the fittest, even if bigness brought greater efficiency. He clearly thought that breaking up the big companies would intensify market competition. In that sense, he wasn't a free marketer. But Woodlock, and later Hamilton, was nonetheless taken with the flamboyant president as were a good many voters.

Hamilton would not be the sole voice of The Wall Street Journal for long. In 1912, when the Journal's finances were getting shaky, Clarence Barron took over management from his wife. Reportedly, the big man with a beard and brush mustache stormed into the newsroom at 44 Broad Street banging his cane on desks and loudly proclaiming that he was now the boss and would tolerate no slacking. For all that fierceness, he was never known to fire anyone, a forbearance unusual for newspaper proprietors of almost any era.

Barron was a large presence in more ways than one. In 1942, Ella Fitzgerald popularized a song about "Mr. Five by Five," who "don't measure no more from head to toe than he do from side to side." That was Barron, who was not five feet wide, but fit the model at five feet, five inches tall with a large girth, weighing somewhere around 300 pounds. It's said he married Jessie Waldron, a widow with two daughters, in part because of his fondness for her cooking when he was rooming at her upscale boarding house on Boston's Beacon Hill.

Although Barron was acquainted with Teddy, the Journal proprietor was more attuned to his own look-alike, the more moderate and steady William Howard Taft, Teddy's handpicked successor in 2008 when Roosevelt chose not to run.

Hamilton and particularly Barron may have started to have second thoughts about Teddy during the banking panic of 1907, in which Barron played an exhausting role in helping J.P. Morgan organize his famous rescue of the banks that were under threat.

A letter from Barron to a friend, quoted in the Lloyd Wendt book, describes his own role in organizing aid from sound banks for those banks that were experiencing heavy withdrawals by depositors. He conducted a marathon of phone calls from his suite at the Waldorf-Astoria hotel. His letter said: "As trouble approached I told President Theodore Roosevelt that it would take $500 million to stop the panic. Later [after the system was stabilized], I footed up the total relief from Washington, London and the New York banks and it was just $520 million.

"Nobody will ever know how hard I worked through many channels to keep the Wall Street fire from spreading. When it was over I went home [to Beacon Street in Boston] and slept for a very long time, and it took nearly a year to recover my nervous energy."

Barron had not only suffered what amounted to a nervous breakdown from the panic but had also lost a lot of money, so much so that for a while he had trouble servicing the notes he had signed to buy Dow Jones. But he recovered and would take over full management of the company and its editorial policies five years later.

Although trustbuster Teddy Roosevelt's antitrust assaults on corporations were never directly connected to the 1907 panic, business confidence certainly was not high during the latter part of his 1905–09 term of office. The October-November panic came on the heels of a stock market slump aggravated by the toll on business inflicted by the horrendous April 1906 San Francisco earthquake. Further anxiety was created by the feared impact on railroad stocks of government's new powers under the Hepburn Act to, through the ICC, set maximum rail shipping rates.

Teddy's early assault on the nation's leading banker, J.P. Morgan, with the 1902 breakup of his Northern Trust railroad holding company was still a fresh memory. It surely must have occurred to Barron that Wall Street was in an uneasy mood before the bank runs began and that maybe Teddy deserved some of the blame.

It can't be certain what the 1907 panic did to Teddy's reputation because he didn't run for reelection in 1908. He had promised not to run for what amounted to a third term and proposed William Howard Taft as his successor. Once elected, Taft continued Teddy's antitrust campaign but on the whole was a steadier hand at the tiller than the famous Rough Rider of Spanish-American War fame. So, in 1912, the party chose to renominate him in preference to Teddy, who had again sought the nomination. Teddy, petulant over the rejection, formed his own Progressive "Bull Moose" party and split the Republican vote in the general election, opening the door for a Democrat, Woodrow Wilson, to become president.

Hamilton was not happy with the Wilson victory, and probably also not with the role his onetime hero Teddy had played in bringing it about. But he made the best of it, writing that Wilson actually was a conservative and that business leaders would welcome his presidency. He may have been right. Wilson, the former president of Princeton University, may have been more of an economic policy conservative than Teddy, who had lost much of his luster in the 1912 defeat and had gone into something of a funk, attempting to regain his self-esteem by launching an expedition to an unexplored region of Brazil's Amazon that almost cost him his life.

Barron, having recovered from his illness, formed a relationship with Wilson as he had with Taft and Teddy and offered him advice when asked. When the United States entered the war in 1917, Barron and the Journal supported Wilson's efforts to mobilize the nation, although he was never as jingoistic as some of the editors of the era, such as the famously truculent Henry Watterson of the Louisville Courier Journal, who ended an editorial on September 3, 1914, marking the outbreak of World War I with the words, "to hell with the Hohenzollerns and the Hapsburgs!" referring to the royal families of Germany and Austria.

The banking panic of 1907 had turned the attention of bankers and the Wall Street Journal to the issue of financial reform. The Journal supported efforts by Morgan and his fellow leading bankers to create the Federal Reserve System, and when Woodrow Wilson signed the Federal Reserve Act on December 23, 1913, Barron gave it a lot of attention in his writings for the Journal. He opened an informative series of articles by writing that "Next to the Declaration of Independence and the Constitution of the United States, the Federal Reserve Act…may be the most important measure ever put before the people of this country. Upon its wise administration depends the good or ill of 100 million and as a nation we shall probably live under it, not only for the 20 years named in the act, but for many generations."

How right he was about that. The act seemed like a good idea, but Barron has certainly been proved correct in qualifying his support by saying its usefulness depended on "wise administration." Congress and the president had insisted, over intense objections by the banks, that the new Federal Reserve Board be under the effective control of presidential appointees, including, of course, the powerful chairman. That control was further strengthened by the New Deal in the Banking Act of 1933.

Barron had hoped that the powers given the 12 Regional Reserve bank presidents, who would be elected by member banks of the region, would actually strengthen states' rights and decentralize financial regulation. But, after the 1933 changes, the regional banks would always be outvoted by the seven presidential-appointed governors on the monetary policy decisions made by the Federal Open Market

Committee (FOMC), as the regional presidents were allotted only five voting members of the committee at any one time.

Even though the Fed was widely billed as an "independent" body and even is to this day, it was at the outset, and still is, subject to strong political pressures. So Barron was justified in conditioning his approval on whether the act would be administered wisely, and he also has been right so far in forecasting that the Fed's decisions would have a powerful influence over the lives of Americans in perpetuity. Proof of what tragedies could occur when the board was deficient in wisdom would arrive 17 years later when the Fed proved ineffective in dealing with the dollar deflation that was an important factor in causing and prolonging the Great Depression.

In his series of columns, Barron set about explaining to Journal readers why the creation of 12 reserve banks and the creation of a national currency (Federal Reserve notes) to supplant bank notes issued by individual banks would improve the workings of the financial system. He was certainly right in predicting that it would bring about cheaper credit, although in our modern age, that has proved to be a dubious blessing. After the 2008 financial crisis, the modern Fed pushed short-term interest rates down to near zero, thus denying savers a decent return on their money and igniting a federal borrowing binge that doubled the national debt in the space of only seven years.

Barron himself had lost his confidence in the Federal Reserve by December 1920. In one of his "Wall Street Sermons" on the front page of the Journal, he wrote, "The Federal Reserve System has to date been a promoter of inflation and of deflation and both have been and are the economic crimes of the war and the peace."

Barron's weight and period of illness didn't slow him down. After his recovery, he was again a human dynamo, not only running the Dow Jones business but also writing extensively for his Boston and New York news services and the Journal. As his views on markets and other issues became better known, he was often quoted by other journalists, and his growing reputation for worldly wisdom expanded the popularity and circulation of the Journal.

His pronouncements were backed by prodigious reporting. His influence on Wall Street gained him wide access to high-level sources, including heads of state. He was on good terms with President William Howard Taft, another 300-pounder to whom he bore some resemblance. Calvin Coolidge was a friend for whom he had a special affection and respect.

Barron traveled frequently to Europe in regal style with steamship cabins for his entourage of family, a nurse and two secretaries. He needed two secretaries because two shifts were needed to handle his constant flow of dictation, as he sent back dispatches to the Journal and his news services on what he learned. He interviewed Nicholas II in Saint Petersburg when the czar was considered to be a powerful leader, only a few years before he was brought down by military defeat in World War I and then assassinated, along with his family, by the Bolsheviks. He had a certain empathy for Kaiser Wilhelm II in those prewar years, but after the bloody World War I conflict began in 1914, he would increasingly regard him, and the German people he governed, as the scourge of Europe.

Barron was one of the first reporters to warn of the dangers of that terrible war as he surveyed the ferment in the Balkan states, predicting that the alliance between Russia and Serbia would ultimately clash with the Austro-Hungarian empire and its ally, Germany. It was, of course, the assassination of Austrian archduke Franz Ferdinand and his wife, Sophie, by a 19-year-old Bosnian nationalist named Gavrilo Princip in Sarajevo on June 28, 1914, that triggered the great war. Austria-Hungary declared war against Serbia, and that brought in Russia and Germany and later France, Britain, smaller European nations and, ultimately, the United States.

The perceptive Barron also foresaw that this would be a different kind of war in that it would be fought with modern machines like tanks, airplanes, and warships and cannons hurling high explosives long distances. It would thus be far more destructive of human lives, including civilians, than wars of the past. He was certainly right about that. It would claim the lives of 9 million combatants and 7 million civilians during its four-year duration.

But Barron's crystal ball also was a bit clouded after the war broke out in late July 1914. With the war a month old, a Journal editorial on August 28 titled "The War to Date" allowed as how "Russia is the only country with something to gain and nothing to lose. Whatever happens, with even the most sweeping victory and the largest war indemnity, Germany is now so bankrupt that it will take her years to recover."

The editorial allowed as how Great Britain and Russia "can feed themselves, while Germany and Austria will starve, at least as long as Britannia rules the waves. This is, in a way, the one ray of daylight in horrible business provoked by what a well-loved German calls the 'Big Brass Hat.' All the allies need to do now is to stand fast, with a sound defense, which includes a vigorous counter attack...What seems to be needed, so far as the leader of the Triple Alliance is concerned, is an international court to issue a writ de lunatico inquirendo."

The editorial was certainly correct in its sarcastic remark suggesting a court inquire into the sanity of the Kaiser and that what had begun would be a horrible business. But it was wrong about almost everything else. Russia's 5.4-million-man army almost matched the combined forces of Germany and Austria, about 6 million. But it was led by a decadent aristocratic class and was no match on the battlefield, suffering mass slaughter at the hands of the Germans.

So, contrary to Barron's forecast, Russia was in fact the biggest loser, not only in casualties but in postwar consequences. The Bolsheviks gained popular support with their promise to take Russia out of the war, overthrew a short-lived representative government headed by Alexander Kerensky, once in power killed the czar and his family, launched a civil war and gave the Russian people 72 years of police state "Communism." Moreover, the Russian people would be ravaged again in the 1940s replay of World War I, better known as World War II.

Also contrary to the Journal forecast, the western Allies in the Triple Entente had a hard time standing fast. The Germans took a large portion of France, almost reaching Paris. Then, three years of bloody stalemate ensued until the United States entered the war and tipped the balance against Germany. The Germans didn't starve, and Britannia did not rule the waves. The editorial had reckoned without Germany's capacity to wage submarine warfare, which took a fearful toll of Allied lives and shipping. So Barron and Hamilton were wrong on about every count. But they certainly were neither the first nor last journalists to misjudge the consequences of a war. It is an occupational hazard.

As it became more and more likely that the United States would enter the war in response to German U-boat attacks on American ships, the Journal carried an editorial deploring the state of American preparedness. It was mainly aimed at Josephus Daniels, the bumbling Populist secretary of the navy. The editorial sounds as if it might have been inspired by the warnings of Teddy Roosevelt and his fifth cousin, a young assistant secretary of the navy named Franklin Delano Roosevelt who was very often at odds with the secretary. Both Roosevelts were on speaking terms with Barron, who had been in frequent touch with Teddy since he advised Teddy on putting down the banking panic of 2007.

Wrote the Journal: "It is impossible to escape the conclusion that those in charge of the military and naval departments are temperamentally unfitted for their task...Mr. Daniels is typical of the handicap a country governed by popular politics carries into a war. He can regard the Navy as a high school for the enlisted man, as a floating branch of the YMCA, as a militant temperance machine, as a carrier of mails or even of cargo. But he cannot regard it as a fighting machine trained to the minute."

On the whole, however, the American expeditionary force acquitted itself well and was sufficiently effective to tip the balance toward a Triple Entente victory, if the devastation and loss of so many young men could be called a victory for anyone.

The Journal didn't think highly of the Bolsheviks then or forever after. The editors were not happy about the Bolsheviks' offer to take Russia out of the war. An editorial of November 16, 1917, scored Leon Trotsky, the Bolshevik foreign minister, for his proposed deal with Germany. Pointedly, the editorial used Trotsky's real name, Braunstein, perhaps to introduce the point that the Ukrainian revolutionary was part Jewish. There's not much evidence of anti-Semitism in early Journal editorials, but given the suspicions of Jews on the Wall Street of that era, it should not be surprising that some crept into editorials from time to time.

The editorial quoted Trotsky as saying the aim of the Bolshevik movement was to gain the "people's right to peace, free life, the land, bread and power." Said the editorial: "It is certain that there is a great deal of land that the Russian people will not get if his program of peace with Germany is carried out." It pointed out that under the deal, the Russians would lose to Germany "a large part of the black soil belt, the port of Odessa, the Black Sea and the mouths of the rivers emptying into it…

"Nor is that all. 'The war indemnity to be paid by Russia must consist largely in the transfer of private titles to land.' It is not to be a transfer of sovereignty alone, but present owners are to be dispossessed in favor of Germans. Pacifism will come high to Russians as well as any other country that meets Germany with it." In other words, the Bolsheviks were not only selling out Russia's western Allies but also a sizable portion of the landowning Russian population.

A Journal editorial about the World War I armistice of November 1918 contained some common sense that would be little heeded by the victorious European Allies, France in particular. The Journal argued that "if the world is to exact, as it unquestionably will, enormous indemnities, which can never be large enough to meet the destruction a national insanity has caused, it must still leave Germany with the tools with which to create the new wealth that will pay those indemnities.

"When we sentence a convict to hard labor, we give him the means for production. We do not expect him to make bricks without straw. The civilized world indeed will take over the receivership of this dreadful relic of the Dark Ages, this monster of greed, rapine, and arrogance and teach him to make a man of himself. An armistice means peace, but peace itself comes later. Recognizing that individual and national punishment of the most severe character is necessary, it is yet the task of civilization to save sixty million people from themselves."

After the armistice, Journal editors were concerned that Germany would go the same direction as had Russia, with a revolution that would bring radicals into power. Their fears were justified, as Hitler would prove 15 years later, but a bit premature. This from an editorial on November 12, 1918: "When the armistice was signed the white flag became the emblem of Germany, and in spirit, at least, her flag for years to come. But with the revolution which forced the abdication of the Kaiser and the German Kings, the red flag was hoisted. However we may flatter ourselves with the prospects of a German Republic, we cannot be blind to the fact that the red flag means anarchy.

"It meant that in the French commune, and, after the world had forgotten that lesson, it meant it again in Russia. Dare we hope that it will not mean the same thing in Germany?"

The editorial was particularly concerned about what would happen in Germany when its soldiers, armed and embittered, returned home. "These men return to Germany armed, exempt from that stern discipline which alone could control them, habituated to rapine and oblivious to all personal controls as represented by religion, continence and honor, such as true civilization alone can breed. They are the creation of Germany, not merely of her war machine but of all the people, who could see nothing in them to criticize so long as they seemed victorious. This monster is let loose, and to what lengths it may go can only be imagined."

"Did civilization fail in Russia? Can it tolerate another failure in Germany?" The crimes of Stalin and Hitler would be the unhappy answer to both of those questions.

One of the most significant effects of World War I was its destruction of monarchial rule on the continent, in Germany, Austria-Hungary and Russia. A Journal editorial on November 9, 1918, worried that good kings like Albert of Belgium and George of England might be swept out along with the bad ones.

"The world is safe for democracy under a king if he is a good democrat in something more than a mere party sense. He may, indeed, when occasion calls be a better democrat than a president." As it happened, both the British and Belgian monarchies survived the war, no doubt in part because they had long ago ceased to have absolute power and were forced to be responsive to democratic institutions.

On January 19, 1919, a Journal front-page article by C.W. Barron told of urging E.J. Dillon, a prominent author and adviser to heads of state, to return to the continent to help out with the post–World War I peace talks at Versailles, outside Paris. Dillon had responded: "There need be no hurry; the trouble has only begun. The problems of the war are as nothing compared with the problems of the peace."

How right he was. As Barron's friend Dillon had predicted, it didn't take long for the Versailles treaty to turn sour over the high level of reparations demanded of Germany. In a speech in Detroit in December 1921, the Journal publisher asserted: "Germany could not pay her debts if she wanted to and she does not want to... She has issued paper money until the value of the mark, which was 23 cents before the war, 12 at the time of the Armistice, eight at the Peace Treaty of Versailles has now fallen to about one-third of a cent. How much lower will it fall? Well, it can't go more than a third of a cent lower. Germany did not want to pay the reparations demanded and she brought about the present situation to prove that she could not. Now she has become alarmed and is asking Washington for help, but that help will not come until she is willing to help herself.

"We might as well admit however, that it is [beyond] the power of Germany to pay 33 billions [in U.S. dollars] of reparations when the whole property of the country is worth only 50 billion. France must take time to cool down and realize that fact. It would mean the slavery of the nation for three generations and the world cannot afford to hold in slavery 50,000,000 people. It took us a long time to find out that slave labor is the dearest in the world, and that free labor is the cheapest and most efficient."

Barron asserted that President Woodrow Wilson's 14-point peace plan "had greatly added to the problems of peace." He quoted the cutting remark of French premier Georges Clemenceau about the 14 points: "the good Lord only had 10."

Wrote Barron: "Close scrutiny of President Wilson's 14 points will show that he is attempting a universal enforcement of only one of the Ten Commandments—'Thou shalt not kill!' The thunders of Sinai and the Finger of Jehovah on the stone tablets of Moses spoke this Commandment no more distinctly than that other Word: 'Thou shall not steal.'

"Man slays his fellow man that he may steal his goods. Nations war upon nations that they may take their lands, their trade and their properties. Stealing, or defense against stealing, is the fundamental aim in individual and national killing."

Barron, as with Clemenceau, clearly thought the American president was naïve in his urgings of disarmament, free trade and the restoration of the status quo ante in Europe in light of the pervasive Allied bitterness toward Germany during the Versailles proceedings. That bitterness and the arrogance of Clemenceau would be important factors in ensuring that another war would engulf Europe 25 years later.

After the war, Barron filed a report on his conversation with a rising young star in the field of economic policy advice who was participating in the Versailles Peace Conference as part of the British delegation. He was John Maynard Keynes, an economic adviser to British prime minister David Lloyd George. Barron discreetly let his readers in on the fact that Keynes was a homosexual by writing that he "didn't seem like much of a family man." But he agreed with Keynes that the harsh reparations demands inflicted on Germany by the French and British would cause problems in the future, as they in fact did.

Neither Barron nor Hamilton agreed with the opinion of some stock traders that wars were good for business, a view often picked up by pacifists and used to damn Wall Street, with cartoons of greedy men in top hats and striped pants as a nest of warmongers. Barron and Hamilton would have none of the "good-for-business" talk.

On October 4, 1912, a Journal editorial attacked the New York Herald for asserting that war in Europe would send Europeans clamoring for U.S. stocks: "Of course, this is only the New York Herald," wrote Hamilton in a haughty English tone, "but there is considerable danger in second-rate thinking for second-rate minds, when the preponderance of second-rate minds is considered…If there is war in the Near East we may make up our minds that it will not mean one penny of investment to the American market that would not come here in any case, while it will involve the liquidation of American securities held abroad…War is a waste. One country cannot dissipate its savings in gunpowder smoke without hurting all the rest of us. In modern conditions of easy communications and international exchange, the misfortune of one is the misfortune of all."

This argument, self-evident it would seem, that war involves massive economic waste would be reflected in many future Journal editorials. Along with the horrible costs in human lives, the loss of physical capital is damaging to national economies.

The argument that the replacement of damaged infrastructure has the good effect of creating jobs was demolished years before World War I in the "broken window fallacy" laid out by the great 19th-century French economist Frederic Bastiat. He held that destruction doesn't advance economic growth. To be sure, a broken window makes work for the glazier, but it subtracts income from the house owner that might have gone to finance more useful endeavors.

But once the United States became involved in World War I, Barron urged that it pursue victory with vigor. That same approach would be taken by Journal editors after the Japanese attack on Pearl Harbor on December 7, 1941. And a version would be expressed by Robert L. Bartley, who set editorial policy for the 30 years ending in 2002, with reference to Vietnam: "Don't get involved in any wars that you don't plan to win."

Some commentators argue, of course, that World War II was a boon to the United States in that it ended a decade-long Depression. But that argument needs a great deal of qualification. Certainly the war ended the unemployment problem, as it pressed nearly 12 million men and over 200,000 women into military service, not to mention the massive ramping up of employment in defense industries. But 407,316 of those soldiers lost their lives, and 671,278 were wounded. The U.S. economy produced massive numbers of tanks, planes, weapons munitions and ships, but most of that materiel was useless for anything other than destruction and had to be scrapped after the war.

The truly important factor in aid of U.S. recovery was that it emerged from the war a victor with its mainland infrastructure and its governing institutions and civil society intact, having had to endure no fighting, other than Pearl Harbor, on U.S. soil, something that no other participant, winner or loser, could claim. It came out with a new spirit of accomplishment and optimism.

World War II also put paid to further New Deal experimentation, which had caused uncertainties among businesses in the 1930s and thereby retarded investment. The nation came out of the war with a new respect for corporate capabilities and a retention only of those New Deal measures, like banking reform, that had proved to be mainly positive in their economic effects.

Moreover, when the United States came out of the war, the U.S. dollar was the dominant currency of the world, and U.S. financing, managerial skills and resources were applied to global reconstruction. World War II as such didn't end the Depression, but the victory gave American businesses and consumers a new confidence and set U.S. governmental policies on a new, more positive course.

If you think war is good for an economy, don't try to tell that to the survivors of World War II in devastated Europe and Asia. Journal editor Hamilton was making a good point when he attacked the "second-rate minds" at the New York Herald.

CHAPTER 3

Hamilton Hates Prohibition

President Harry Truman was right in a sense when, in a 1948 campaign speech in Chicago, he said that The Wall Street Journal was the "Republican Bible"—but only in a sense. Truman, of course, was applying the old FDR formula of identifying Republicans with the hated tycoons of Wall Street, while at the same time taking a swipe at the Journal, which had given him mixed reviews.

Yet being called by the president the "Bible" of a party representing roughly half the electorate, even if it applied only to the editorial page, must have had some benefits in gaining the Journal national attention when it was still a relatively small newspaper. The Journal of 1948, which for over a half century had supported free-market capitalism, certainly had more admirers among Republicans than among Democrats. With the advent of the New Deal, the Democrats had become infatuated with a more radical version of Teddy Roosevelt's "Progressive" politics. Its guiding theorists were experimenting with laws that attempted to control market transactions through federal regulatory interventions that were shaking the confidence of business owners and investors. The Journal deplored much of what the New Deal was attempting.

But Truman was wrong if he was trying to suggest that the Journal was a party newspaper. With one unfortunate exception, it adhered to the Charles Dow injunction against endorsing political candidates. The exception came in 1928 with an editorial by Hamilton, ordered up by the dying C.W. Barron, that endorsed Republican Herbert Hoover. Barron apparently feared that the election of Democratic New York governor Al Smith would undo the economic achievements of his good friend Calvin Coolidge.

What Barron didn't seem to realize—although it may have made no difference—was that although Hoover was a Republican, he was not cut from the same cloth as Coolidge or the earlier William Howard Taft. His penchant for market interventions was almost as intense as what would later be displayed by the New Deal Democrats. For example, he signed the excessive and ruinous Hawley-Smoot Tariff Act in 1930, which had a lot to do with deepening and prolonging the 1930 recession, turning into what we know now as the Great Depression. It scuttled many businesses and almost did in Dow Jones itself. The Journal never again endorsed a political candidate.

But the Journal's free-market ideas usually have been more compatible with those of Republican candidates than Democrats over the years, or at least more compatible with what Republicans *professed* to believe, even if they were less dedicated in practice than in their rhetoric. The Dow policy of no endorsements has served the Journal's opinion editors well because it has freed them to criticize Republicans, often more fiercely than Democrats, when they have strayed off the free-market path.

Republicans, with the exception of the election of Democrat Grover Cleveland to the presidency in 1884 and for a second term in 1893, had controlled the White House for 37 of the 45 years leading up to the election of Woodrow Wilson in 1913. Even Cleveland, a former New York governor admired for his probity and conservatism, was of a different ilk from the statists who would later become a powerful wing of the Democratic Party.

But there was one extremely important issue on which the Journal would differ sharply from the prevailing opinion in the conservative wing of the Republican Party: Prohibition. In the late teens of the early 20th century, there was a groundswell of anti-alcohol sentiment in the country—fanned among other odd things by a World War I animus against German Americans and their prominence in the brewing industry and their fondness for beer.

The Journal was against Prohibition, even though it got much of its support from conservative Republicans. But the Journal's opinion counted for little against this avalanche of do-goodism. The 18th Amendment passed and was implemented on January 16, 1920, by the Volstead Act. New York mayor Fiorello La Guardia estimated that enforcing it in his city alone would require 250,000 additional cops and a like number of investigators to police the cops. As Clarence Barron had foreseen, the results were disastrous, with the act giving rise to bootlegging, the rise of criminal gangs and widespread lawlessness and corruption.

In a fiery editorial in 1921, the Journal castigated Republicans for their support for Prohibition, writing that the party had succumbed to Prohibitionist bigotry when it should be the party of freedom. "You cannot ameliorate a cesspool by sowing the surface with forget-me-nots and daisies," the Journal editorial said.

At the beginning of the 1928 election campaigns, the Journal even saw fit to briefly suspend its Republican leanings and pass a left-handed compliment to Democratic candidate Al Smith for advocating repeal of the 18th Amendment. A Journal editorial, presumably written by Hamilton and referring to the governor's annual message to the New York legislature, archly praised him for his attacks on Prohibition while at the same time criticizing him for his support for government ownership of electric utilities. Publicly owned versus privately owned electric power utilities was also a big issue in those days, and the Journal was, of course, a defender of private ownership against political involvement in the provision of a vital service.

* * * *

But there were other momentous happenings as America entered the 1920s. A Journal editorial on September 17, 1920, shortly after the 19th Amendment to the Constitution forbade "sex-based discrimination in state and federal elections," correctly predicted that the vote of women would swing the November presidential election to the Republicans. The Republicans had pushed the amendment through Congress in 1919 against Democratic opposition, so it was natural that suffragettes would favor Republicans when their right to vote was guaranteed nationally. Moreover, wrote the Journal, "the country is tired of Wilson, his uncompromising autocracy, his monopoly on all the political virtues, the inefficiency and extravagance of his administration." The Journal was right. Senator Warren G. Harding won in a landslide over Democrat James M. Cox, with 404 electoral votes to Cox's 127.

The president who Barron formed his closest attachment to was Calvin Coolidge, the Vermonter who ascended to the presidency on the death of Warren Harding in 1923. Barron had met Coolidge at a dinner party given by H.B. Endicott, a prominent New England industrialist who was father-in-law to one of Barron's two stepdaughters, Martha Endicott. Coolidge was then governor of Massachusetts, where he would become famous for his firm suppression of the 1919 police strike in Boston, proclaiming in a reply to a message from American Federation of Labor president Samuel Gompers that "there is no right to strike against the public safety by anyone, anywhere, anytime."

Coolidge and Barron had a long conversation at the dinner party and developed a liking for each other, even though their two personalities could hardly have been more opposite. Barron was an extroverted, garrulous newspaper tycoon, whereas Coolidge was a taciturn, flinty Vermonter serving as governor of a populous eastern state that had once been one of the most influential 13 colonies. What they had in common were keen intellects focused on public policy issues and a shared belief that allowing markets to do their work in resolving economic dislocations produces better results than government interventions. Barron thereafter promoted Coolidge's political career. He rode on the delegate campaign train to the June 1920 Republican convention in Chicago where Warren Harding was nominated for president and Coolidge for vice president. He gave the Republican ticket praise in the Journal but held to the Charles Dow stricture against endorsing candidates.

After Coolidge became president in 1923 on the death of the scandal-tarred Harding, Barron continued as his friend and counselor. The new president proved to be particularly resistant to the pleadings of lobbyists, particularly the powerful farm lobby, for subsidies and import protections. The economy soared in the Roaring Twenties as automobile sales and housing starts burgeoned and American industry brought forth labor-saving household appliances like motorized washing machines and vacuum cleaners. Radio came into its own, and in 1927, the first "talking" motion picture, "The Jazz Singer" starring Al Jolson.

The Wall Street Journal prospered along with the new Barron's weekly business newsmagazine introduced in 1921 at the suggestion of Hugh Bancroft, husband of Barron's other stepdaughter, Jane Bancroft, and a proper Bostonian. Bancroft, a lawyer, had had an off-and-on relationship with Barron and Dow Jones over the years, but for all practical purposes was the company's business manager at the time he proposed the magazine launch.

Barron displayed his admiration for Coolidge in a late 1924 interview with the Boston Traveler, saying that the fundamental factor in the outlook for 1925 was "the strength of the government in Washington." He went on to tell the interviewer that there had been a great deal of "sloppiness" in government over the last 50 years, but for the first time in a generation "we now have a firm hand at the helm and a man who stands for plain speaking and fundamental principles in national security and defense."

He said that since Coolidge had delivered his first State of the Union address to Congress early in 1924, the outlook for business had steadily improved. Barron was right again; the economy soared to new heights in the mid-1920s. Incidentally, his reference to sloppiness encompassed a half century that included the incumbency not only of Warren Harding, who was indeed sloppy, but also Teddy Roosevelt, whose genuine achievements, such as the Pure Food and Drug Act, had no doubt been forgotten by Barron in his resentment of the 1912 election debacle that put Wilson in the White House.

The Journal's growth in circulation and prominence in the 1920s was in large part due to Barron's fame and popularity. But some of the credit should go to the talents of his new protégé, a large young man from Indiana named Kenneth C. "Casey" Hogate. Barron had come upon

Hogate during Barron's quest for an interview with Henry Ford. Ford had rebuffed his requests, perhaps because of the unkind treatment the Journal had given Ford's World War I "peace ship." Barron had termed the 1915 mission to Europe by Ford and other amateur statesmen hopeful of arranging peace negotiations among the warring powers overly altruistic. It failed, as he predicted.

To patch things up, Barron was advised to work through the 24-year-old Hogate, already at such a tender age editor of the Detroit News, who had had an interview with the reticent auto tycoon. The portly Barron and the young Hogate, who nearly matched Barron in weight but was better proportioned with his pounds spread over a six-foot, two-inch frame, dined together in Detroit in 1921, and Hogate's intercession with Ford got Barron his interview.

Barron took an instant liking to Hogate, once telling a friend that he regarded him as the son he never had. He offered him a job as Detroit bureau chief for the Journal, which seemed like a big step down from editorship of the News. But Hogate could foresee that the Journal opened opportunities for him to enlarge his audience from local to national and that bureau chief was just the entry door to this wider realm. He was right. Late the next year, Barron made Hogate managing editor of the Journal.

Hogate, whose father had owned a newspaper in Danville, Indiana, a small college town just west of Indianapolis, had graduated from DePauw University in Greencastle, Indiana. He had earned his degree in three and a half years and had won a Phi Beta Kappa key. He was so well liked and admired at the Journal that the existing managing editor, Walter Barclay, willingly stepped down to a lesser position to make way for him.

William Peter Hamilton would continue writing editorials under the new Hogate regime, and Barron would continue to be the true voice of the paper with his frequent columns. But clearly Barron intended for Hogate to be the future custodian of a newspaper that had achieved national prominence as the font for Barron's prolific, forthright and often prophetic writings. Under Barron, the paper's reach had advanced far beyond the small but attentive audience it had had under Dow. Circulation had risen fivefold, to 56,000 in the 1920s from 11,000 when Barron took over. It was still small relative to mass circulation metropolitan dailies, but its readers were important decision makers in business and finance, and to some degree, in politics. So its influence was far greater than its circulation numbers would suggest, and for that reason it had little difficulty in attracting advertising, a "demographics" advantage that still serves it well.

The ease of getting ad revenue from the Journal was fortunate in the Barron years because it enabled Dow Jones to support the owner's elaborate and expensive lifestyle. He was a man who traveled first-class, sometimes in a private railcar to accommodate his retinue and family. He repaired to Florida, one of his favorite holiday destinations, on a private yacht, stayed in the best hotels and traveled on ocean liners in royal style for his frequent visits to Europe. In addition to his Beacon Street mansion in Boston, he had a summer home at Cohasset, Massachusetts.

But he was hardly idle during all this luxury living. While he moved about, he dictated thousands of words in the form of articles, letters and staff memos to his two secretaries. He also employed a male nurse and masseur and made frequent visits to the sanitarium of Dr. John Harvey Kellogg in Battle Creek, Michigan, to try to cope with his weight problem, with only limited success.

Barron's lavish style paid dividends for The Wall Street Journal. It made him conspicuous, and his air of royalty combined with his assertive and logically persuasive writings persuaded heads of state and industrial tycoons that he was a man to be reckoned with. It certainly impressed lesser journalists, who often called on him for comment on financial developments, thus enhancing the Journal's reputation and authority among readers of large-circulation metropolitan newspapers.

But all this had to come to an end, and on October 2, 1928, C.W. Barron died at the Battle Creek Sanitarium at age 73. He was by then so famous that his picture appeared on the front page of the New York Times. Eulogies poured in from all over the world and were duly printed in the Journal by Casey Hogate. The Saturday Evening Post, at that time one of the nation's most widely read magazines, called him the "father of financial journalism." And Calvin Coolidge wrote, in a telegram to Barron's stepdaughter Jane Bancroft: "To me it is a personal loss as I valued his friendship and his counsel."

An article by Ken Hogate announcing his death said: "The staff of the Wall Street Journal bows in reverence to the high principles ever enunciated by Clarence Walker Barron and in appreciation of his sweet personality and lovable, warm-hearted regard for them—which personality—so virile and endearing—can never die in their affections."

Jane Bancroft was Barron's principal surviving heir. So Hugh and the Barron-anointed Casey Hogate would carry on the business after Barron's death.

Barron scattered some pithy aphorisms in his lifetime of reporting on major events. So great was his fame in the 1920s as a financial guru that the Illinois Merchant's Trust Co. chose him to supply two of the eight epigrams to be inscribed on the walls of its new Chicago bank building along with the writings of such classical philosophers as the Roman Cicero and the 16th-century Lord Chancellor of England, Francis Bacon. The lines he provided:

"All Progress of Men and Nations is Based Upon the Sacredness of Contracts." And "A Wealth of Nations is Not in Prices, But Production and Reserves in Store and in Service."

Barron's daily outpouring of wisdom could be described as overly loquacious, not so surprising when you consider that he was dictating stream of consciousness observations to his secretaries. But he left future writers some useful guidelines: "The soul of all writing and that which makes its force, use and beauty is the animation of the writer to serve the reader. Never write from the standpoint of yourself but from the standpoint of the reader."

That last bit of advice would be embraced by Hogate and his successors and would guide Journal writers thereafter, with excellent consequences.

CHAPTER 4

Kilgore Dissects the New Deal

The Dow Jones board met four days after Barron's death. It consisted of three people: Jane Bancroft, now the principal owner; her husband, Hugh; and Casey Hogate. Hugh was elected president and Casey vice president and general manager with authority to write checks on the company's accounts and access to its safe deposit vault. With that, the post-Barron phase of Wall Street Journal history was launched.

From the beginning, the Bancrofts would follow a principle of leaving the news and editorial policies in the hands of a talented professional journalist, perhaps because they knew that it was the abilities of a fine journalist, Clarence Barron, that had built Dow Jones to its present status. That would be the practice down through the years. Their descendents would leave the running of the newspaper, and ultimately the entire Dow Jones, up to a series of editors who had won their spurs initially as writers. It would serve Dow Jones and its employees and owners well.

Casey Hogate was the first in that series, and no doubt his talent and personality helped strengthen the Bancrofts' decision to leave management up to the professionals. Hogate and Bancroft, who by then had proved himself as a talented executive, immediately set about to bring order to the loosely coordinated Dow Jones subsidiaries, such as the Boston and Philadelphia news bureaus. Casey also searched for talent to beef up the Journal's editorial staff. William Peter Hamilton died in December 1929, leaving a big gap, and was replaced by 52-year-old Frederick Korsmeyer, a thoughtful Nebraskan who had been his understudy but who couldn't match the force and bite of Hamilton's editorials.

Hamilton had based Journal editorials on the liberal ideas of 18th-century philosophers such as Adam Smith and John Locke. The former had created the logical base for letting markets find the most efficient employment of resources and the latter the arguments upholding the principle of "natural rights" of man that had so influenced the authors of the Declaration of Independence and the Constitution. Like Barron, Hamilton was an astute market analyst. They agreed on the principle that "The market represents everything everybody knows, hopes, believes, anticipates."

In 1926, Hogate had recruited a former United Press reporter from Ohio, William Henry Grimes, to take over the Washington bureau from the aging and alcoholic John Boyle. In 1929, Hogate hired a bright young man from his alma mater, DePauw University, named Bernard "Barney" Kilgore into the New York office. Grimes and Kilgore would prove to be inspired choices, both playing key roles in the future development of Dow Jones. Also in 1929, Hogate and Bancroft pursued the Journal's claim of being a "national" newspaper by opening a West Coast Wall Street Journal in San Francisco. The timing wasn't propitious. It was eight days before the stock market crash.

The Journal had warned, after a setback in the market in 1928, that stock buying with "call" money borrowed from banks at 12% interest rates (marginal borrowing) plus the huge inflow of buying orders from abroad was of concern. But it didn't shout it from the rooftops.

In May 1929, Journal editors weighed into what proved to be a historic dispute between the New York Federal Reserve Bank, supported by its private member banks, and members of the Federal Reserve Board Washington, political appointees of the president. The New York reserve bank, presiding over the nation's banking center, had dominated monetary policy through the 1920s with excellent results under the leadership of Benjamin Strong. But Strong had died in 1928, and that had touched off a power struggle between the New

York Fed, with its focus on sound banking, and the more politically minded board in Washington.

Concerned about the speculative fervor in the New York markets fueled in part by the easy availability of margin loans, the New York Fed wanted to raise the "discount" rate it charged on loans to banks to 6% from 5%, this being the Fed's traditional way of damping down credit excesses. But the governors in Washington were resisting.

"Why will not the board follow the advice of practical men of affairs?" demanded the Journal. Washington finally gave in and raised the discount rate to 6% in August, but not before it had established that the politically selected board in Washington, not the New York Fed, was now in charge of monetary policy. The results for the next few years would not be pretty, as the Fed failed to adequately respond to the 1929 market crash through the traditional means that had worked well after the 1920 crash, seeing to it that the banking system had sufficient liquidity. It thus bore heavy blame for bank failures and damaging deflation. Economist Milton Friedman in his 1980 book "Free to Choose" would call this one of the major causes of the Great Depression.

Herbert Hoover in his memoirs described the board of that time as "a body of startling incompetence." Clarence Barron had been quite right in conditioning his optimism for the Fed on his hope that it would exercise "wise management." That, unfortunately, was not to be once the system came under the domination of political appointees rather than what the Journal chose to call "men of affairs."

Having endorsed Herbert Hoover, the Journal's editorials were rather muted in offering criticisms of his performance, a timidity that vindicated Charles Dow's warning that a good newspaper should never tie itself to a politician of either party. The Journal went out of its way to praise some of the measures of the president, such as the creation of the Reconstruction Finance Corp., essentially a government bank.

But the editors couldn't help noticing that the hyperactive Hoover was making some colossal mistakes. For one thing, he and the Republican Congress raised income taxes to "balance the budget," not a particularly wise measure during a time when the relatively well-to-do Americans, the only people who at that time paid income taxes, had just been shocked by the crash and were uncertain about economic recovery and thus wary of new investments.

The Journal's free-market principles were violated when Hoover bowed to heavy lobbying by farmers and industry and signed the notorious Hawley-Smoot Tariff Act, one of the greatest protective tariff increases in American history. When the nation's trading partners retaliated in kind, Hawley-Smoot brought about a virtual shutdown in world trade, hitting American farmers, who accounted for a large share of American exports, hardest of all. That, along with the hapless Fed's inability to arrest deflation, worsened the Depression. A petition signed by 1,028 leading economists urged Hoover to veto the measure, to no avail. Under heavy political pressure from protectionists, he ignored their advice.

Republicans were excessively committed to their efforts to "help" the farmer. An editorial on April 15, 1930, probably written by Korsmeyer and titled "A Tariff Banquo," attacked a proposed export subsidy for farmers that William Edgar Borah (Rep., Idaho) wanted included in the Hawley-Smoot bill. The editorial likened the provision to Banquo's ghost in that it popped up repeatedly in Congress and was hard to banish. The editorial calculated that for cotton alone, the provision would cost the Treasury $80 million a year, and the subsidy would also defeat efforts by the government to curb crop acreage to support prices of farm products. Farmers would respond by increasing their production with the "certainty of a future collapse making their condition worse than ever."

As for the tariff bill generally, the Journal said on April 1, 1930, that the "pending tariff bill has been constructed on the good old theory that this country can make its own living standards and let the rest of the world roll by." The editorial challenged the popular idea (still existent today but more dangerous then) that an export surplus, enforced by high tariffs, is a good thing for the economy. It cited a book titled "America Looks Abroad" by banker-economist Paul Mazur about the fundamental inconsistency of that view.

Said the editorial: "America looks abroad, wrote Mazur, because she can't help herself. She seeks an answer to the not altogether new question how she may continue to collect $1,000,000,000 of annual interest on foreign loans and still preserve a merchandise export balance of nearly as much. With due conditions and qualifications, Mr. Mazur's conclusion is that it cannot be done."

This editorial was not the first and would not be the last time that the Journal would have to point out that the flip side of an export surplus is a foreign investment deficit. Americans in the 1930s frequently grumbled over the failure of our European Allies to pay their World War I debts. Mazur and the Journal were pointing out that high tariffs made it difficult for the Europeans to earn the dollars to make those payments, even with the best of intentions.

The damage from Hawley-Smoot wasn't long in coming. A Journal editorial on December 30, 1930, noted that exports of autos and parts for the 10 months ending in October had dropped to $249 million from the $488 million in the like period a year earlier. "This is not an isolated instance but is only one of many of our export trade. When there is a great falling off of foreign demand for the products of labor, whether cotton or machinery, there must be a falling off in employment that reacts upon all industry and trade," said the Journal.

On January 28, 1930, the Journal examined a proposal by Irving T. Bush, founder of the Bush Terminal Co. in Brooklyn, that, to prevent future financial crises, bankers should be licensed. Mr. Bush had written that the public accepts as a matter of course that doctors and lawyers be licensed, but when it comes to financial well-being, "we place our affairs without reservation in the hands of any person who chooses to open an office and call himself a banker."

Replied the Journal: "'We do nothing of the sort. Some of us do, to our sorrow. The majority of us do not even trust the storage or forwarding of goods or their passage through the customs to any person who chooses to open an office and call himself a forwarding agent. We turn, rather, to expert and reliable organizations like the Bush Terminal Co...."

The Journal pointed out that banking is a business and that each party to a banking transaction asserts the right to act on his own judgment; "if what Mr. Bush calls 'the guiding hand of greed' too often controls the seller, the same motive actuates the buyer even more frequently."

A Journal editorial on December 31, 1930, marked the "End of a Trying Year." Trying to put the best face on things, the writer struck a hopeful note by offering that "there are good reasons to believe that such impedimenta as 1930 leaves behind can be disposed of more easily and quickly than could that which remained at the close of 1929. The country is now in a realistic frame of mind. It has rid itself of the last of its illusions and is both willing and able to reckon with the facts. Quite possibly it has swung too far away from the light-minded credulity of early 1929 and is now disposed to exaggerate its fears, just as it was inflating its hopes beyond all reason less than two years ago. At any rate, men everywhere recognize the necessity of sober calculation, of cold scrutiny of all business projects in relation to the inherent soundness and usefulness."

But a short while later, the Journal was notably cool toward Hoover's 1931 State of the Union address, criticizing him for a lack of leadership in signing Hawley-Smoot. An editorial said the message was "in fact disappointing," betraying Mr. Hoover as "a man whose mental vision is apt to become focused on what he wishes to see."

As the Depression deepened the Journal's support for Hoover waned further and although it still leaned toward Hoover over FDR in the 1932 presidential race, there were no more enthusiastic endorsements. The Journal's editorial position was equivocal, deeming both parties to be, in effect, antibusiness. Indeed, an editorial on July 1, 1932, favored the Democrat platform plank as being the "most honest" on the repeal of Prohibition, which even in the depths of a Depression, it described as the "most important issue facing the nation."

But as the election neared, the Journal was furious at FDR for lending his own support to high tariffs and other political capitulations to the farm lobby. An editorial on November 3 stated: "Governor Roosevelt has unreservedly pledged himself to continue and extend the same impossible effort to afford tariff protection to export surplus producers which gave birth to the Hawley-Smoot and worse to the Agricultural Marketing Act and its $500,000,000 farm board folly."

The latter was a reference to the 1929 law passed by the Republican Congress and signed by Hoover that lavishly refunded the 12 federal farm loan banks created by the Federal Farm Loan Act of 1916. The federally preferential loan terms offered by these banks probably had a lot to do with the overproduction that had held down farm prices, giving rise to farmer demands for import protection. Farmers paid a very high price during the Depression for the federal measures they had lobbied so hard for, and the Journal's editors recognized the damage caused to the economy by these federal interferences with the normal workings of markets.

But after Roosevelt and the Democrats won a landslide victory, the Journal granted them a honeymoon, no doubt partly because the editors were themselves anxious about the state of the U.S. economy. An editorial praised the rapid-fire New Deal creation of legislation during FDR's first 100 days by opining that the new administration had "superbly" risen to the occasion.

"It and the country still have incredible tasks to perform before they can afford so much as a pause for breath. But together they have a good beginning and there are times when a beginning is nearly everything."

FDR and Hogate were in fact neighbors, with adjoining farms in Dutchess County, New York. They knew and liked each other, despite the differences in their political views, and often had long talks at their country places and in New York. Hogate had prevailed on Governor Roosevelt, apparently with some success, to give the New York Stock Exchange some slack, letting it have a try at self-reform.

Roosevelt, after his inauguration as president on March 4, 1933, immediately responded to the banking crisis, caused in part by Fed incompetence, by temporarily shutting down the nation's banks, thereby freezing depositors' funds. The Journal was only mildly critical. It even advised against the use of bank clearing house scrip, normally narrowly employed in the settling of interbank accounts, as a kind of substitute money, fearing it would lay the groundwork for inflation.

The Journal may have been wrong about that. Given the state of the banking system and a Fed that was little more than a bystander, a substitute money might have been useful in providing liquidity. Yet fears of inflation were a powerful force in that era, a time when the world had recently seen a German economy collapse under the weight of hyperinflation and when the British had in 1931 abandoned the international gold standard in their desire for more flexibility in the manipulation of money.

Although the Journal seemed to accept that some sort of emergency action was needed, it did point out that shutting down the banks was a further blow to an already weak economy and urged the government to end the "bank holiday" quickly. The government was less than responsive to that demand, as some bank inspections and depositor freezes dragged on until the end of the year. When the bank holiday ended, only 12,000 banks were permitted to open. In mid-1929, the nation had had 25,000 banks.

The Journal, however, supported two New Deal measures. It backed the Federal Deposit Insurance Act, which had an important influence on stabilizing the banking industry in the 1930s and thereafter by giving depositors more confidence in banks and reducing bank runs. And in a front-page editorial on April 4, 1934, it gave strong backing to the Securities Exchange Act, which created the Securities and Exchange Commission. The editorial said that "not only owners and users of investment capital but the investment bankers whose fortune it is to bring these two interests face to face, should welcome the legislation."

For one thing, the Journal's editors liked the idea of legal requirements that would bring about greater transparency in corporate reporting. They had historical memories of the Dow and Jones days when some companies, including the economically dominant railroads, didn't even deign to issue public annual reports. Reporters like Jones and Bergstresser had to fight for information about the true financial condition of the companies that were the subject of large bets being made by Wall Street investors. Hogate and others likely felt that the securities act would go a long way in restoring public trust in Wall Street, and quite likely they were right.

The Journal even offered some initial support for what, along with the revolutionary Agricultural Adjustment Act (AAA), was an equally revolutionary New Deal experiment, the National Industrial Recovery Act. The act set up the National Recovery Administration (NRA), whose job it was to organize the entire American business community into industry cartels, with separate "codes" for each industry.

The Journal even joined other newspapers in displaying the NRA's eagle symbol on its front page to show that it was a subscriber to the publishing code. But that sharp and uncharacteristic deviation from the newspaper's traditional free-market policies would be short-lived, thanks in part to the rising influence of Hogate's young protégé, Barney Kilgore.

The initial embrace of the NRA could be attributed to the fact that Dow Jones, along with the rest of the country in 1933, was facing hard times. Circulation and advertising had dropped sharply. Hugh Bancroft died in October of that year after a long illness at age 53. His widow, Jane, owned or controlled roughly 90% of the shares of Financial Press Companies of America, the family holding company that owned Dow Jones. She in essence turned the company over to Hogate, whom she much admired, telling him to do what was best for the company and "Don't you and the boys worry about dividends." Jane and her late sister Martha had loved their stepfather C.W. Barron, and Jane shared his trust in the abilities of the young man from Indiana.

Hogate worked tirelessly to keep Dow Jones afloat and focused much of his attention on rebuilding readership, in part by broadening the Journal's scope, not only as a national financial newspaper but a national business newspaper as well. To this end, he endeavored to liven up the Journal and make it more readable. He and Bancroft in 1930 had brought back Thomas Woodlock, the Journal's editor of a quarter century before, to write a front-page column. The Review & Outlook column originated by Charles Dow was moved from the front page to page 8 and became the official purveyor of the Journal's institutional opinions, which it remains to this day.

As mentioned previously, after leaving the Journal, Woodlock had become a railroad analyst, and in 1924 Coolidge had appointed him a commissioner of the ICC. In 1930, Hogate correctly surmised that a talented wordsmith like Woodlock in his waning years might want to do something more interesting than reviewing railroad petitions for rate increases. He proved to be right. Woodlock accepted the offer and was soon back in the role of offering Journal readers front-page commentary on everything from the performance of Herbert Hoover to the philosophy of Spanish essayist and poet George Santayana. His philosophical pieces gave the Journal class but were hardly the trenchant observations on current events that had gained Barron fame. In short, he was not the voice of the newspaper.

Whereas the return of the 63-year-old Woodlock was an evocation of the Journal's past, young Barney Kilgore was the embodiment of its future. He was moving up quickly as a protégé of Hogate, just as Hogate had been a protégé of Barron. Like Barron, he was a prodigious producer of intelligent, engaging copy. He wrote, as Barron had advised in his essay on good writing, with the reader foremost in mind and would later, as Dow Jones CEO, establish that principle as a Journal hallmark, which likely contributed to its remarkable ability to attract readers throughout the last half of the 20th century.

Kilgore started on a mundane job in New York in late 1929, just before the crash, checking the performance of the Dow Jones news service, delivered by broad tape "tickers," designed in house, to customers around the country. His role was to keep tabs on how often important stories ran on the ticker before competing wire services offered them and how often the competitors won the race, and by how many minutes or seconds. In the wire service business, a few seconds is a win; 20 seconds is a major victory. Though a routine job, it taught Barney a lot about business news coverage.

Hogate pushed him ahead quickly, shipping him to San Francisco to be news editor of the West Coast edition. It was there in March 1932 that Kilgore started writing what he called his "Dear George" column in the form of a letter to a fictitious correspondent about issues of the day. Hogate soon picked it up for the New York edition, putting it on the editorial page and explaining in an italic precede: "This series of letters in so far as persons mentioned therein are concerned, is fiction, of course. But the problems discussed are real."

The first column was about deflation, perhaps the foremost problem of 1932, the year the U.S. economy sank to its lowest point in the Depression. Wrote the 23-year-old columnist: "Did you ever stop to think what deflation is? It isn't a thing more than a bull market in money...Right now prices are low and dollars are high. And what that does to a lot of people is plenty."

He would add in a later column that the "problem with inflation or deflation is not one of condition but of a change of condition...it is a change in the value of the dollar that wreaks havoc with the economic order." The Kilgore column generated a spate of approving letters from readers, particularly after Barney invited his fictitious correspondent to write him with his own thoughts, thus provoking letters from readers.

The Journal had found a new voice in this talented writer from Indiana, one who spoke to the reader in a plain, conversational tone and explained complex issues in simple terms. Kilgore biographer Richard Tofel wrote that the column was "an extraordinary breath of fresh air in the musty precincts of financial journalism, and newspaper journalism generally." Tofel went on to write that "Kilgore's new column assumed that its readers were interested but not expert, eager to understand but currently confused, particularly as the economic order seemed to collapse around them."

C.W. Barron would have been pleased with the emergence of this young man who consciously or unconsciously adhered to the maxim Barron had laid down years before: Put the reader first. Indeed, Barney in one of his columns, would repeat an observation about the stock market that both Barron and William Hamilton had made in various ways during the Journal's earlier years, instructing "George" that the market "is a place where all knowledge about everything that has the slightest thing to do with business and trade is brought to bear eventually upon the price of securities representing equities in that business and trade." It was another way of saying that Charles Dow's creation of indexes that would measure market sentiment had been a marvelous invention.

Kilgore was brought back to New York and started a new editorial page column, Reading the News of the Day, which was more explicitly journalistic in that "news of the day" meant exactly that. Along with a wide range of subjects, he addressed the issue of barriers to trade, warning cotton farmers in the South that, because of their dependence on foreign markets, they had better "think twice before taking up the cry, 'Buy American.'" In another column, he wrote that the history of helping the farmer in the last few years "has been a process of trial and error, with some pretty good-sized errors."

As Kilgore's fame spread, it was not long before he, as with Barron, was being interviewed by other journalists. He made guest appearances on NBC's nationwide Red Network, something that thrilled his parents, Tecumseh and Lavina, in South Bend when they picked it up on Chicago's WMAQ.

Kilgore, although from a Republican family, was initially friendly toward the New Deal. He was particularly impressed with the quiet conversational tone of Franklin D. Roosevelt's fireside chats, which also were broadcast on network radio. He initially was hopeful about the National Industrial Recovery Act, which attempted to form businesses into cartels that could raise prices and, so it was hoped, put business on a sounder footing. The NRA was set up to implement codes governing prices and wages for individual industries.

But Kilgore decided to make a tour of cities to question people about how the NRA was working, an innovation that would give rise later to the popular Journal technique called the news "round-up," which anticipated the modern craze for opinion polling by sending reporters out on the streets to buttonhole citizens and get their views on a particular topic. As he surveyed the impact of NRA rules on individual business, he became more and more skeptical and said so in his writings. The New Deal's efforts to regiment business was not lifting them out of depression but instead sowing chaos, particularly with its efforts to raise wages while at the same time, in contradiction, trying to control prices.

The NRA, headed by a thin-skinned army general named Hugh Johnson, was not pleased with Kilgore's reports. In a speech to the American Federation of Labor in Washington, General Johnson left little doubt that he was attacking The Wall Street Journal when he declared that "the idea of a Wall Street journal going out to demonstrate through the little fellow the failure of a great social regeneration is one of the grimmest, ghastliest pieces of humor of all the queer flotsam of our daily work."

The general's fit of temper was probably a reflection of his own realization that the NRA was something of a mess. The Journal was the least of his problems. The NRA, which some later historians would call an experiment in proto-fascism, was short-lived. In 1935, the Su-

preme Court issued a ruling striking down the NRA as an unconstitutional exercise of government power. By that time, there was little
enthusiasm in Congress for trying to salvage any parts that might
have passed court muster. It died a timely death as a two-year-old.

The period of grace granted by the Journal to the New Deal
withered away quickly. Even as early as April 1933, only a month
into FDR's administration, Journal editors were beginning to have
doubts. They opposed FDR's decision to take the United States off the
gold standard, call in monetary gold at the traditional price of $20.67
and then raise the exchange price for gold in central bank transactions to $35 an ounce. FDR's controversial Executive Order 6102
exacted a $10,000 fine and a potential prison term for any American
citizen caught "hoarding" gold.

FDR's move was intended to devalue the dollar in international
exchange markets to reverse the deflation that had begun with the
1929 crash and to create inflation instead. A dollar was now worth
only one thirty-fifth of an ounce of gold in international exchange,
whereas it would buy over one-twentieth of an ounce before FDR's
unilateral devaluation.

This disturbed the Journal's inflation hawks. An editorial observed
that "Just as the United States was the first nation to abandon gold
voluntarily it is now the first to deliberate publicly on the expediency
of debasing its currency in the absence of the traditional compelling
reason thereto. For certainly the national budget could be balanced
within a reasonable time without it. We are a nation calmly discussing inflation 'as an instrument of national policy' whereas heretofore
it has always been begun stealthily by finance ministers desperate
to conceal national bankruptcy from the people or from an armed
enemy at the gates."

The Journal was, of course, referring to the age-old practice of
governments deliberately cheapening their currencies, thereby exacting a tax from savers and consumers in the form of a lowered value
of their money and savings. What Barney Kilgore would have called

a "bear" market in money effectively lowered the cost of paying off government debt, thereby easing the path to greater indebtedness. Whether FDR could have ended deflation by less drastic measures would be much debated. It would have helped to have had a central bank better attuned to the nation's monetary needs.

The Journal had also become skeptical of the ideas of the British wunderkind, John Maynard Keynes, and would remain so thereafter. Keynes was not a member of FDR's "brain trust," but he influenced policy. He wrote an open letter to FDR in late 1933 suggesting that the government could cure the Depression by borrowing more and spending more. The Journal attacked this theory with the same argument it would continue to use thereafter against Keynesianism: How is it economically "stimulative" when the government takes money from one person, the taxpayer, and gives it to another?

The Journal also challenged Nicholas Murray Butler, the president of New York's Columbia University, an institution that had contributed two of its faculty members, Raymond Moley and Rexford Tugwell, to FDR's original three-member brain trust.

After Butler had deplored the "the profit motive," a Journal editorial asked: "What is this profit motive that is suddenly become fashionable to decry. The profit motive is simply the common aspiration of all men to better their material status through individual exertion...How many members of the Columbia University faculty have exerted themselves beyond the requirements of their inadequately salaried duties to make contributions to literature and the technological arts for which the world is glad to pay them?"

The New Deal's Banking Act of 1933 gave the Fed board in Washington more clearly defined monetary policy power by creating an FOMC to conduct the Fed's money-creation activities. Putting to bed the days when those powers were often exercised at the discretion of the New York Fed, the act made political control over monetary policy more explicit by dictating that the FOMC would be made up of the seven politically appointed Fed governors and only five regional presidents, whose membership would rotate from year to year. It is doubtful that greater political control improved the Fed's performance.

First with Hoover and then with the New Deal, the center of the nation's economic decision making was shifting from New York to Washington. The Federal Reserve Board in Washington had won its power struggle with the New York Federal Reserve Bank. Board members even got titles, able to call themselves "governors" in the manner of the governor of the Bank of England, whereas the heads of the regional banks would remain bank "presidents," implying that their responsibilities were mainly regional.

With this power shift going on, Hogate saw the need to beef up the Journal's Washington bureau. The man he chose to do it was the 25-year-old Barney Kilgore, whom he appointed manager of the bureau in early 1935. The able William Henry Grimes had been promoted from bureau chief to managing editor of the Journal in September 1934 and had moved to New York.

Hogate was responding to the massive change the New Deal had wrought on the origins of news as it spread its influence over economic transactions far and wide. Washington was now in charge of the economy, or was at least boldly and recklessly attempting to be. For better and for worse, the Journal had to cover that capital city's outpouring of ukases.

Barron had thought so little of the Journal's Washington bureau that he seldom visited it, preferring to deal directly with presidents. His good friend Coolidge had once invited him to spend a night at the White House. When he did consult with the Journal's Washington reporters, there was something of a communications problem. According to the Wendt history, Barron's corpulence precluded his climbing the steep stairs to the Washington bureau. So he would get out of his chauffeured limousine below the bureau's window and shout up to the longtime bureau manager, John Boyle, "Boyle, Boyle! Come down here!"

Boyle, who somehow despite Prohibition, managed to supply his large thirst for alcohol, also was averse to climbing, either up or down, those steep stairs. So he would stagger to the window and yell, "You come up." The standoff was resolved by Barron shouting his instructions from his position on the sidewalk to Boyle in the window. He was willing to tolerate Boyle because he didn't assign much importance to the bureau.

But that was certainly not true after FDR's first 100 days of legislation to totally reorder the American economy, from acts (Glass-Steagal) that separated commercial and investment banking, to farm legislation that authorized the government to try to raise farm prices by paying farmers to burn part of the cotton crop and slaughter baby pigs. The Journal found it difficult to even record what was happening, let alone offer sufficient commentary on the wisdom of the acts. Hogate was a friend of FDR but not a confidante. One thing they had in common, though, was a mutual admiration for the young Barney Kilgore.

Early in his administration, FDR had publicly recommended to reporters that they read a Kilgore column to get a better understanding of the monetary and budgetary issues involved in paying World War I veterans a cash bonus. He said, "I don't agree with the story all the way through but it's a good story. It is an analytical story on an exceedingly difficult subject, the question of issuing currency to meet the government's obligations. I think that Kilgore could have gone just a bit further than he did."

FDR, like Hoover, was a believer in a balanced budget, and though some of his programs were radical, they weren't extravagant. For example, his farm act proposed to pay for farm subsidies with a tax on food processors, a provision among others that prompted the Supreme Court in January 1936 to scuttle it and necessitate a rewrite. The court ruled that the AAA included unconstitutional infringements by the federal government on powers reserved for the states.

As to the nettlesome bonus issue, a 1924 act had granted veterans bonus certificates, but they were not redeemable until 1945. A large "bonus army" consisting in large part of unemployed veterans descended on Washington in the summer of election year 1932 demanding immediate cash payments. Hoover paid a high political price when he refused on budgetary grounds and ultimately ordered the army to disperse the protesters.

Roosevelt also refused to pay but partly defused a similar protest in 1933 by offering the veterans jobs in the newly created Civilian Conservation Corps, which employed young men primarily to maintain national parks and forests. Congress finally passed a bill in 1936 to grant the bonuses nine years early and overrode FDR's veto. So naturally the president was grateful for Barney's dispassionate analysis in 1933.

A Journal editorial deplored the 1936 Bonus Act, arguing that it and farm subsidies would further expand the federal budget deficit in fiscal 1937. It said this had raised the question, in acute form, "whether there is to be any control over spending and borrowing?"

The Roosevelt administration had been running large deficits throughout the depressed 1930s, with the gap between revenues and outlays rising to a high of 5.4% of Gross Domestic Product (GDP) in fiscal 1936, which happened to be an election year. One might argue, as did Keynes, that deficit spending had a bearing on the limited economic recovery from 1933 through 1936. But that theory would be subject to some doubt when, in 1937, the U.S. stock market and economy suffered another crash, ushering in what has been called the second Depression.

In 1934, Kilgore was becoming increasingly skeptical of the New Deal's programs and voiced his doubts on the Journal's front page. He wrote that, since the New Dealers came to power in March 1933, they had had "a definite political philosophy...They have had, too, a vague social philosophy...But they have lacked and continued to lack any economic philosophy whatever."

Of the NRA, he wrote that after six months of reporting on its efforts, he had concluded that "because of its haste in pursuing the objective of a code for everyone and everyone under a code, and to the degree with which it succeeded in attaining that objective, it now finds itself with an enforcement problem on its hands that staggers the imagination."

Some New Dealers may have breathed a sigh of relief after the Supreme Court put the NRA out of its misery in 1935. Democrats in Congress were sensing that the public was becoming a bit weary of great social and political experiments. To be sure, FDR sought to retaliate against the court with his euphemistically titled Judicial Procedures Reform Bill of 1937, which would have given him the power to expand the 9-member court to as many as 15 members with his own appointees, a move that quickly became identified as an effort to "pack" the court.

One would have expected the Journal to rain hellfire on this proposal, but instead it came up with a short and rather badly written editorial equating the president's scheme to an effort to install umpires who would favor the home team. Maybe the mildness of the Journal's response reflected some knowledge that the effort had little chance of becoming law, Roosevelt's landslide reelection in the preceding year notwithstanding. Indeed, the bill died in the Judiciary Committee of the Senate when even the Democratic majority had little stomach for an all-out assault on the third branch of government, separate and equal to the presidency and Congress.

Barney Kilgore's tenure as Washington bureau chief brought more of his thoughtful analysis. With regard to the New Deal's efforts to jack up farm prices by destruction of crops and farm animals, Barney attacked the New Deal's price-fixing efforts, writing that such efforts "invariably fix prices at uneconomic levels."

He also applied his logical mind to Keynesian theory: "No government ever really creates purchasing power. It merely has the power to redistribute it. Hence, despite all claims that the New Deal has no intention of robbing Peter to pay Paul, the fact is slowly emerging that it must either tax Peter to pay Paul (which amounts to about the same thing) or it must tax Paul to pay Paul (which is even more patently a ring-around-the-rosey game)."

On one of Kilgore's periodic trips to sample grassroots opinion about the New Deal in September 1934, he quoted a "shrewd observer" in Cleveland as saying, "If the administration really wants to plan a recovery all it has to do is quit planning." But nonetheless, he reported that FDR still enjoyed widespread popularity, as would be evident in his 1936 victory.

As 1936 passed into history and the 1930s wore on and Kilgore made vigorous use of his post as Washington bureau manager, things began to turn sour for FDR. His effort to pack the court fell flat. The crash of 1937 dashed any claims he might have of economic policy success. And in the 1938 midterm elections, the Republicans made a strong comeback in Congress. On top of all this, the global outlook was beginning to look increasingly dangerous. The Spanish Civil War broke out in 1936 and soon became a proxy contest between Hitler on the side of the rebellious Francisco Franco and Stalin on the side of the Loyalists, thus providing a foretaste of the massive struggle between the two that would come later. In 1937, Japan invaded Manchuria, starting a war with China. And in 1938, Hitler annexed Austria and, after getting a pass from Britain's Neville Chamberlain, also took over a German-speaking part of Czechoslovakia called the Sudetenland.

Americans were averse to any involvement, and Congress passed a series of Neutrality Acts beginning in 1935 mainly forbidding arms shipments to warring powers. The Journal was well disposed toward these laws, but they were gradually being eroded as Roosevelt sought ways to aid China, a victim of Japanese aggression, and Britain and France, who were threatened by Germany. In October 1937, Roosevelt proposed to "quarantine" countries that violated treaties, which would have the effect of allowing the United States to embargo aggressor nations, an act of war.

The Journal opposed that idea in an editorial titled "We Could Muddle Into War." While it recognized that Americans opposed aggression, it argued that the president's proposal was "strongly suggestive of forcible measures against nations that wage aggressive warfare, declared or undeclared. Does anyone believe that public opinion in this country can be marshaled to support the United States in measures of international force?"

During the 1940 presidential election, Kilgore was impressed by the enthusiastic public reception a fellow Hoosier, Wendell Willkie, was getting as he campaigned for the presidency on the Republican ticket against Roosevelt. Kilgore thought the election would be close. But he hadn't accounted for the effective political machine the Democrats had created. FDR won 55% of the popular vote. Kilgore wrote a column apologizing to readers for being carried away by the noise and excitement of the Willkie campaign.

But Kilgore would soon cease to be the most prominent Journal byline writer. In early 1941, he and Grimes had a long discussion in New York during which Grimes offered to step aside and let Barney become managing editor. Grimes would become the new voice of the Journal, although an anonymous one most of the time, by taking over editorial opinion responsibilities with the title of editor. Hogate approved of the change.

It was a felicitous change. Barney could apply his creative talents to the continuing efforts to make the Journal more interesting and readable. And Grimes, while retaining some responsibility for the overall quality of the paper, would apply his sharp intellect to the task of making Journal editorials more assertive and exacting. Working as a team, they both succeeded in that endeavor, judging from the increased prominence of the Journal as a source of news and opinion.

Grimes' editorials would continue the Journal's long-standing opposition to involvement in foreign wars in 1941 even as Europe was being set ablaze by Hitler's tanks and bombers. At one point, a rather defensive editorial expressed resentment over having its position described as "isolationist," saying that "it does not help clear thinking to invent words with a sinister meaning and then proceed to hurl them at people." But the Journal had a long antiwar tradition and, right or wrong, was adhering to that tradition.

CHAPTER 5

Pearl Harbor's 'Stark Reality'

All the debate about going to war would end suddenly on December 7, 1941, when the war came to America. Some 360 bombers and fighter planes launched from six Japanese aircraft carriers that had stealthily slipped to within 220 miles of the U.S. territory of Hawaii came streaming through the Kolekole Pass in the northern Oahu mountains to attack the U.S. fleet at Pearl Harbor. The Japanese admirals had picked Sunday morning for the raid, correctly assuming that it would be a time when the Americans were in their lowest state of readiness.

The Journal's coverage displayed the Journal's new team at its editorial best. Bill Kerby, a Kilgore protégé who had been made assistant managing editor, was on duty when news service teletype bells began jangling at 3 p.m. on that Sunday afternoon alerting editors that there was big news coming. When reports of the attack started coming through, Kerby summoned Kilgore and Grimes. In short order, with a contribution from Washington bureau chief Eugene Duffield, they were remaking the Monday front page to meet the Journal's press deadline, only three hours away. It was a superb achievement. Kerby's lead story, written with Kilgore looking over his shoulder and offering suggestions, correctly predicted that the attack would mean a massive mobilization of American industry for the production of weapons and munitions. Duffield supplied the news that the president and Congress would put the United States on a war footing within hours.

Grimes, for his part, wrote an editorial saying that, with the Japanese attack, the war debate had ended. The Journal had been critical of FDR's "lend-lease," which involved, among other things, lending 50 U.S. destroyers to Britain and Canada in return for basing rights on British Caribbean islands. The Journal had feared that Roosevelt was leading America into the European war in violation of the American Neutrality Acts.

But on December 8, under the headline "We Have a Duty," a Grimes editorial told of the "stark, horrible reality that American territory has been attacked" and that Japan had declared war on the United States. It said that everything had changed once the news of Pearl Harbor had set the teletype machines clacking on Sunday afternoon:

"In that moment, the events of last week seemed to have been removed to some remote era of antiquity. The things that business and finance discussed last week seem now to have no relation whatever to tomorrow nor to the many days to come after tomorrow...Every citizen has and knows his duty...It will be heavy for all...We say that the sacrifices will be made. The duty will be performed."

Writing in short "takes" of five-by-eight copy paper sent immediately to the typesetters down below in the Journal building at 44 Broad Street, the editors totally remade the Monday edition in three hours. The new front page had three decks of banner headlines stretching across the top, something Journal readers had not seen before. The Journal was on a war footing.

With Roosevelt's dramatic speech to Congress the next day declaring war and declaiming that December 7 was a "day that would live in infamy!" the administration became more realistic in its attitude toward business. Big corporations, which FDR had scolded with his populist rhetoric in the past, were suddenly urgently needed to mount the war effort. New Deal schemes to reorder the economy were set aside to unleash the creative and productive forces of a capitalist system. The problem of financing the war effort through bond issues was given serious attention. So was the danger of inflation as huge new demands were placed on the nation's productive capacity.

The private sector responded magnificently to this new urgency, converting plants previously making autos and home appliances to the production of tanks, warplanes and munitions in a matter of weeks.

Journal editorials and editorial page articles offered advice to policy makers. On December 17, a Journal editorial surprised readers by departing sharply from traditional free-market arguments to support price and wage controls. It argued, rather disingenuously it would seem in hindsight, that the question was "simple." Would controls aid the war effort and "help sustain the morale of the fifty million or more who must sustain themselves to equip, clothe and nourish our fighting forces? We believe a thoroughgoing price control will serve those ends."

No doubt Congress and the administration didn't feel they needed the Journal's imprimatur, but they surely welcomed it. They quickly set up the Office of Price Administration to put ceilings on consumer prices. It worked reasonably well, although that was probably mainly due to the fact that the sale of war bonds was soaking up a lot of the extra cash civilians soon were earning by working overtime in defense plants.

Three years into the war, however, the Journal made it clear that its support for controls applied only to extraordinary circumstances. On February 28, 1944, almost three months before the Normandy invasion and 18 months before the war's end, the Journal was arguing that all wartime restrictions on the economy should end when hostilities ceased.

In 1942, Hogate was incapacitated by a stroke. He decided to name as general manager a veteran executive named Joseph Ackell, who had invented the new high-speed ticker, consolidated the Dow Jones wire service into a nationwide web and was running the Journal's production operations. Grimes objected on grounds that the appointment would weaken the power of Kilgore and that the company had always been run by newsmen. According to an account by Bill Kerby, Grimes called the Bancroft family business adviser in Boston, Jack Richardson, and told him that if the Ackell appointment went through, Grimes, Kilgore and Kerby would probably resign. The upshot: Kilgore became general manager of Dow Jones, Bill Kerby became managing editor of The Wall Street Journal and Buren McCormack, another DePauw graduate, became assistant managing editor. Grimes would remain editor and have general supervisory authority over news operations.

Barney had been a Hogate protégé, so the Kerby story is a bit puzzling. But although Hogate was very ill, he was still head of the company and may have felt that turning over routine management tasks to Ackell would not preclude his choosing a successor at some later date. He remained in nominal charge of the company, despite frequent absences because of successive strokes, until his death in 1947 at the young age of 49. At that point, his title was chairman. Barney had become president in 1945, but his elevation was not made public at that time. He became CEO on Hogate's death.

Hogate's early death was attributed by some of his associates to the heavy workload he had carried during the Depression out of devotion to the task of keeping Dow Jones alive. Hogate had literally worked himself to death, they felt. There is little doubt that he justified the faith that Barron and the Bancrofts had invested in him in 1928. He had built a solid journalistic organization.

Faced with newsprint shortages and other limitations, Dow Jones continued to struggle during the war, but Journal circulation rose, to 64,400 in 1946 from 35,395 in 1942, thanks no doubt in part to Kilgore's efforts to make it more readable and concise. Editorials gave full backing to the war effort, although at one point the Journal cautioned against excessive rationing of consumer products beyond products, such as automobile tires, that were vital to keeping the military well supplied. It argued that there should be as little distortion of the normal workings of the market as possible so that production and distribution of nonessential goods would proceed normally.

Grimes set editorial policy. He was a scrappy, no-nonsense little guy with a talent for clear, logical argument. He had tutored young

Barney Kilgore, his successor as Washington bureau chief, in the ways of Washington and the New Deal, and they remained close. As editor and chief editorial writer, he would bring crispness and cogency to the opinion page's views on public policy questions.

A framed copy of the signed editorial Grimes wrote marking the opening of the Journal's new Midwest edition in Chicago on January 2, 1951, still hangs on the wall of the editorial board's conference room in New York to remind present-day writers of the direction set long ago. It's titled "A Newspaper's Philosophy." The last paragraph sums up editorial policy with, "...we make no pretense of walking down the middle of the road. Our comments and interpretations are made from a definite point of view. We oppose all infringements on individual rights, whether they stem from attempts at private monopoly, labor union monopoly or from an over-growing government. We are not much interested in labels, but if we were to choose one, we would say that we are radical. Just as radical as the Christian doctrine." Grimes' declaration sounds a lot like what William Peter Hamilton had written a half century earlier when he asserted that there were not two sides to every question.

On July 8, 1944, a little more than a month after the successful Allied invasion of the European mainland, a Journal editorial offered an assessment of the government's war finances, pointing out that only 33% of what the government spent in the most recent fiscal year was borrowed, whereas the percentage was 71% of a considerably smaller amount the year before. "We have, then, improved the financing of this grossly expensive war. But it is none too good yet." The Journal was worried about the inflation that might be induced by war financing combined with price controls and the potential postwar transition from a wartime to peacetime footing as pent-up consumer demand overwhelmed the capacity to produce consumer goods.

The Journal also took note of deliberations on a postwar international monetary system then under way at Bretton Woods, New Hampshire. It noted that some proposed provisions of the planned exchange rate stabilization fund (later named the International Monetary Fund [IMF]) might raise eyebrows in Congress. One proposal would direct a country to lend to the fund when its currency was in short supply among trading partners. The Journal observed that this would mean that the Federal Reserve, not investors or banks, would be indirectly financing U.S. exports. The Journal would support exchange rate stabilization in principle over the years to come but would have much more to say about the actual workings of the IMF, a lot of it critical, in the future.

One of the most significant events of the century, the dropping of atom bombs on the Japanese cities of Hiroshima and Nagasaki, would be treated in the kind of matter-of-fact tone that characterized Journal editorial writing. An editorial on August 7, 1945, was titled "The Power of the Atom" and referred to the long-standing hope, going all the way back to before World War I, that as weapons became more destructive, men would cease to wage war. "Between the destructive powers of armies of 1914 and those of today, there is probably as much difference as those of the Civil War and Caesar's legends. President Truman's announcement of the discovery and use of the atomic bomb raises the prospect that by tomorrow today's explosives may seem like so many popguns."

But the editorial contained a note of hope, anticipating what future president Dwight Eisenhower would call an "atoms for peace" plan as atomic fission was employed as an energy source. "The force that today blasts a city into dust may soon be harnessed to render obsolete all gadgets big and little. From the oxcart to the automobile, from the treadmill to the steam engine and the dynamo were but a brief few hours in history and the world as we know it now moves even faster."

Raymond Moley, a member of FDR's original brain trust who had broken with Roosevelt in 1936, was writing a column for the Journal in 1945. He noted that news services were carrying jokes and puns about the bomb, such as a line that the United States had sent Japan an "atomized statement." That might sound shocking today, considering the thousands of Japanese civilians incinerated by the bombs, but most Americans in 1945 thought that no fate could be worse than the Japanese deserved after their sneak attack on Pearl Harbor and their barbarous treatment of American prisoners of war. There was also joy to be found in the prospect that the bomb would likely end the killing, as it in fact did.

Moley had a serious point to make: that the bomb should impel intelligent men to think more clearly about the political arrangements this new destructive force would necessitate. "Political and economic devices result from, they do not cause, scientific discovery. They are conditioned by the known facts of the physical world. They do not anticipate. They follow."

By forcing a Japanese surrender on August 15, 1945, the bomb did spare the lives of countless U.S. soldiers and both Japanese soldiers and civilians. Before that, the Journal had also turned its attention to the latest summit meeting on the future of Europe, where the war had ended with the surrender of Germany on May 8. The meeting at Potsdam, a suburb of Berlin, was the first for Harry Truman, who had ascended to the presidency after the death of FDR on April 12, and also for British Labour Party leader Clement Attlee, who had become Britain's prime minister on July 26, after defeating wartime leader Winston Churchill. The other participant, Russia's Joseph Stalin, was a veteran of wartime summits.

The Journal was skeptical of such "Big Three" proceedings and was hopeful that Potsdam would be the last, as it indeed proved to be. While the editorial writer admitted that there had been a certain glamour to these secretive meetings of the Allied chieftains, "there was about the practice a suggestion of personal government which was certainly alien to the traditions of both the United States and Britain." As that sentence implied, Joe Stalin was no stranger to "personal government."

The Journal decried the practice of lasting international decisions made by the "sudden inspirations of men whom circumstances have clothed with extraordinary power. However wise these men, they cannot in a period of days have all the information they should have..."

The editorial remarked that, after the death of Roosevelt, his successor, Harry Truman "discovered that there was no one who could tell him exactly what went on at the Yalta conference [February 4–11, 1945] and what agreements were made there." Many historians have argued that FDR, in failing health and not in full command of his faculties, had in effect ceded the future of central Europe to the imperialistic Stalin.

The unsigned editorial, which bore the fingerprints of Grimes, concluded with a small bouquet for Harry Truman for negotiating machinery that would bring about more systematic negotiations by lower-level officials. "How expert Mr. Truman may be in foreign affairs, we don't know. Whether he could beat Stalin in a game of poker, we don't know. Whether Mr. Stalin liked him, we don't know. We don't think they make any difference. What makes a great deal of difference is that Mr. Truman seems to understand the process of government administration."

After K.C. Hogate's death in Palm Springs, California, in February 1947, Dow Jones was firmly in the hands of Barney Kilgore, who would proceed with his plans to turn The Wall Street Journal into a compact, readable, national business newspaper.

Later in 1947, Grimes won the first Pulitzer Prize awarded the Journal. His entry was a series of editorials in 1946 that, among other issues, deplored the postwar spread of dictatorships to much of the world, particularly in the nations of central Europe that were falling victim to Soviet imperialism. His editorials were again an expression of the Journal's long-standing adherence to a belief that the preservation of personal freedom was of paramount importance in the conduct of both foreign and domestic policy.

Grimes in 1946 also had aimed a feisty and very brief parting shot at former vice president Henry Wallace, a leading New Dealer and early fan of Soviet collectivism who helped craft the 1933 farm bill that regimented farmers into a system of quotas and subsidies. Wallace might have become president if Democratic Party elders had not forced FDR to drop him from the ticket in 1944. After Truman fired him as Commerce secretary in 1946, he joined the left-leaning New Republic magazine. Wrote Grimes: "Henry Wallace has become editor of the New Republic. We suggest it serves both of them right."

Grimes would guide policy through Truman and Eisenhower years, which were the early years of the Cold War with the Soviet Union, a war that quickly became a hot war when a Soviet-backed North Korea invaded South Korea in 1950 and Truman acted to protect the South. The Journal approved of Truman's spunk in establishing a "containment" policy to curb Soviet imperialism. World War II evidently had destroyed any belief at the Journal, as it had for most Americans, that the United States could isolate itself from the troubles of Europe and Asia.

An editorial on March 13, 1947, had said that the president had not tried to hide the difficulties his containment policy would entail for the American people. But the "alternative is to withdraw from world affairs and see Europe and the Middle East, at least, come immediately under Russian domination. That means deportations, firing squads and the wholesale transfers of peoples. It means for a great many years at any rate the Christian idea of dignity of the individual will have to live underground if it lives at all, in a great part of the world."

The editorial went on to say that the Soviet-U.S. conflict was not one for power or territory but a conflict of ideas. "The idea that man is an individual with inalienable rights and that one of these is the right to associate with other men in forming institutions of their own making is on one side. On the other is the idea that man is a cog whose function is to be part of a great machine built and engineered by the most ruthless and powerful...Between these two ideas there can be no compromise."

That marker laid down by Henry Grimes would be a core Journal policy throughout the Cold War. The Journal supported the Marshall

Plan, which provided economic aid to Europe to successfully counter efforts by Soviet-backed Communist parties to take over governments. There would, however, be differences between the Journal and Truman and his successors on Cold War tactics.

After North Korea invaded South Korea in 1950 and Truman sent American troops to counter the Soviet-backed invasion, the Journal cautioned against extending the war to China, a position that was mooted when China entered the war on its own. In December 1950, Grimes wrote that "if there must be a war then it should be fought with Russia, the inspiration and the brains of world aggression. It would be silly to fight China or any other Russian satellite. Undoubtedly, that suggestion will shock some of our readers, but we think logic will support it."

The Journal's reservations about war, and particularly U.S. involvement in wars in Asia, would apply later to Vietnam, when it opposed JFK's plan to send American advisers to aid the South, the first step toward what would become an enormous American involvement. But when the United States was once engaged in wars, the Journal supported whatever was needed to prosecute them successfully.

On domestic policy, Grimes was suspicious that Truman might resurrect some of the high-handed policies toward American industry that had characterized the New Deal. But, as mentioned earlier in this book, it was Truman who chose to bring the differences between the two out into the open. During his 1948 campaign for reelection against Republican Thomas Dewey, Truman fired up an audience in McAlester, Oklahoma, by attacking the Journal as the Republican "Bible," saying "they used half their editorial columns giving me hell because I am for the people!"

Grimes, of course, welcomed the challenge. What could be more fun for an editor than to have a public slugfest with the president? Wrote Grimes: "If President Truman is a consistent reader of this newspaper—as we certainly hope he is—he must be aware of the fact that our loyalties are to the economic and governmental principles in which we believe and not to any political party. We regret he chooses to distort this newspaper's position."

That was certainly true in principle, but Truman had a point. Although the Journal learned from its bad experience with Herbert Hoover that endorsing candidates can come back to haunt you, its defense of free-market capitalism had always had more adherents among Republicans than Democrats and still does.

When Truman, in response to a steel strike during the Korean War, issued an edict putting the mills under federal control on grounds that the strike endangered the war effort, Grimes had one of his fits of temper. His leading editorial writer, Vermont Connecticut Royster, writes that he was planning to ask Grimes for a raise. But when he peeked into the editor's office, he observed Grimes jumping up and down on his hat in fury over this arbitrary exercise of presidential power. Royster decided to pick a better time. The hat didn't look much different after the abuse. Grimes' battered, gray fedora was one of his trademarks, marking him as a member of that ancient tribe of newspaper veterans contemptuous of personal decorum.

Royster, newly returned from war duty in the Pacific, became part of the Grimes editorial writing team in 1946. "Roy," as his friends called him, had joined the Journal in 1936 and had been assigned to Kilgore's Washington news bureau. But the navy upgraded him from reserve status to active duty in early 1941 and assigned him to an aged destroyer based in Panama for what he thought would be a short cruise. Pearl Harbor extended the cruise for five years, during which he prowled both the Atlantic and Pacific, finally with his own command of a destroyer escort. Kilgore was happy to have him back, perhaps sensing, correctly as it happened, that Roy would be at his best as a writer of opinion, rather than news, and had the potential to succeed Grimes as editor, which also proved to be correct.

Roy grew up in Chapel Hill, North Carolina, the son of a lawyer who had also taught Greek and Latin at the University of North Carolina (UNC). His father was teaching Roy to decline Latin verbs before he was in first grade, and he was further schooled in the Latin and Greek classics at the austere little Webb School in Bell Buckle, Tennessee. He later reflected that at UNC the classics were snap courses that helped him keep up his grade average.

That early training must have been partly responsible for the smooth flow of Roy's writing. Like Kilgore, he gave readers the impression he was sitting them down for a little chat, presenting his views in a modest, sometimes self-deprecating and frequently witty way. His range of subjects was broader than those that had been addressed by Kilgore, who usually stuck to political economics and finance. Royster sometimes ventured into more philosophical areas of the type that Woodlock, whom he admired, had explored. On any given subject, he might quote Euripides or Aristotle or bring the conversation down to the earthy wisdom of Huckleberry Finn.

He also had the grit to stand up to Grimes on matters of editorial policy. When in April 1951 Truman fired the world-famous five-star general Douglas MacArthur, who had led America's victory over Japan and was at that time conducting the Korean War effort, Grimes, like a lot of other Americans on the right, was shocked. But Roy stood up for Truman on grounds that the general had flouted civilian authority when he publicly threatened to attack China. Grimes gave in and told Roy to write the editorial. Roy graciously noted the arguments of Grimes and many others against the Truman shocker, but presented his own case that the president is commander in chief, and uniformed troops, even generals, risk chaos or worse when they disobey orders. Irate letters poured in from Journal readers loyal to MacArthur, and Grimes assigned Royster to respond to them, perhaps in retaliation for having to cede the argument to his junior editor.

Royster also was responsible for the Journal's May 20, 1954, editorial after, in a unanimous decision, the U.S. Supreme Court struck down racial segregation in public schools (Brown v. Board of Education) on grounds that segregation violates the Constitution's guarantee of equal protection under the law. Grimes had doubts based on his concern that the South would not accept the decision, but Royster, himself a southerner, argued otherwise and had little difficulty this time in persuading Grimes. In a May 20 editorial titled "Society and Law," Royster wrote that the decision was inevitable. "The justices have not so much made history as followed it."

He continued: "The philosophy of racial distinctions under the law could not have forever survived, in any event, because it does not comport with the majority view of the equity of government." But in deference to the concerns of Grimes and others, he wrote that it was wise of the court to defer implementation of its decision because it "does not comport either with the equity of government to require the people of a large region to tear down overnight the whole social structure which, though we are apt to forget it today, is rooted in ancient social necessity."

He wrote that for many southerners the concern over ending school segregation was not a matter of racial prejudice but rather "an honest conviction that their children will be injured in many areas by submergence in a culture that has not had time fully to mature... Laws and court decisions can give impetus to change when the pattern of society is changing, as it is now in the South and elsewhere. But laws and court decisions can avail little until the majority of people who must live under them are able to accept them." That went partway toward explaining what Royster meant by "ancient necessity," but only partway. The most likely explanation might be that Roy was being deliberately vague in an effort to cut his fellow southerners some slack.

The Royster editorial pleased almost nobody, and he was again assigned to handle the heavy flow of mail, most of it critical. But it was perceptive and prophetic. Many in the South did refuse to accept the ruling, and the federal government had to use force in some cases to gain access to formerly all-white schools for blacks. Freedom riders from the North were killed. Martin Luther King was martyred. But ultimately the rule of law prevailed, and many Americans today,

North and South, regard Brown as the greatest victory for equal protection and civil rights in the history of America.

Royster had written earlier affirming his belief in the democratic process. On March 17, 1950, he had attacked the idea that American politics lacks an adherence to principles. "The Civil War could have been avoided by a compromise which retained slavery in half this country (which is what Lincoln favored) and the upheavals of the late nineteenth century over free silver could have been prevented by a compromise with inflation. A clash on principle brewed one revolt and almost a second one. But would we have been a better, greater nation for such compromises? And is it true the people refused to face an issue of principle when it was set before them?

"Perhaps politics and principles don't mix. But the men who believe so don't seem to have much faith in the democracy they are busily defending."

Yet another event in 1954 would be of little moment for the country, but of enormous importance for the Journal. Henry Gemmill, in charge of the Journal's news side as managing editor, was a large, personable young man born in Toledo, Ohio, with the talent and desire to fulfill Barney's goal of making the Journal a more readable and interesting newspaper. He was as irreverent toward big business sacred cows as Grimes was of government pretensions.

What could be more interesting than the auto industry in a postwar era in which young families were buying houses and cars? The news from Detroit was that the auto companies were planning major redesigns of their 1955 models as GM, Ford and Chrysler competed for the dollars of an increasingly affluent public; disposable income had burgeoned by 70% in a decade. The American love affair with cars was resurgent after having gone unrequited during the war.

Gemmill and Page One editor Jack Bridge assigned Detroit bureau manager John Williams to do a story about what the new models would look like, supplying pictures if possible. This was in May, four months before the auto makers would unveil the 1955 models with their usual show business hoopla.

Gemmill, Bridge and Williams knew that the Detroit press, at the behest of the companies, had long observed a code of omertà about new models. It may sound strange to modern ears, but auto companies had significant influence with newspaper and magazine publishers back then because of their large ad budgets. Their self-serving argument was that if important model changes were heavily publicized, consumers would postpone their buying until the new models arrived. Dealer sales out of existing inventory would suffer. So new model information, pictures especially, were guarded like a military secret.

It was a dubious argument in that it assumed customers were so stupid that they weren't aware of the "planned obsolescence" game the auto companies had been playing for years. Dealers had for years been discounting current models as the advent of new models approached. Gemmill and his colleagues decided that the Journal would not be a part of this Detroit keep-them-in-the-dark game.

Johnny Williams was faced with a tough assignment, but he knew that auto companies always have spies checking out the future designs of their competitors, and he found what he wanted from one of the smaller companies, probably Studebaker, which operated out of South Bend, Indiana, not Detroit. No one will ever be sure of the source because Johnny held steadfastly to his pledge not to reveal it, even to his wife, Jerri.

On May 28, the Journal ran Johnny's front-page story. Necessarily, and in a departure from the long-standing Journal practice of offering nothing but gray type and charts, it included pictures. Readers got reasonably accurate images of the 1955 Dodge and Chevrolet sedans and an accurate sketch of the 1955 Ford.

General Motors was furious. The company and its affiliates withdrew advertising from the Journal worth $250,000 a year, a big sum for the Journal at that time. It shut off Journal access to its press releases and public relations flacks. It claimed that the Journal had stolen GM property.

GM no doubt expected an abject apology, which might have been forthcoming if a Detroit paper had committed such a sin. But Kilgore didn't cave. Rather he ordered his editors to intensify their coverage of General Motors, using the Journal's national network of skilled reporters. The Journal covered everything from the complaints against GM by the company's independent dealers to strikes in local plants. It cadged sales and production statistics from subscribers to trade journals like Ward's Automotive Reports.

The point Barney wanted to make was that a tough news organization didn't need press handouts to cover a major corporation. It was a replay of something prodigious reporters Eddie Jones and Charles Dow of the original Dow Jones team had proved over a half century earlier in their coverage of the rampant and secretive railroad moguls.

Grimes waded in with a response to the several letter writers who sided with GM. An editorial titled "A Newspaper and Its Readers" reminded the writers that they themselves presumably read the Journal to get news. "Would they wish us to print only the banking news approved by bankers, only steel news approved by steel officials, only the real estate news approved by real estate agents? If we followed that practice would they not soon wonder how much information was not being printed and begin to doubt the usefulness of this newspaper's service?

"The fact is that it would be of no use whatever. If our readers thought that every story in The Wall Street Journal was censored by the industry or the company which it is covering, they would not have confidence in it. Nor would the situation be any better if we ourselves undertook to censor the news by our ideas of what is 'good for business.'"

The editorial concluded that "when a newspaper begins to suppress news, whether at the behest of its advertisers or on pleas from special segments of business it will soon cease to be of any service either to its advertisers or to business, because it will cease to have readers."

That good sense didn't move some Detroit reporters angry at having their conformity with advertiser dictates exposed. At a meeting of the local chapter of Sigma Delta Chi, the professional journalism society that Kilgore had worked hard to promote, a motion to support The Wall Street Journal was voted down by a majority of the large number of members who turned out to join the issue. Johnny Williams was crushed by this betrayal by his fellow journalists. The Time magazine correspondent who led the opposition to the support motion was later rewarded with a job at GM. But he paid a price in the form of lost respect from many of his former colleagues and was not very highly regarded by his new associates at General Motors as he accepted his sinecure.

In the end, however, it was GM that caved, denying that it had attempted to influence Journal news policy. The matter was settled at a meeting in Detroit on July 7, 1954, between Barney and GM president Harlow H. Curtice, a crusty little man who had little use for journalists and was uncommunicative even at press parties hosted by the company. The Journal agreed to print an exchange of letters between the two.

I was a Journal reporter, having joined the staff in Chicago in March 1952 after a stint at the Muncie (Indiana) Press. Our little crew in Chicago glanced at the Curtice letter, which voiced his familiar complaint that our story had hurt GM sales. But it was Barney's letter that we seized on. We were not disappointed. He wrote that while the Journal certainly welcomed advertisers, its news columns were not for sale.

The effect on news staff morale was electric. We were working for an honest newspaper! Advertisers noted as well, and advertising manager Donald A. Macdonald would later observe, that the "response from our readers and advertisers and the public was magnificent! Our future was assured!" Indeed, it was. After that, the Journal's readership began a rapid climb that would make it the nation's largest-circulation newspaper and also the most trusted, according to many opinion surveys asking readers to list the publications they regarded as most reliable.

Its poor-mouthing notwithstanding, GM didn't suffer either from the Journal's advance disclosure. In 1955, production of Chevrolets surged far ahead of rival Ford to a record 1.7 million, a number that wasn't exceeded by anyone until 1962, when Chevy broke its own record with an output of over 2 million cars.

CHAPTER 6

Royster Counsels JFK

G rimes retired in 1958 after a heart attack, and Royster became editor. In March 1959, Roy discoursed on the Journal's philosophy in an interview with business writer John Brooks for an article in Harper's: "Basically we are for minimum government. We believe that the primary reason for government is to provide police power—to keep me from knocking you over the head. In foreign affairs, we don't think the United States can run the world, or even the Western world."

In his memoir, "My Own, My Country's Time," Royster wrote, "I think of myself as a radical, for there is much I would like to change in both society and politics. I have no desire to return to the nineteenth century romanticized as the pinnacle of an enlightened age. Yet I do believe our heritage from the past contains many values worth preserving as we approach the end of the 20th century."

Royster further revealed his personal philosophy in what he called a "Forewarning" rather than a foreword, to a 1967 collection of his writings titled "A Pride of Prejudices" (Alfred A. Knopf): "I have been called a 'conservative' and something referred to as a 'nineteenth century liberal.' Both labels are, I think, inaccurate. Anyway, if conservative means, as it often seems to nowadays an opposition to change for opposition's sake or a disposition to return the country to some imagined halcyon past, I beg to be excused. This is more an awareness that the past is as romanticized in history as youth is in memory than any want of awareness about the imbecilities of the present. My prejudice is that we might often better things by changing them.

"There is much to be said for the nineteenth century, but who, really, would want to take the world back to it? Besides the latter part of it marked a reversion among the intellectuals to the medieval philosophy of the all-wise king and his ministers who should manage all the people's affairs in proper fashion. That century's seminal thinkers, let us not forget, included the Fabian socialists and Karl Marx, all of whom were self-styled liberals....

"I am often pessimistic about the immediate future, waxing indignant sometimes when our long heritage is abused or past lessons ignored. Who can avoid pessimism, looking at the state of the world and the behavior of the people in it? About the long future, however, I am stubbornly optimistic. Although mankind does forget old lessons to its pain, just as young people do those of their fathers, it always relearns them. It is comforting to remember that the Dark Ages only lasted five hundred years."

That last line, with its amusing irony, was pure Royster.

The Journal editorial writers were not enthusiastic about Richard Nixon in the 1960 presidential election campaign, but they also had doubts about John F. Kennedy, even though both Royster and Joseph Evans, his chief editorial writer, knew and liked JFK from their prewar days in Washington. They were afraid that JFK was too much under the influence of neo-Keynesians like John Kenneth Galbraith and historian Arthur Schlesinger, Jr. Nixon at that point didn't seem to have neo-Keynesian deficit spending tendencies. That would come later after he, in 1968, actually won the prize he failed to get in 1960, the U.S. presidency.

On January 20, 1969, shortly before his inauguration as president, JFK invited Royster to lunch at the Carlyle Hotel in New York. The presidential floor of the hotel was so chaotic, Royster reported, that it only belatedly dawned that someone was supposed to order lunch. JFK scolded Royster for an editorial criticizing the president-elect's announcement that he would appoint his brother Robert as attorney general. But he also asked Royster to help him allay fears in the business community that he was fiscally irresponsible.

He also was worried about the situation in Indochina. He had hoped for a resolution of the crisis while his predecessor, Dwight D. Eisenhower, was still in office. Whatever decision was made on U.S. involvement or withdrawal would be unpleasant, he told Royster, and added, "I don't have the confidence of the people the way Eisenhower does."

And so it went, Royster wrote, "on Cuba, on the farm problem, on domestic economics, on the foreign balance of payments. He appeared to be a young man suddenly appalled at the complexities of the job he had won, and yet so engaging in his uncertainties as to stir instinctive sympathies."

The new president would certainly have welcomed Royster's sympathy as a series of crises beset him shortly after he took office. Sometimes he got it; sometimes he didn't. Certainly he didn't when he blundered into the Bay of Pigs crisis only three months into his presidency. Beginning before JFK took office, the CIA had been training a small army made up mostly of refugees from the Castro revolution, to invade Cuba and install a U.S.-friendly government. The invasion was badly managed. Castro knew it was coming and easily repelled it, capturing the survivors. The Journal was scathing in its criticism:

"With the apparent collapse of the Cuban invasion, the U.S. finds itself in a sorry mess. The only sure thing is that our troubles with Communist Cuba are not over. About the only hope is that we might learn something from the debacle and proceed accordingly.

"This country is reviled around the world for participating in an invasion in which it did not in fact participate and which all too plainly it did not control. But we suspect that the deeper feeling, especially in the capitals of international Communism, is one of astonishment at U.S. weakness—its failure to deal with this threat on its own doorstep.

"This reaction will compound our difficulties with the Communists everywhere. Meantime the Communists in Cuba emerge stronger than ever, harder for anyone to topple, better able to peddle their Red revolution elsewhere in Latin America."

How true that was. The Bay of Pigs fiasco persuaded the bumptious

Soviet dictator, Nikita Khrushchev, that the new American president was not only young but inexperienced and weak and thus could be counted on to give way when subjected to further tests.

The first test would come the following August when the Soviet-backed East Germans set about building a high, barbed wire–topped concrete wall sealing off the Soviet zone of Berlin from the British, French and American sectors. These zones, plus a similar partition of Germany itself, had been agreed to by FDR, Winston Churchill and Joseph Stalin at the 1944 "Big Three" conference in the Soviet Black Sea resort called Yalta. Or at least that seemed to be the deal. After FDR's death in April 1945, his successor, Harry Truman, seemed to have little knowledge of what deals FDR had made. But at any rate, the former capital of Germany, Berlin, was now deep within Soviet-controlled and -fortified borders of what came to be called East Germany with access from the West only through agreed-upon narrow corridors. And now, with the building of the wall, East Berlin would also be inaccessible, except under conditions tightly controlled by the Soviets.

This was in a sense an aggressive act, as there had been no agreement under the Yalta pact or any other negotiation that East Berlin could be fortified. But its true purpose was not aggression. Rather, the Communist regime in East Germany was concerned about the number of German workers fleeing to the West to gain jobs and opportunities not available in the moribund, party-directed, centrally planned economy that had been established, under Soviet compulsion, in the East. The wall wasn't direct aggression, but it was a case of Khrushchev thumbing his nose at the new American president and suggesting something more sinister: that Russia might at some point try to eject the Americans, British and French from Berlin altogether.

The Journal's commentary on the erection of the Berlin Wall included a long, thoughtful piece titled "Berlin: Background of a Crisis," written by John F. "Jack" Bridge, who had a short time earlier switched to the editorial page staff from his former job running the Journal's front page. Referring to the partition plan, originally designed by a committee headed by British Socialist Clement Attlee and agreed to at Yalta with very little debate or discussion, Bridge quoted something Harry Truman had written: "This shows conclusively that heads of state should be very careful about horseback agreements, because there is no way of foretelling the final result." Bridge thought that the statesmen of 1961 would do well to ponder that thought.

Berlin, with its small western enclave surrounded by Soviet-controlled territory, would remain a Soviet hostage throughout the Cold War. Its tenuous circumstances would play a role in the strategic calculations involved in the Cold War's most dangerous face-off, the Cuban Missile Crisis. Fidel Castro, after seizing control of the Cuban government in 1958, had sought Soviet protection, which the Soviets willingly but slyly provided. In 1962, word began to filter out of Cuba that the Soviets were installing launching sites for medium-range missiles capable of delivering nuclear warheads to a large number of U.S. cities. At first, it seemed to Khrushchev that he had been right, that the Americans were "too liberal" to block his daring gambit.

But as confirmation of what the Soviets were up to became clearer, JFK and his aides realized they had a major problem on their hands. Fear of the Soviet missiles was spreading across the United States. In a televised speech to the nation on October 22, 1962, JFK announced that he was "quarantining Cuba" and demanding that the Russians withdraw their missiles. That bold challenge alerted the nation that we might be on the verge of a nuclear war. It created a bull market in bomb shelters.

I was a rewrite man on the Page One desk when, on the morning of October 23, Royster ambled over to our area and asked in his North Carolina drawl, "Waal, are we all going to get blown up?" None of us clever wordsmiths had a flip answer for that question. We were too scared. The next day, the Journal had a long editorial, following up on the short vote of support Royster had given Kennedy on deadline the night before. It was reminiscent of the "we will do our duty" editorial Grimes had written after the Pearl Harbor attack in December 1941.

Royster wrote: "The President has now committed the nation to the proposition that we will not permit the Cuban island to be turned into a threat to the safety of our country and of the Western Hemisphere. On that proposition the whole nation is prepared to support the president at whatever risks, now or hereafter. There should be no mistake about that.

"It is precisely for this reason that it would be unfortunate to have the President's decision beclouded by doubts as to his judgment, suspicion as to his motives or uncertainty as to his resolution to carry through with the other decisions this decision may demand.

"Yet there is no denying that such clouds exist and that the President must work diligently to dispel them."

Having given the president support in this moment of extreme danger when the American navy was already stopping ships on the Atlantic to search for arms bound for Cuba and a shooting war with Russia might break out any time, Royster discussed the long delay that had occurred before the administration had brought the missile crisis to a head. He wrote that we could pass that over but for the fact that the naval blockade was not the end but the beginning of the hazards and its outcome was uncertain. We didn't know if the Russians would counter with some move on Berlin, for example.

"When any nation embarks upon a course so hazardous, it must have the trust not only in its destiny but in those who lead it...

"What the President has now done is, we believe, well done. But we have no illusions about what it entails. So in what comes hereafter he is going to need the full confidence of the country, and it is imperative that the country have full confidence in the President. Assuring that is a task in which he must not fail."

Whether Kennedy in the heat of a crisis read the Journal editorial is not known. He had become increasingly annoyed at Journal editorials as he passed into his second year in office, and he probably would not have liked the implication that he was slow to react to the missile crisis. But in the event, he did not fail. When Khrushchev realized that the United States was mobilizing its massive air and sea power in preparation for an attack, he backed down and agreed to pull the missiles out of Cuba in return for a U.S. guarantee that it would not invade Cuba short of a major provocation. The United States also agreed to pull some obsolescent missiles out of Turkey, a part of the deal not publicized at the time. As Secretary of State Dean Rusk put it: "We were eyeball to eyeball and someone blinked."

By the end of the month, Royster was able to write that the Cuban Missile Crisis seemed to be ending in a "significant victory for the U.S. and President Kennedy in particular." The editorial went on to say that when the United States was willing to deploy its power, it could put the enemy on the defensive and even on the run.

But there was a lesson for peace as well: "Some people around the world did a good deal of hand-wringing at the forceful American policy on Cuba and the Kremlin; anything, including surrender, it seemed to them, was preferable to the high risk of war. But the truth is that the Soviet missile installations were a threat to peace and only by our risking war could peace be preserved."

JFK had indeed won a major battle, but the Cold War was by no means over. And, there are some plausible interpretations of his assassination just over a year later that suggest that his success in embarrassing Fidel Castro and Nikita Khrushchev might have cost him his life. No one will ever know for sure what motivated the assassin Lee Harvey Oswald, but his Soviet and Cuban connections will always give credence to the theory that his death was a consequence of a Soviet desire to extract vengeance for its missile crisis defeat. The KGB was capable of any imaginable atrocity.

Both Royster and his second-in-command, associate editor Joseph E. Evans, had direct knowledge of the Communist world. Evans, after army service in World War II, had stayed on in Europe as a journalist, writing articles from Germany, France, Belgium, Holland, Italy, Czechoslovakia and Poland during that turbulent period when the Soviet Union was tightening its grip on Europe by helping the member parties of the Communist International (Comintern) to subvert existing government and seize control.

In February 1948, Communists took over the western-leaning government of Czechoslovakia. A prominent non-Communist Czech, Jan Masaryk, stayed on as foreign minister, but on March 10, 1948, Masaryk's dead body, clad in pajamas, was found in the courtyard of the foreign ministry underneath a window of a ministry bathroom. Many years later, in 2004, the Prague police finally concluded that what many people in the West had suspected at the time was true: that Masaryk had been defenestrated by KGB agents.

The foreign minister's murder was of importance to Joe Evans because he had met and fallen in love with a beautiful, redheaded young Czech army officer named Marie Petrachkova who was attached to the Czech diplomatic mission in the Soviet sector of East Berlin. She had been an aide to Masaryk. As it became clear that the Czech foreign service was falling under Soviet control, Joe helped her defect by smuggling her out of the Soviet zone into West Berlin. After her flight, the KGB twice broke into her apartment in the American sector to try to kidnap her. Luckily, she was not at home both times. Joe bought a gun and took her to live with him. She became his wife.

After his return to the states, Joe became Journal foreign editor and then Washington bureau chief of the Journal, before joining Royster on the editorial page. He would continue to make reporting trips abroad. A compilation of articles about a tour of Russia, titled "Through Soviet Windows," was published by Dow Jones in 1957.

As for Royster, he also had no illusions about Soviet treachery. In an essay about Stalin on October 6, 1949, Royster wrote: "It is not that all men who play with power—call it Communism or Statism or what you will—have bad intentions. What ends in tyranny may have begun with a vision. Nothing is so corrupting to a man as to believe it his duty to save mankind from men. He comes to evil because he must first usurp the rights of man and finally the prerogatives of God.

"So the evil that is Stalin is no enigma, whatever his personality be.

One may even surmise that his disciples are correct when they attribute to him the seeds of greatness; certainly a dream of remodeling the earth is a majestic dream. The monstrous error which condemns all such men is the fruit of one forbidden tree. Satan was an archangel who dreamed, too, of playing God."

Royster had made a tour of the Soviet Union in the summer of 1962, just before the Cuban Missile Crisis. In an August 22 essay in the Journal, he wrote that he had found Russia to have retained many of the characteristics of a feudal society. He reported that on his departure he was chatting with a newfound Russian friend: "My friend asked me with a smile if I was now convinced that in time the Soviet Union would catch up with the Western World.

"My Soviet friend was an intelligent and sensitive man whom I had come to like, and the temptation was to avoid hurt feelings and an angry rebuttal by speaking some vague politeness. Instead, I replied, as softly as I could: 'never in your lifetime or in mine.' The expected explosion didn't come. A shadow passed over his face, we shook hands silently and he left me. The next morning I got on the plane for Paris and never saw him again."

The Journal editorial page would have few illusions, then or ever, about the nature of the Russian empire, and has none today at a time when Russia again is ruled by yet another feudal czar.

The Journal gave JFK full backing during the missile crisis, but earlier in 1962 it had been more critical. In April, John F. and his brother Bobby, the attorney general, had reverted back to the command-economy practices that had done so much to destroy business confidence during the New Deal. U.S. Steel, after negotiating a labor contract, had raised prices 6%. JFK claimed the company had broken an agreement with the government to hold prices steady and demanded that the increases be withdrawn.

He asserted that "a tiny handful of steel executives whose pursuit of private power and profit exceeds their sense of public responsibility" had shown "utter contempt for the interests of 185 million Americans."

An April 13 Journal editorial titled "Business in the Doghouse" said that obviously this portrayal of business "is considered the way to put oneself on the side of the angels, just as it was 30 years ago."

But the Journal argued that times had changed since the New Deal. "The market economy has proved itself a vast cornucopia for the people. It has brought about a vast improvement in working conditions. Instead of tycoons owning companies, we have today salaried managers of publicly-owned corporations, and everyone knows their contributions to the local communities and the national culture.

"The owners alone number many millions today. The number of people who own U.S. Steel is far greater than the number of people who work for U.S. Steel. And both the owners and workers throughout the nation have a better understanding than they used to have of the role of free enterprise in a free society.

"Perhaps, in the supercharged air of the moment, many Americans agree with the President's denunciation of business. But on further reflection, it is possible that they might find distasteful a rabid new Government onslaught on the free economy."

JFK won his fight with steel, but at the cost of alienating business, just as the Journal suggested. He himself seems to have decided that demagoguing business wasn't quite the winning formula it had been 30 years earlier. But that didn't mean it wouldn't be tried many times again by the Progressive wing of his party, particularly in periods of recession when both the government and the people wanted someone to blame.

Evidence of a change of heart came on January 24, 1963, when Kennedy announced a major tax reform with significant benefits for business. It cut the high income tax rates for middle- and high-income families. Said the president: "This will restore an idea that has helped make our country great—that a person who devotes his efforts to increasing his income and wealth, should be able to retain a reasonable share of the results." Thus, the reform would cut the corporate tax rate to 47% from 52%, and owners of small businesses would get a rate reduction of 27% on the first $25,000 of net income (the equivalent of $193,000 in 2015).

The tax program had no doubt been vetted by the president's chief economic adviser, University of Minnesota economist Walter Heller, and Treasury secretary C. Douglas Dillon, former head of the Wall Street security house, Dillon, Reed & Co. Years later it would be cited by Wall Street Journal editorial writers as proof that it was a Democrat, not a Republican, who in the modern era had initiated a supply-side tax reform of the sort the Journal was promoting.

But in 1963, Royster's men were more cautious. They liked the tax reform, but they didn't like the overall fiscal 1964 budget because the tax rate cuts were combined with large spending increases. The editorial writers were concerned that the administration was planning to run the highest peacetime budget deficit in American history. An editorial titled "Leeches to Cure Anemia" challenged Professor Heller's Keynesian contention that deficit spending was now "the main stream of economics." It was also once thought, said the editorial, that it was possible to cure "every human ill from gout to pernicious anemia by bleeding the patient. The few who questioned the practice of leeching met this crushing retort that they were challenging the main stream of informed medical opinion. And so they were."

How wonderful it would be, said the Journal, if all that was required for prosperity and growth was for the government just to increase the money supply and spend it—but can that be true?

"Is it true that chronic deficits are harmless?" Does a nation solve the problem of a large trade deficit, a steady loss of its gold reserves, a heavy defense burden and a public debt larger than the world has ever seen "by printing more money to spend abroad as well as at home, making its public debt even larger and giving our creditors more reason to trust the value of our gold than the value of our dollars?"

The Journal would weigh in again after Secretary Dillon outlined details of the tax plan. A February 7 editorial remarked that the administration seemed to be working at cross-purposes. It praised the president for saying that the burden of taxation was one of the heaviest weights on the economy and that government should hold down nondefense spending, reduce government employment and aim toward a balanced budget.

"Yet when the promised tax program is presented to Congress it turns out to propose taking a million people off the tax rolls entirely, to keep corporate tax rates 'temporarily' higher... increases the steepness with which taxes rise with income, and to deliver new blows to the accumulations of capital by putting double taxes on estates and soaking pension funds with stiffer tax treatment... all too often some sound beginnings have been made to good policies only to be annulled by what comes after. And it is hard to see how such star-crossed purposes can, in the end, serve any purpose at all."

The Kennedy budget, complete with tax reform, would be enacted after his death, and it did seem for a time that what Professor Heller chose to call the "new economics" (in fact, the old 1930s economics of Maynard Keynes) did seem to be working, most likely because of what survived of the cuts in high marginal income tax rates did stimulate investment. U.S. real Gross Domestic Product (GDP) grew 25% from 1964 to 1969, and it looked as if Professor Heller had discovered a magic elixir. But then things started going badly wrong, as the Journal's editorial had suggested they would eventually. More about that later.

Race was still a big issue when JFK assumed the presidency in 1961, despite the gradualism that Royster had recommended after the Brown v. Supreme Court desegregation order. On September 30, 1962, a riot broke out in Oxford, Mississippi, when James H. Meredith, backed by a federal court order, endeavored to became the first black to be admitted to the University of Mississippi. A mob resisted the federal marshals who escorted him onto the campus. Two men were killed before federal troops put down the riot and forced Mississippi's governor and the university to obey the court order.

The mob had been shouting "Never, No Never." Royster wrote: "Neither the courts nor presidents have tried to replace evolution with revolution. But there can be neither patience nor understanding when a mob arises to say to other men that their future is only hopelessness. For any man to say this to another man is immoral. For an institution of government to elevate it to a policy of state is something that good men cannot tolerate. And the true lesson of Mississippi, whatever the constitutional lawyers may say, is that they will not."

Scenes like the one in Oxford, broadcast live on network television, and powerful editorials of the type penned by southerner Vermont Royster and some other brave southerners like syndicated columnist Ralph McGill, who also was editor and publisher of the Atlanta Constitution, and Hodding Carter II of the Greenville (Mississippi) Delta Democrat-Times would turn national opinion against the tenacious segregationist "culture" that Roy had referred to in his 1954 editorial about Brown v. Board of Education. Southern elites began to see such scenes as the one at Oxford as a frightening display of a redneck reaction that was foreign to them and thus began to swing to the side of the courts and the federal government. In a few more years, official racial segregation would become a thing of the past.

But, of course, President Kennedy would not see that day. He was assassinated on October 22, 1963, by Oswald, an ex-marine who had had suspicious associations with the Soviet Union and Cuba. Royster, in an editorial that appeared the Monday after the Friday shooting—the Journal had no Saturday edition at the time—acknowledged the Journal's policy differences with the president, but wrote that "all who knew him even slightly, as we did, could sense his statesmanship and see what an engaging and thoughtful man he was."

Clearly, Royster was concerned that there might be an eruption of violence or demands for vengeance in response to the killing. Because of the racial tensions of the times and the fact that the president had been murdered in Dallas, many people initially feared that he had been victim of a "red neck" plot. Those suspicions were mostly dispelled—although some would linger for decades—after Oswald was caught, himself assassinated by Jack Ruby, and his identity and background became public knowledge. But initially, conspiracy theories ran riot.

Royster wrote that Kennedy's sense of history "would have told him that all such murders were the work of individual hysteria, just as was the murder of the assassin...So, we believe, he would not have made the occasion of his own tragic death the opportunity for a new witch hunt of either the left or the right without ascertaining the facts. He would not have been so quick as some politicians and commentators to jump to conclusions. All the more shame on those who were so ready to attribute his assassination to some organized diabolical plot of the so-called radical right."

Below the Kennedy editorial, the Journal had kind and hopeful words to say about the new president, Lyndon B. Johnson (LBJ). It pointed to his successful 30-year career in politics and his importance on the 1960 Democratic ticket in eking out a narrow victory—one-tenth of a percentage point in the popular vote—over Richard Nixon and his running mate, former Massachusetts senator Henry Cabot Lodge, Jr. As Senate majority leader, LBJ had been famous for his ability to negotiate legislative compromises between the two parties.

Wrote Royster: "We are, right now, a nation almost equally divided on many great issues. We made our choice at the last election only by a hair's breadth, and it was from this division among the people, deep and sincere, that grew many of President Kennedy's great difficulties. That the nation is now one in sorrow and outrage does not alter the fact that, as a nation, we are still undecided about the shape of our national society and about the means of molding it.

"To confront this kind of task, now made even more difficult by the shock of assassination and the consequent political disruption, it would be hard to imagine a man of more suitable qualities." Those Johnson qualities included, so Royster wrote, the common sense to "distinguish between the important and the less important, and the realization from his lifetime of political experience that where the people are divided there is wisdom in the way of reconciliation."

The third editorial that day remarked on the remarkable ability of an American system of a rule of law that in a crisis could effect a quick and orderly transfer of power from a fallen president to his successor.

Having given LBJ a kind and thoughtful welcome, the Journal soon reverted to its traditional role as a critic of Democratic Party policies. Royster was prophetic in a March 1964 column expressing skepticism about LBJ's War on Poverty, suggesting that it would lead to inflation, which it did.

"What will sooner make poorer those handicapped in life than a still further cheapening of those dollars? What more cruel to those who must live on social security, a pension, an insurance policy or a lifetime's savings?

"Still, we find this poverty program utterly fascinating. First time we ever heard of a party running for re-election by running down what it's done for the country and telling the folk they never had it so bad."

But however strange that may have sounded, LBJ would win a resounding victory over the Republican candidate, Arizona senator Barry Goldwater, in the 1964 presidential race. The victory could be attributed partly to an economy that was humming along nicely, to sympathy for a president who was thrust into terrible responsibilities at the speed of a fatal bullet and to his ability to restore confidence that the government was fully functional after such a shocking event.

The Journal referred to the Goldwater defeat, which also took down some able Republican lawmakers, as a debacle. It was highly critical of the Goldwater campaign, saying that he came across not as a conservative but as a radical. It argued that an essential characteristic of a properly understood conservatism is not to rush into change for change's sake, "and this includes a reluctance to quickly change long-established institutions. Especially if it includes a reluctance to remove or drastically alter them until better alternatives are thought out." The writer apparently was referring to those institutions of the New Deal that had survived either Supreme Court or legislative demolition. Most prominent among those surviving laws were those that provided governmental safety nets for the poor or indigent.

In a separate Thinking Things Over column, Royster wrote that perhaps Goldwater's greatest error was a misunderstanding of the nature of the uneasiness felt by many Americans. "These people, in number yet unknown, are made uneasy by a Government ceaselessly growing bigger and more powerful, by doubts that relentless depreciation of money is the magic potion of prosperity, that the good society is built on dubious public morals, or that a nation's safety lies in the eager wooing of its enemies."

Royster cited opinion data from the Harris Poll, which at that time was the Democratic Party's favorite sampler, showing that half of the electorate agreed with Goldwater that there was too much corruption in government, and 60% agreed about the demoralizing effect of some of the government's welfare and relief programs. "Finally, there is a deep significance in the revealing statistic that six out of every ten voters agreed with the central thesis of Mr. Goldwater's philosophy—namely, that the power of the Federal Government should be trimmed."

Those numbers gave some support to the Journal editorial's insistence that there was a widespread concern in the country about the increase in governmental centralization and the federal assumption of power. It argued that the electorate might have responded favorably and perhaps decisively to a campaign that hadn't promised a "semi-revolution but simply a halt to the Governmental power trend and an intelligent re-examination, in an atmosphere of calm and deliberation, of the structure and uses of Government in our time. But such was not the choice they were being given by Senator Goldwater."

There may have been some wishful thinking in that paragraph, but in a mere four years LBJ would be out, and the voters would elect as president a Republican, Richard Nixon.

A hint of the problem that would bring down LBJ could be found in a postelection piece on foreign policies by the Journal's diplomatic correspondent in Washington, Philip Geyelin. To wit: "Almost all the President's counselors agree the struggles in South Vietnam cannot be allowed to drift on in deadly deterioration indefinitely; with a new government in Saigon [U.S. operatives had helped bring down the old one] the President will now be urged to press a stepped-up military effort, including over-the-border reprisals against North Vietnam. The betting is he will give a cautious go-ahead—and thus accept a risk of 'escalating' the little war into something bigger." The speculation about the president's likely course was right on both counts.

At the luncheon at the Carlyle just before his inauguration, JFK told Royster that he would soon have to make some difficult decisions about Vietnam. The decision he made was for more U.S. involvement. As part of the long-standing U.S. policy of containing Soviet expansionism, the United States was already supplying financial aid to the government of South Vietnam to help them fight Viet Cong guerrillas, backed by North Vietnam, which was in turn backed by the Soviet Union, under Nikita Khrushchev's pledge to support "wars of national liberation." JFK in his inauguration speech in January 1961 had reaffirmed U.S. resistance to the Soviet expansionism with his stirring words, "we shall pay any price, bear any burden, meet any hardship, support any friend, oppose any foe to assure the survival and success of liberty."

Having made that commitment, in May 1961, JFK decided to send 400 Green Beret military advisers to train the South Vietnamese army in counterinsurgency warfare. By October, the number of advisers had expanded to 12,000. The Journal was critical of this tactic. An editorial observed that the war was nonetheless going badly for the South, but wondered whether sending advisers was a practical military approach.

"Nobody wants a full commitment of U.S. fighting men, but to win a stalemate in Korea, the U.S. did have to fight along with the South Koreans and the U.S. was in charge. Elsewhere we have deterred Communist aggression with the implicit threat of nuclear retaliation. The

Vietnam business by contrast looks like a military mishmash...Perhaps we should all realize that there are certain things that the U.S., for all its military power, cannot do. One is to reshape the nature of peoples' radical values."

The Kennedy administration didn't heed that advice, becoming more and more enmeshed in the Vietnam War. In the fall of 1963, the United States, through the CIA, gave a go-ahead signal to generals plotting the assassination of South Vietnam president Ngo Dinh Diem, by assuring them that the United States would not interfere and aid would continue after such an event. Diem was assassinated on November 2, just 20 days before JFK himself would be murdered. Some historians, looking back, cite the Diem assassination as the day the United States took ownership of the Vietnam War. At the time LBJ took over as president, promising not to lose Vietnam, there were 16,300 American advisers in South Vietnam, and the government there was getting $500 million in annual U.S. aid.

The Journal voiced its continued skepticism about the American Southeast Asia policy after the Diem coup. An editorial on November 4 reminded readers and the administration in Washington that the United States normally deplores military coups in defiance of a solemn constitution when they occur in Latin America. "Moreover, the U.S. Government was heavily involved in it, whether it engineered the overthrow or not. At a minimum, the U.S. Government used its pressures to encourage an uprising."

The only hopeful thing the Journal could find in this was that it might end domestic quarreling in South Vietnam and allow the country to get on with the main business of fighting a war. But, "what is less edifying is the drift which we have permitted for years in Southeast Asia. We gave up in Laos, which is understandable in the circumstances, but the U.S. Government didn't have to try to fool the people by calling it a sound settlement.

"In Vietnam the U.S. couldn't seem to figure out what it was doing. It is at least conceivable that a more adept diplomacy, plus the same kinds of pressures used in the present instance, could have softened the Vietnamese political troubles and hence averted the coup. ...

"We profoundly hope the Vietnam coup will turn out to be a victory for the Vietnamese people and the struggle against Communism. It is difficult to see it as a manifestation of far-sighted American foreign policy."

That was the situation in Southeast Asia that LBJ inherited when the necessity to make world-shaking decisions was suddenly thrust upon him. And with his landslide election in his own right in 1964 and a compliant Democratic Congress, he would have a mostly free hand to follow his own best judgment in how to proceed further. Unfortunately, things would only get worse as he escalated America's involvement in the war.

The Soviets, quietly fueling the conflict with their material support of North Vietnamese Communist leader Ho Chi Minh, would use their highly effective international propaganda apparatus to vilify the United States for its involvement, an offensive that would gradually turn Americans and their allies against the war and play no small part in the ultimate U.S. defeat.

On a reporting trip to the Soviet Union as a Journal foreign correspondent in April 1967, I found that my KGB minders were practically chortling at how well things were going for their side in Vietnam. On a conducted tour of Moscow's Palace of Young Pioneers, where youngsters were indoctrinated in collectivist doctrine, I was subjected to a lecture from a bright, pretty 12-year-old girl about the evil things my country was doing in Vietnam. I tried to explain to her that in wars lots of bad things happen, but the script that had been prepared for her left no doubt that it was America that started the war, not Soviet imperialism. I marveled at the chutzpah of the Soviets in employing this innocent child as a spokesperson for a corrupt regime.

The other war that LBJ chose to escalate was what he called his "War on Poverty," announced in his State of the Union address in 1964, just after he had assumed the presidency. The address energized his

Democratic Party base and no doubt convinced a lot of independent voters as well that this hard-nosed master politician from Texas had a soft spot for the poor and elderly. It probably played a role in winning him his big victory in November of that year.

But fighting two wars at the same time, each with escalating costs, is expensive. Johnson had remarked when he assumed office at what a marvelously powerful country the United States had become. But that was at the height of the business cycle in the early 1960s. With the benefit of hindsight, it seems that Johnson totally overestimated how much of an income transfer burden this marvelous economy could sustain. The Greeks would have called it "hubris," an attitude of excessive self-confidence that has brought down many a great man.

Federal outlays from fiscal year 1965 to fiscal year 1970 rose 65%, to $195.6 billion from $118.2 billion, or an average of 13% a year. When the business cycle turned down in the late 1960s, the government began running large deficits. In fiscal year 1968, the government had to finance 14% of its budget, and that had consequences for the dollar and the health of the global economy, just as Royster had predicted it would in 1964. It was in the late 1960s that the dollar-based Bretton Woods international monetary system began to break down because of the weakened dollar.

The 1964 election had installed a solidly Democratic administration and Congress that presumed a mandate from the voters to bring into being large visions. LBJ was determined not to lose Vietnam while at the same time not to lose this opportunity to build what he called "The Great Society," or, in less grandiose terms, a major expansion of the welfare state. The building blocks of that society would be federal aid to supplement the traditional state support of public schools, an expansive program of public housing, federal health insurance for the elderly, called "Medicare," and medical insurance for the poor, Medicaid—all of them expensive.

The program that would have the greatest potential for budget busting was Medicare, which has become increasingly unsound actuarially over the years as greater longevity has greatly expanded the elderly population, and the high demand generated through insurance programs like Medicare and Medicaid has ballooned the cost of medical care. To make matters worse, the Obama administration further extended subsidized medical insurance with the Affordable Care Act (ACA) of 2010, committing the government to even greater budgetary outlays.

In an editorial titled "An Unhealthy Climate" on April 27, 1965, the Journal acknowledged that Medicare would surely be enacted within a few months. It cited the alacrity as remarkable given the experience of other nations with nationalized health care. Yet it acknowledged that Congress wasn't going as far as Britain's socialists had gone with the all-encompassing National Health Service, which was at the time in a state of crisis with the availability of care deteriorating and doctors threatening to quit over low pay.

The Journal wrote that American doctors were not so much concerned with an abstraction called "socialized medicine." But they were concerned with the prospect that, once Medicare was under way, "the Government will assume increasing control of more and more aspects of health services...

"Whatever anyone calls that kind of setup, it unquestionably brings in its train practical problems of grave import—problems of excessive and possibly insupportable cost, unwieldy administration, deteriorating services and discouragement of entrants into the medical field."

The Journal's fears were unduly pessimistic because the government's difficulty swallowing the big bite of the health insurance industry it took in 1965 would postpone anything resembling the British National Health for decades, and even ObamaCare didn't extend to an attempt at total federal management of the health care system, even though that may have been the long-range plan of its designers. When the dismal results of what Washington did run directly, Veterans Administration (VA) hospitals, became evident in 2014, it dampened any public enthusiasm that might have existed for health care totally under government control, known as a "single payer" system. The discovery of the VA's mismanagement and long waiting lists for veterans seeking care vindicated Journal cautions against nationalizing medical care.

The Journal on July 27, 1965, had a thoughtful editorial on a broader issue that gave rise to the 21st-century tea party movement and was still very much an issue as the 2016 elections approached. Its title was "The Cult of Coercion," and it was a riff on a line in a book titled "The U.S. Economy" by the noted business author and editor John Davenport: "Government by its very nature is coercive." This observation was so self-evident, wrote the editorialist, "that it is all the more remarkable to find free Americans permitting a steady accretion of coercion."

To be sure, "there must be Governmental institutions for the sake of order and the protection of the society as a whole. Order, in turn, means force and the power to compel: The power to put a man in the armed forces for a prescribed period, to take his substance in taxes, to imprison him if he violates the Government's laws and, in our time, much else besides.

"The reconciliation of freedom and order was the paramount concern of the men who created the American political framework, and what they devised is the nearest thing to perfection in political history. Precisely because they understood that government must be coercive, they set about to keep the Government limited and disperse its powers."

But alas, for every benefit government grants, there must be coercion. Medicare means that all who work must pay for the benefits to a particular group. Innumerable subsidies to agriculture and industry must come out of the taxpayer's pocket. Grants to educational institutions come with federal oversight.

"We grant that it is difficult to fashion an effective brake on the trend. We further grant that, thanks again to the intelligence of the original framework, our nation is still far freer than many others. Such solace is diminished, however, by the realization that liberties need not be lost overnight; if they go gradually, they are as surely lost.

"Unfortunately a continuing loss is more likely when both politicians and ordinary people so often seem confused or disingenuous about the inherent nature of government."

The Journal was concerned not only with the present costs of the Great Society but the future costs as well. "How many billions will Medicare, for example, be costing five or 10 years hence? The tab for the new housing and urban legislation is estimated at some $8 billion for four years. If history is any guide, the chances are excellent that long before that it will be much higher. Each new departure—like rent subsidies—sets a precedent for fresh raids on the Treasury."

What worried the Journal was the likelihood that overspending would generate inflation and weaken the dollar's international standing, a fear that proved to be prophetic. In a May 11, 1965, Thinking Things Over column titled "Cassandra's Credentials," Royster cited the concerns of the respected French economic commentator, Jacques Rueff, about the effects of U.S. fiscal and monetary policy on the Bretton Woods international monetary system, which was anchored by a U.S. dollar backed by gold at a fixed price of $35 an ounce. Royster quoted Rueff as fearing that, with U.S. debts piling up and the dollar's value weakening, other central banks would ultimately demand gold, rather than dollars, in settlement of debts. That would force an embargo on gold, a declaration of bankruptcy for the U.S. dollar and an economic debacle.

Rueff was exactly correct, although it took some time. Six years later, President Richard Nixon would be forced to abandon the dollar's gold backing or, as some put it, "close the gold window," thereby scuttling the Bretton Woods monetary system. All currencies, including the dollar, would become fiat currencies backed only by government promises. The inflation the Journal had feared for so long would not be long in coming thereafter.

The other big issue of the 1960s was, of course, the war in Vietnam. President Johnson, in keeping with his promise not to "lose" Vietnam, was steadily expanding U.S. involvement with bombing raids on the

North and a buildup of combat troops to help the South Vietnamese defeat Viet Cong guerrillas. By the end of the year 1965, the United States would have almost 185,000 troops in Vietnam.

With this commitment having overridden the Journal's earlier reservations, the newspaper softened its objections, as it had done in previous wars once the battle was engaged. Its editorials became more reflective about the practical problems of the Truman Doctrine of containing Communist expansion, particularly as they related to Asia as opposed to the largely successful application of the doctrine in Europe.

Meeting the Communist thrusts in Greece and Berlin had yielded marked success. "But with the real war in Korea, our purposes collapsed into sorry confusion." Here, the Journal was no doubt referring to the failure of Truman and his secretary of state Dean Acheson to draw a bright line making it clear to the Communists that the United States would defend South Korea in the event of an attack. In the case of Vietnam, the Journal thought that LBJ had been "commendably explicit about the basic political objectives which justify our commitment." Consistent with the long-standing containment policy, they were aimed at "deterring aggression by blunting an aggressor's thrusts and by convincing friend and foe we will continue to do so."

"Unfortunately, this clear basic purpose does not automatically translate itself into specific war aims necessary for analysis and planning. Particularly, even the clearest statement of ultimate political goals is little help in deciding how much military force is required. Someone must first specify the military goals required to secure the political ones." The editorial ended with: "the history of American wars rings with a warning: When we send our troops to fight, much of their sacrifice may be in vain unless our leaders have a clear idea of what, exactly, we are fighting to accomplish."

As it turned out, the North Vietnamese would be a particularly tenacious foe. A reporting trip for a front-page piece on the fumbling Soviet effort to attract tourist dollars took me to Tashkent in Soviet central Asia in April 1967. My Russian handlers, no doubt with mischief aforethought, one night seated me in the hotel dining room with two English-speaking North Vietnamese editors from Hanoi. Compatriots of these wiry little men were trying to kill Americans, and Americans were trying to kill their fellow Vietnamese and maybe even them if they were unlucky enough to be near a bomb blast when they returned home.

Instead of exchanging fire, we were only exchanging words, although not in a particularly friendly fashion. I told them that a major power like the United States could not afford to lose a war to a small country like Vietnam. Their answer, delivered with some bitterness, was, "We'll never give up." They were right. Despite terrible punishment from the U.S. military, the Vietnamese Communists didn't give up. We did, and South Vietnam was delivered into their hands.

I had reckoned without the rising antiwar mood in the United States, fueled in part by Soviet propaganda. Although bona fide college students were exempted from the wartime draft by decree of Congress, student protests against the war were already beginning in 1965. A Journal editorial on October 27 of that year was titled "On Throwing Tantrums." It began with the words, "Even after all the discounting is duly done, the current rash of youthful demonstrations against the Vietnam war must puzzle the mind and conscience of thoughtful men. Is it a case of young people failing society or the other way around? Or some of both?"

The editorial conceded "that this is a peculiarly messy, disagreeable war, despite its broad objective of containing communism." But the writer thought that the "contemporary liberal philosophy which has dominated the intellectual fashion of a generation" had contributed to the rise of protests. It deplored the evidence that a variety of "free speech" that "is devoid of intellectual content, invites no debate, tolerates no rebuttal, trades on emotion, bases its appeal on sheer numbers of demonstrators and beckons to exploitation—has become so accepted it is employed by dissatisfied groups of every description."

Maybe so. But those "tantrums," as the Journal called them, would play a significant role in bringing about the eventual U.S. withdrawal from the war. Even the Journal editorial page would acquiesce in that decision. As early as 1965, the Journal was acknowledging that protests are an expected accompaniment of war. On October 25, 1965, Royster wrote: "Almost every war we have ever got in has brought them forth. Even the idealism of the original revolution wasn't unmarred by protesting riots; neither was Mr. Madison's war with England or the Civil War among ourselves."

CHAPTER 7

Forecasting a Vietnam Defeat

On February 8, 1966, Royster was clearly having doubts about the conduct of the war in Vietnam. After a visit to Michigan State, he wrote: "Quickly you discover it's not the fear of fighting that discourages the young or the old. It's the thought of fighting for an uncertain purpose and with no prospect of a victory to end it. Suppose we did beat the Vietcong, so the question runs, what then? A man who fought in the jungles of Guadalcanal and thought he knew why, asks if his son dies in the jungle of Vietnam for what purpose will he have died?"

On May 24, 1966, Royster felt it necessary to counter arguments that the press coverage of the war was partly to blame for the antiwar protests: "A journalist owes nothing to those who govern his country. He owes everything to his country. This is as true, when you think about it, in war as it is in peace, and it applies as much to the frontline correspondent as to the editorial writer pondering the policy of nations in his littered sanctum. The difference is that in peacetime there is rarely any difficulty, either for the reporter who writes or for the reader who reads, in deciding when the interests of the authorities and the interests of the nation collide. Most of the time they are the same, but in peacetime the journalist need never hesitate to write something that may injure the one if it serves the other.

"In war it is not always so simple, as both editors and readers are rediscovering now that the nation is once more engaged in fighting on a distant battlefield and when—once more—the news sometimes deals with battlefield reverses, planning mistakes and logistical snafus. All of these things, one way or another, have lately been in the news about Vietnam."

He concluded: "Every reader, if he will pause to reflect, will recognize that a newspaper serves illy when it keeps silence about the bunglings of generals or the ineptness of other officials, even if that may include the President. The reporter or editor who does so out of kindness to the individuals concerned, or out of some mistaken idea of 'responsibility' to the government, is not merely being cruel to those risking the hazards of battle. He is being irresponsible to his country's cause."

The Truman Doctrine that set about to contain Soviet expansionism and was central to the Cold War was broadly approved in principle by Americans. But it was the specifics, such as whether to fight wars against Communism on the Asian mainland, that was proving to be the divisive issue in American politics of the mid-1960s. A Journal editorial on May 25, 1965, titled "Policeman of the World" explored that question, which happens to be as heavily debated today with our latest wars as it was then. The Journal thought that, while there was abundant reason for disquiet about this seemingly new role, the dangers of an alternative course also have to be faced.

It was clearly the Soviet objective to try to foment Marxist revolutions in underdeveloped areas of the world. In trying to combat these efforts under the Truman Doctrine, "Will the U.S., as has been facetiously suggested, run out of Marines? Will it, like the Roman Empire, become so overextended it helps bring about its own downfall?"

These were good questions, the editorial conceded, and it allowed that it would take a great deal of restraint and intelligence to "continue opposing Communist aggrandizement and somehow avoid getting sucked into little wars all over." Yet the picture was not as bad as it might look. Communist insurgencies were not succeeding in some countries, such as Brazil, even without U.S. help. And America had the advantage of being able to pick its spots and then inflicting sufficient damage on the Communists to possibly cause them to "tire of their gruesome game."

The editorial concluded: "We can neither police the entire world nor abandon all responsibility in it, for in the end that means abandoning responsibility for our own institutions and interests. To find the dividing line between dangerous overextension and necessary action will be the key to policy and the measure of its wisdom."

The Middle East was an arena of conflict in 1967 as it has been pretty much ever since. The Soviets were involved there as well, backing an Egyptian strongman, Gamal Abdel Nasser, who was trying to divert attention from a failing economy by making aggressive moves toward Israel. On June 5, the Israelis launched a preemptive strike, an air attack that wiped out most of Nasser's air force on the ground. The Six-Day War was on.

In my then role as a Journal foreign correspondent, I had been to Israel a short time before and had sensed the tension. But when the attack came, I was in London. I caught an El Al flight out of Heathrow for Israel. The DC-8 was piloted by El Al senior executives because all their young pilots were fighting the war. The flight was unusual because in place of several seats, it was carrying a shrouded jet engine, presumably from Rolls-Royce, to replace the damaged power plant of one of its fighters. The passengers were mostly reporters, although there was one teenaged American Jew who was going to join the Israeli Defense Forces. We landed at what was then Lod Airport in a blackout, and everyone cheered when the middle-aged El Al executives brought us in safely. Before leaving London, well aware of the complications of Israeli censorship, I had filed a front-page piece quoting predictions of military specialists at Jane's Intelligence Review in London that Israel would try to make it a short war because of its enormous inferiority in numbers against the nations it was fighting: Egypt, Syria, Jordan and, nominally, Iraq. That certainly proved to be the case; the war was half over by the time I got there. I was soon busying myself reporting on its aftermath, asking some Israeli soldiers if they planned to return the Arab land they had captured. Their unsurprising answer: "No way!"

The Journal editorial at the outset of the war carried the exasperated title: "The Madness Breaks Out." It noted that since the creation of Israel by the United Nations in 1948, a birth marked with an Arab attack that tried but failed to kill the new state in its cradle, the United States had tried to straddle the gulf between the two sides. It faulted the United States for trying to prop up Nasser with economic aid and getting only insults in return, not to mention the dictator's turn toward the Soviets for military aid. Since the editorialists had no way of knowing how things would turn out, they raised the real questions of whether the Soviets would intervene and whether the United States would get sucked into a larger conflict at a time when it was heavily occupied in Vietnam.

The editorial concluded: "It is saddening that at this stage in human history certain states refuse to recognize the right of another to exist, especially when the Israelis have given numerous indications that they would, if permitted, cooperate with their Arab neighbors in building a better life for the whole area." The Middle East remains a cauldron today, although in different ways from 1967. With the added dimension of a hostile Iran's quest for a nuclear weapon, and Jihadist Arab warriors practicing seldom-paralleled acts of brutality, the new ways are no more endearing.

Another event in 1967 saddened Journal employees. Dow Jones CEO Barney Kilgore, who had engineered the remarkable success of the newspaper we were working for, died at the age of 59. A Journal editorial called his a "Horatio Alger story," reminding us that he was born in little Albany, Indiana; was a Washington columnist for the Journal at age 24; bureau chief at age 26; and Journal managing editor at age 32. By age 37, he was Dow Jones president and well on his way toward building Journal circulation to more than 1 million copies printed in eight plants around the nation, from a circulation of 33,000 just before he became managing editor.

The Journal editorialist, Royster no doubt, wrote that no one had ever seen Barney lose his temper or engage in flamboyant gestures. Despite his gift for self-containment, "there was a demon in him about what he wanted to create; his pride in his newspaper was as great as that of a composer for his symphony, and so was his jealousy for it . . . his friends can only tell you that he had a touch of genius and was to a full measure a gentleman. Such men are rare."

The Journal's skepticism about the Vietnam War deepened as the troubled world entered the year 1968 and antiwar protests became more intense and widespread. An editorial on February 23, 1968, titled "The Logic of the Battlefield" was controversial at the time and is debated even today among military historians and even members of the Journal editorial board.

It began thusly: "We think the American people should be getting ready to accept, if they haven't already, the prospect that the whole Vietnam effort may be doomed." It argued that the South Vietnam government we were supporting seemed increasingly hapless, whereas North Vietnam, adequately supplied with manpower and a large supply of Soviet and Chinese weapons, seemed prepared to carry on the war indefinitely.

The writer, Royster's deputy Joe Evans, thought our current military tactics were "sad to see." He wrote of "the wholesale destruction of towns and cities in order to 'save' them, killing or making homeless refugees out of thousands more civilians...Hence the question: Are developments on the ground making a hash of our original, commendable objectives?"

Joe acknowledged that losing in Vietnam would be "a stunning blow to the U.S. and to the West in the larger struggle with international communism." At home "it will be a traumatic experience to have lost a war in which thousands of Americans died in vain."

He concluded with: "Conceivably all this is wrong; conceivably the Communists are on the brink of defeat and genuine peace talks are about to begin. It doesn't look that way, and as long as it doesn't everyone had better be prepared for the bitter taste of defeat beyond American power to prevent."

The editorial was sadly prophetic. South Vietnam would ultimately be abandoned by a U.S. Congress under pressure from antiwar demonstrations and would come under Communist rule, with further casualties as some South Vietnamese were liquidated or sent to "reeducation" camps. Many others, called the "boat people," died trying to escape to Thailand in small boats. Worst of all, Cambodia would suffer a massive genocide at the hands of the Khmer Rouge, a particularly brutal Communist Party. American generals who fought the latter stages of the war would insist that all this need not have happened, that they had stalled the Communist offensive before Congress jerked the rug out from under their efforts. It would take Americans a long time to get over this defeat.

As if the Vietnam protests weren't trouble enough, on a Thursday night, April 4, 1968, the world-famous civil rights leader Martin Luther King, winner of a Nobel Peace Prize for his nonviolent protests against racial injustice and a prominent opponent of the Vietnam War, was shot dead as he stood on a balcony of the Lorraine Motel in Memphis, Tennessee. James Earl Ray, a white escaped convict, confessed and got a life sentence. The murder stirred up shock and racial rioting across a nation already unsettled by student demonstrations against the war.

Because the shooting came too late for Friday editorial page comment and there was no Saturday Journal at that time, Journal editorial commentary didn't appear until the following Monday after a weekend of rioting. It said that King had become a special symbol of the civil rights movement because he offered the common man the opportunity to participate in his demonstrations while at the same time warning that they would be truly successful only if violence was avoided.

"Dr. King was the first to recognize that his tactics, however necessary he felt them, undeniably brushed with the dark impulses buried within men. Always he sought to awaken the conscience he knew also lay somewhere within men of every color.

"It's especially sad that the act of one madman overwhelmed the good conscience of others and released in them dark impulses to violence. The injury is not only to his cause and to his nation, but also to the memory of a man who symbolized the way of non-violence."

An editorial the following day took a tougher line toward the weekend of rioting and looting, pointing out that the principal victims were residents of black neighborhoods. It said the perpetrators were "not even remotely representative of the vast majority of the Negro people; the burning, the pillage, and killing were the work of those with little regard for Dr. King and with little thought of making a civil rights protest. They were looters and vandals, pure and simple."

The editorial said that when "law and order are abdicated to hoodlums it's all society that suffers, and those that suffer most grievously are the forgotten Negro people."

A further comment on April 10 addressed the question of whether the foundations of American democracy itself were threatened by the widespread outbreak of civil disorder. Some voices were arguing that the American "experiment," unique in world history, might finally fail. But the writer argued that "so far our political institutions are withstanding these severe shocks remarkably well—shocks likely to topple governments in other lands.

"And if it is thoroughly understood that the alternative to making the system work is anarchy and regimentation, then American democracy can still confound the predictions of downfall. In the future as in the past, we the people are capable of showing that a free society, for all its vulnerability, can be the strongest of all."

During all the turbulence of April 1968, the Journal's Vietnam correspondent, Peter Kann, checked in with an article about how there was a sense of unease among those conducting the war that major events affecting the war's progress are being shaped elsewhere, "in Washington and Chicago, Moscow and Hanoi, and maybe Geneva."

He reported with irony that combat soldiers were writing worried letters home asking after the safety of the endangered families in places like Newark and Detroit. There were dark jokes about President Johnson asking for more troops to open Route 1 between Washington and Baltimore. "While Washington burned last weekend, Saigon was safe and secure—outwardly back to normal. Pretty Vietnamese girls in white ao dais strolled in the park, shielding themselves from the sun with painted parasols..."

In a Thinking Things Over column titled "Man of the South" on April 16, Royster wrote about King's unique perception about the nature of the civil rights struggle, that it had to be won through men's hearts. He intuitively understood what was not so readily apparent, that there was among his white neighbors in the South a "great, if hidden, reservoir of good will, compounded both of a tradition of Christian charity and of a deep-seated guilt feeling about the past. The problem was to tap it," and this he did "with the touch of a man who knew his people...

"In the rest of the country...there has been among the people no deep-seated guilt feelings about the past that could involve their hearts as well as their minds. There the relationship between black and white may be more correct but it is less personal. In the south a peaceful march to the rhythm of spirituals disturbs men's hearts; elsewhere, unless it's disruptive, it's just another parade."

An April 26 editorial took note of the positive ways that civil society was responding to the racial upheaval. Henry Ford II of Ford Motor Co. was heading a presidential task force determining how to create more urban jobs. J. Howard Wood, president of the American Newspaper Publishers Association (ANPA) and publisher of the Chicago Tribune, had proposed that the ANPA promote scholarships enabling young blacks to study journalism and had offered $100,000 from the Trib to start the ball rolling.

Said the editorial: "This is preeminently the American way—surmounting difficulties and building a better society through thousands on thousands of private efforts. Acts of good will and of good business, they interact and feed on each other until presently what had seemed impossible begins to look attainable after all. It is demonstrably more effective than massive Federal programs, which so far have done little good and not a little harm."

That last point, if a bit jarring, might have been referring to such issues as public housing projects, which Journal editors argued often replaced viable urban neighborhoods with sterile apartment blocks in which crime often thrived and which, in many cases, lacked easy access to the service establishments, like dry cleaners or hardware stores, that populate normal neighborhoods.

Following on the heels of the King assassination came, just after midnight on June 6, the killing of Robert F. Kennedy, Jack's brother, at a Los Angeles hotel by Sirhan Sirhan, a 24-year-old Palestinian from Jordan. Robert was campaigning for the presidency. The wave of violence seemed almost too much, but there was more to come, this time in Europe.

In August 1968, my wife Jody and I and our three children were visiting Jody's family in Franklin, Indiana, enjoying the paid home leave from the Journal's London base that I rated every two years. But news doesn't recognize a reporter's entitlement to a holiday. The Soviet Union invaded Czechoslovakia. It was a nasty business for a while, as was the case for just about every Soviet power play of that era, and indeed some that the Russians are still pulling off today.

But after it was all said and done, the Journal in an editorial called it a "Defeat for Moscow." The Czech people had resisted the Soviet invasion, and the Soviets had left Czech Communist Party first secretary Alexander Dubcek, who had attempted a liberalization reform known as the "Prague Spring," in place. The editorial said the "Soviet failure to install a new puppet government and return Czechoslovakia to the Stalinism of the Novotny regime is both astonishing and encouraging. It requires no great perception to see that the Russians drastically miscalculated the reaction to the invasion within Czechoslovakia and throughout the world.

"The Soviets are not notably sensitive to world opinion, but the outcry from practically everywhere, including other Communist states and parties, must have sounded deafening to them." The Journal called the outcome "a victory for the Czechoslovakian people and for human freedom."

Although the editorial was quite valid, perhaps its tone was too optimistic. The Soviets left Dubcek in place only temporarily, then quietly shunted him aside and then expelled him from the Communist Party in

1969, clearing the way for the party to return to its old Stalinist ways. He wound up working in the forestry service. It would not be until 20 years later, when the Velvet Revolution overthrew Communism, that the Czechs would finally be free. When Dubcek appeared with Vaclav Havel, author of the overthrow, on a balcony overlooking Wenceslas Square, he was greeted with enthusiastic applause.

The trials and disappointments of LBJ's four years in office had persuaded him not to run for reelection. The Democratic candidate in 1968 was his vice president, Hubert H. Humphrey, an engaging former senator from Minnesota. The Republicans nominated the man who had lost to JFK in 1960, Richard M. Nixon. Nixon won in a close contest that came down to a few votes that swung Illinois his way. The race was complicated by the presence of two other strong candidates, peace crusader Eugene McCarthy, who attracted youth votes, and states' rights defender George Wallace, who had strong defenders among southern white conservatives.

The postelection Journal editorial thus found it impossible to read any definitive mandate, "especially so against the background of this political year, a year of wrenching developments." The whole public mood had been one of "vague but intense dissatisfaction," said the editorial. Moreover, Nixon would face a Congress controlled by Democrats.

Yet the Journal chose to be hopeful, suggesting that the very indecisiveness of the polity created an opportunity for "a leader who can start to define precisely what it is the public wants. If the new President can rise to that unique challenge, he can reap the unique reward of putting his stamp on the political alignments and the political relevance of a new era.

"How it will work out in history depends on the incoming President's vision, skill and luck, but a potential is there. The mandate the American people have given him is that most tentative but most powerful sort. It will be what Richard Nixon can make of it."

On July 20, 1969, Americans, depressed by war news and racial and antiwar protests throughout the nation, finally got some good news for a change. On a Sunday evening, millions sat glued to their TV sets to witness the amazing spectacle of the lunar lander Eagle descending to the surface of the moon. Not just Americans, but people all over the globe, were able to watch this feat. At our flat in London, Jody and I and our three children had our TV on at 2 a.m. to see Neil Armstrong and Edwin "Buzz" Aldrin in their white space suits and globe helmets becoming the first humans to have set foot on any soil other than that of Mother Earth. America displayed to the world that we were not a clumsy giant but a nation capable of remarkable technological achievements, just as JFK had intended when he set the Apollo moon program in motion in 1963.

The moon shot had been described by some cynics as a highly expensive publicity stunt to prove that Americans could beat the Soviets at their own game. The Soviets had begun the game on October 2, 1957, when they had launched the first artificial satellite to orbit the earth, making sure that the shiny Sputnik I was visible for all to see as it circled the planet and displayed Soviet technological prowess. The cynics had a point, but it was a powerful demonstration in a political sense. The moon shot proved American technological superiority. Any perception, here or abroad, that the Soviets were winning the Cold War at that point needed reconsideration.

The Journal editorial on July 22 was titled "Triumph of the Mind" and wondered if future historians would see the moonwalk as a singular achievement or the first of a series of "pointless extraterrestrial visits, of little benefit to man while his earthly condition deteriorates."

But it argued that no amount of caviling about the cost "diminished the fact that human ingenuity, and the toil of thousands on the ground, devised near-perfect instrumentalities for the purpose." The astronauts themselves displayed high courage in undertaking this most dangerous of explorations and richly deserved the world's applause.

Vice President Spiro Agnew suggested trying for a manned landing on Mars by the end of the century, a far-fetched vision then but one that still stirs the imagination of space travel enthusiasts. The Journal cautioned against such grandiose ideas that would entail even greater risks and diversions of resources, commending a less feverish approach. "Apart from knowledge as an end in itself, what if any is man's purpose in space…No one has given satisfactory answers and there may be none…

"Meantime, in praising the Astronauts the world in fact pays tribute to the wonders of the human brain and spirit."

Whatever the practical arguments might have been pro and con, America and the West certainly needed the psychological lift the successful moonwalk provided. In the space of 20 years, the Soviets had responded to the American containment policy by enticing America into costly wars with Soviet proxies. The Korean War had been something of a draw, but it had saved South Korea, which would become a dramatic example of how market capitalism raises living standards that would contrast sharply with the Communist stagnation of North Korea.

In Vietnam, the United States lost, but perhaps gave other Southeast Asian leaders a warning of what could happen to them if they didn't do a better job of winning the trust of peoples in their own lands and thereby inoculating themselves against Communist insurgencies. Whatever the reason, Thailand, Malaysia, the Philippines, Indonesia and Taiwan all moved in the direction of more democratic governance and avoided the fate of their Vietnamese, Cambodian and Burmese neighbors. Geopolitics in the 1970s would remain dodgy for the Pax Americana but not as problematical as in the turbulent 1960s. The "Soviet containment" stand the United States made in Vietnam could perhaps at least claim that achievement.

CHAPTER 8

Joining the Fray

In early 1970, I had lunch at the Savoy Hotel in London with Warren Phillips, who had just been promoted to general manager and editorial director of Dow Jones, which positioned him for his accession to CEO in 1975. I told him that I was ready to return to the United States. The biggest story in the world was happening in the United States. With race riots and antiwar protests, it seemed to be undergoing what my wife, Jody, described as a national nervous breakdown.

We had been shocked one morning to read on the front page of the London Daily Telegraph about a particularly violent race riot in Plainfield, next door to Westfield, the town we had left behind in 1966. One Friday, our 14-year-old son Jim had asked our permission to take part in an antiwar protest being organized at the American School in London for the following day. If we had been told that a politically adept American graduate student at Oxford named William Jefferson Clinton, fresh from a trip to Moscow, was helping organize such rallies, his name would have meant nothing to us. Then, he was just one of many American youths with student exemptions from the Vietnam draft who were protesting the war. We told Jim we didn't think it a good idea to demonstrate against your own country on foreign soil in a time of war, and he took that as a no.

I told Warren that my stateside job preference would be editorial writing. He advised me to get in touch with Joe Evans, whom Warren had first met when they were both European correspondents in the late 1940s. I did, and Joe, surely with Roy's blessing, welcomed me to the page.

Hence, in August 1970, I became one of the writers who would help carry on the philosophical debate that Grimes, Woodlock and their fellows had conducted. Royster was presiding over the editorial meeting my first day on the job. The other participants were Evans, features editor Stephen McDonald, arts editor John J. O'Connor, chief editorial writer Lindley H. Clark and editorial writer David Anderson. Another editorial writer, Robert L. Bartley, had been posted in Washington to sharpen his wits in engagements with politicians and the Journal's Washington news bureau, which at that time was not well disposed toward the editorial page.

I was hoping to sit back and listen on that uneasy first day. But the England I had left behind had just held a national election. The Conservatives, led by Edward "Ted" Heath, had returned to power, scoring a victory over the incumbent Labourites. Roy chose to address the editorial writer who, having just arrived from London, would presumably offer a brilliant analysis of that outcome.

"So what do we think about the British election?" he asked me.

"My God," said an inner voice, "I'm supposed to know what WE think?" I stuttered out that I didn't believe things would improve under Ted Heath. Frankly, after watching the pitiful performance of both parties over the preceding four years, I didn't think the story was even worth much attention—although I didn't say that. The British empire was gone. Its military power had been vitiated by the ravages of World War II and postwar socialism. The romance of England had worn thin with me.

I said I didn't think things would change very much. The answer I gave turned out to be right. England went from bad to worse under Heath, and he has since been ranked among the most ineffectual prime ministers ever to have been given sleeping quarters at Number 10 Downing. But in the immediate moment, I'm sure Royster expected me to come up with a better idea than I had offered by providing a detailed description of why Mr. Heath won, what he had to offer and where Britain would go from this particular turning point. Since I had been more engaged with events in places like Africa and France than in England, I was not really up to speed on the election, except for my distrust of Heath. Other members of the London bureau had covered it. My answer didn't sound like much of a story to Roy, which surprises me not at all in retrospect. I should have been better prepared.

"Waal," said the famous editor resignedly in his trademarked North Carolina drawl, "sounds like we're going to have an interesting page tomorrow." I was acutely aware of both the sarcasm and the message: If you're going to write for this page, you had better start coming up with something more forthright and interesting than the nonstory you just offered. I've been trying to do exactly that ever since, having been chastised by a master of the art.

But despite that bad start, I soon felt a sense of liberation. We were a small staff, unlike the news department, and I could range widely in my writing. I also was finally free to express ideas in a forthright manner rather than hiding them, as most reporters do, behind the veil of "interpretative reporting" and quoting sources who support a story's theme. Editorial page precedents, which I mostly agreed with, were not a constraint.

And, of course, opinion page writers are allowed and expected to explore the endless world of ideas. Why, for example, are dictators so often dangerous? As a recent visitor to the Soviet Union, I was assigned to review "Khrushchev Remembers," a 1970 book advertised as having been derived from the taped memoir of Nikita Khrushchev, the Russian leader whose testing of JFK in the Cuban Missile Crisis raised widespread fears of nuclear war. Khrushchev, in 1956, shortly after coming to power, had exposed the massive crimes of his predecessor and mentor, Josef Stalin, to a secret gathering of top Communist Party officials.

Although Stalin's horrors were well known by the time Little, Brown published the book and Life magazine excerpted it in December 1970, the insider revelations were something of a sensation. How they got into the hands of Strobe Talbott, the editor and translator of the book, wasn't revealed at the time, but there's one plausible theory that they were seized from the aging Khrushchev by the KGB and leaked to Talbott by Khrushchev successor Leonid Brezhnev to put down any danger of a Stalinist uprising in the party.

Talbott, a friend of Bill Clinton in their Oxford days, would years later join the Clinton administration as an ambassador-at-large dealing with the breakup of the Soviet Union. Some of his writings drew charges from critics that he was a dupe of the KGB.

I focused my review not so much on all the intrigue surrounding the tapes and the question of whether they were authentic but on what seemed to me an important lesson to be learned from the book's exposure of Stalin's reign of terror: One reason dictators so often commit mass murder is fear. Men who achieve great power without legal process or popular support are aware of their own illegitimacy and knowing that they themselves used violence to succeed, they are fearful that some rival might do likewise. They "are suspicious—morbidly so in Stalin's case—of all rivals and opposition." They ease their anxiety by disposing of ambitious underlings and sowing enough fear to scare off other potential challengers.

Another subject that fascinated me in the early 1970s was the phenomenon of the corporate dropout, perhaps because I had seen one or two cases among the upwardly mobile strivers in Westfield, New Jersey. In a piece about "existential man," I wrote that these dropouts were willing to abandon their chances for higher incomes, living standards and status to go in search of a new, less taxing "life style." An author then in vogue named Walter A. Weiskopf had come up with a concept called "existential scarcity" that went beyond life's basic necessities to include such things as love, friendship and "the experience of beauty, worship, the pursuit of truth and of the good."

In retrospect, I think I was a bit too friendly toward these arguments. The "rat race" critics were in fact posing a false dichotomy. There is no reason why employees of a corporation need suffer "existential scarcity" if they strike the proper balance in their lives between earning a living and enjoying the companionship of family and friends and sampling what culture, in the broad sense, has to offer. In fact, most people do that, even individuals who devote the large amount of time and effort that is needed to rise to top corporate jobs.

I also didn't detect that this might be simply a new manifestation of the old back-to-nature philosophy that has popped up in odd moments of history. Lurking beneath the platitudes was something that would be called the "Limits to Growth" movement, which was premised on the notion that industrial development was exhausting the world's resources. That notion, which was fundamentally elitist and dismissive of the world's poor, caught on with President Jimmy Carter and was one thing that cost him reelection. I warned CEOs that other anticorporation screeds might be coming down the pike in company with this yearning for "the simple life."

The disregard among the intellectual elite for those who engage in common toil would provoke a counterattack that I wrote about in the 1970s. The counterattack was called the "sagebrush rebellion." Self-declared "environmentalists" had picked a soft target, western ranchers and lumber companies with leases on part of the federal lands that compose about 60% of the American West. The environmental lobby in Washington had won new laws setting aside huge tracts as "wilderness" areas off-limits to any kind of human activity, including human efforts to prevent forest fires. They had also pushed through bans on controlling natural predators, such as coyotes and mountain lions, with the result that sheep ranchers were being put out of business by the loss of livestock.

Rural westerners were up in arms over these threats to their livelihood from groups like the World Wildlife Federation and Sierra Club. These organizations had mustered funding and political backing from eastern urban liberals—with no stake whatever in the economy of the West—through propaganda depicting those westerners dependent on the land for their livelihoods as despoilers of the beautiful landscapes easterners could see pictured in National Geographic.

I flew out to Wyoming to have a look, touring the region mostly by light plane. Flying over the Yellowstone area, I noticed the sharp contrast between the well-tended conifer forests owned by Weyerhaeuser Co. and the adjacent government woodlands with dead growth and blackened fire sites. The back-to-nature movement had been promoting a policy called "natural burn," which called for letting forest fires on government land burn themselves out as they did a thousand years ago. The only problem was that a thousand years ago there was little demand for sound lumber to build human dwellings, and there also were fewer humans around to accidentally ignite or be forced out of their homes by forest fires.

On Wyoming's high plateau, I talked with Marvin Applequist, who had chosen ranching over a career as a symphony musician but whose ability to grow alfalfa for cattle was being threatened by tighter restrictions on the runoff of waters he used for irrigation. "I love this country, but I suppose the people back east think I'm marginal," he said. Indeed, I was witnessing the early stages of a shift in political power from rural producers to urban elites.

But there were bigger things brewing in the early 1970s than the troubles of Mr. Applequist. When Richard Nixon closed the gold window and slapped on wage and price controls in mid-August 1971, free marketers had a right to expect the Journal to stomp on his policies with both feet. But while making our objections known, we initially took a gentle approach. I wrote the first draft of an editorial, later improved upon by Lindley Clark, that appeared on August 17, 1971, that said, "As Mr. Nixon surely knows a wage-price freeze will not end inflation, even if it is uniformly observed." But we allowed that a temporary freeze, which was what Nixon had initially promised, might have a "helpful psychological effect, since it will give everyone breathing room."

However, we warned that the Federal Reserve under Chairman Arthur Burns had been adding to the money supply at a rapid rate, "increasing fears that more inflation lay ahead." We ended with these soothing words: "These are difficult times, and Mr. Nixon has faced up to what must have been, for him, difficult decisions."

In an August 26 editorial, we hardened up our stance against wage and price controls: "Neither a wage-price freeze nor a full set of mandatory controls is a cure for inflation. At best either will buy a little time while the underlying price pressures are brought under control. If the freeze doesn't provide that breathing space, or if those involved don't make proper use of it, formal controls over everything, and perhaps for a long time, have to look like a real possibility."

Lindley, the only formally trained economist on the staff, followed up our initial editorials with a much tougher one in October when it was becoming evident that, just as we had feared, the initial promise of "temporary" wasn't being fulfilled. Renewing our long-standing objections to price controls, he wrote that using government police power to fight market forces was a recipe for disaster. The Journal had long asserted that state interference with the price mechanism crippled the market's ability to adjust supply to demand and efficiently allocate resources.

A few years earlier, I had seen such damage firsthand in my visits to the crippled Soviet Union, which had fixed prices and wages for years under its central planning doctrine, reaping economic stagnation. Shortages were so bad that people queued up just to buy a pair of shoes from surly clerks in state stores.

On Nixon's behalf, it should be remembered that LBJ and a Democratic Congress had destroyed the dollar as an international standard, and Nixon still faced a Democratic Congress making strong demands for price controls. We pointed that out at the time, unwilling to let the Democrats off the hook by blaming only Nixon for one of the most serious economic policy errors of the post–World War II era.

Lindley was our leading specialist on Bretton Woods and, because he understood its flaws, was relatively sanguine about its passing. He pointed out that the original plan worked out at Bretton Woods, New Hampshire, in 1944 did not envision permanently fixed currency exchange rates and made provision for regular consultations to decide on rate adjustments. Their objective was to promote "the freest possible flow of trade and investment. In a free market, the value of anything, even a nation's currency is always subject to change," Lindley reminded our readers, no doubt an opinion influenced in part by economist Milton Friedman, an advocate of floating exchange rates.

But under Bretton Woods, Lindley wrote, nations proved reluctant to change exchange rates. Britain's socialist governments, for example preferred to seek bailouts from the system's International Monetary Fund (IMF), rather than take the politically embarrassing step of devaluing the pound to reflect the diminishing export capability of their stagnant economy.

The United States ran huge trade deficits in the early postwar era, but that was no problem because the recovery from the war created a strong world demand for dollars. "More or less accidentally, the world went on a dollar standard," Lindley wrote. But when excessive U.S. government spending made the dollar and its low-priced link to gold suspect, the system crashed, and Nixon ended the sale of gold to other central banks at the long-standing price of $35 an ounce, thus taking the world off the dollar gold standard.

Wrote Lindley: "It would have been better if the system had been reshaped through voluntary international action, instead of being compelled by the U.S. move. There was no assurance, however, that the other countries were ready to offer such cooperation. The best that can be hoped for is that the U.S. and other nations will now work together toward an arrangement without the inflexibility that spelled doom to the old system." That didn't happen, although even today a lot of countries peg their currencies to the dollar formally and informally. As we entered the fall of 1971, we would have more to say about Nixonomics, but as the year drew to a close, our thoughts would be interrupted by an upheaval on the editorial page itself.

CHAPTER 9

Kissinger Scolds Bartley

My comfortable feeling of working under the tutelage of such veteran editors as Roy, Joe Evans and Lin Clark was short-lived. In October 1970, Roy came down to our editorial meeting from his perch on the executive floor (he was also a vice president and director of Dow Jones & Co.) and announced that he was retiring. He was only 53 but had had cancer surgery and had never enjoyed the managerial part of his job entailed by his executive duties.

"I'm a writin' man," he told us. So he was heading back "home" to Chapel Hill to teach at the University of North Carolina and practice the craft he loved—writing. Roy's departure meant that Joe was in charge, but Joe also had health problems, in his case heart trouble. A little over a year after Roy left, Joe had a heart attack on his way home to Westchester and died. He was only 52. Lin Clark wrote a touching obituary and stepped into the breach to keep us going.

Warren Phillips, the rising young star of the executive suite who would soon be Dow Jones president, undertook the job of selecting the next editor, working with Roy. They chose the 34-year-old Bob Bartley, an Iowa boy Roy had plucked out of the Philadelphia bureau eight years earlier on the basis of some muscular book reviews written for the editorial page. Bob would later prove that Phillips and Royster had made an excellent choice, but his elevation was not popular with the rest of the staff. Bob was cut out to be a leader, not a Mr. Congeniality, and had not gone out of his way to win friends at the Journal. The fact that he could outshine us all as a writer didn't add to his popularity.

The announcement came as a particular shock to Lindley, who

had good reason to believe he was next in line after a distinguished record at his jobs at the Journal, including a stint as a sure-handed manager of the Journal's front page. He was by far the most productive writer of solid, thoughtful economic and political analysis.

Lindley had been my patron. In 1961, he had asked Warren to bring me onto the Page One desk, a launching pad for other good assignments, after assessing my work as Atlanta bureau manager. We lived in the same town, Westfield, New Jersey, and shared a common memory of Muncie, Indiana, where Lindley grew up and where Jody and I later had worked as reporters for the Muncie Press. A confession he once ruefully made to me told me of the passions behind his calm exterior. He was a delivery boy for the Indianapolis Star in November 1936 when FDR was elected for a third term. Lindley was so furious at the news that, instead of delivering the papers, he tossed them into a creek.

It thus didn't surprise me that Lindley told Warren he couldn't continue to work on the page after being passed over. He switched back to the news side to cover economics. J.J. O'Connor had already left for an illustrious career as a New York Times theater critic. Steve MacDonald, who had also thought himself a candidate for editor, followed Lindley to the news side. Anderson drifted away.

It was beginning to look as if we might not have an editorial page staff. But Lindley advised me to stay on, and Warren took me to lunch to make the same request. With his usual persuasiveness, Warren said that this was an opportunity to work with an extremely talented young man. I was impressed that he put matters on that level, suggesting that there was professional satisfaction to be gained. I agreed to stay on. I had nothing against Bob, I had a family to support and I felt I had found my calling in writing editorials for the Journal. I had never thought of myself as a candidate for editor after such a short time on the page, and I recognized that Bob's assertiveness resulted from his own passionate ideas about how the world should be ordered. Finally, I was in a very good position to bargain for more money and status, which I did with some success.

My relationship with Bob was rocky at first. When this brash young man undertook to give me writing lessons, I told him that I had doubts about whether we were going to be able to work together. I think Bob, for all his self-confidence, also had some uncertainty about how to manage a veteran newsman. But we eventually smoothed out the rough edges and began to work as a team. In 1973, Warren fulfilled the tacit bargain we had made over lunch, and I was promoted to deputy editor of the page, a title I would retain, with some later modification, for another 33 years. Being a professional second man has its trials but also its beauties. It spared me from many of the administrative duties that accord with being a part of the upper-echelon corporate hierarchy.

With Bob leading the way, we would engage in bruising battles over the years in our defense of individualism and private property rights in a world where those principles had been under heavy attack for several decades. The United States, after its brief experiment with New Deal dirigisme in the 1930s, had recovered its balance during World War II and had emerged as the world's strongest military and economic power. But there were new problems straight ahead.

The combination of price controls and the Fed's easy money gave the U.S. economy a short-term boost. Jody and I drove to Indiana in the summer of 1972, and the highways were choked with prosperous vacationing Americans. Bob and I covered the Republican Convention in Miami that summer, and Nixon was a hero to the party, if not to the anti–Vietnam War rioters outside the convention hall that the police were trying to disperse with tear gas. When I left the convention that night, my eyes were stung by the tear gas still lingering in the air. In November, Nixon was reelected over George McGovern in a landslide.

I would meet McGovern 30 years later when we were both on the program of an agricultural conference in St. Louis. We rode into town from the airport together in a car laid on by the sponsors and checked into our hotel, the lobby of which incorporated the waiting room of the city's venerable Union Station, a onetime Midwest hub for train travel. George told me about passing through that station in 1943. He and his wife, Eleanor, had just been married in South Dakota and were on their way to his air force post, with their meager belongings in a single suitcase.

"Someone stole our suitcase," he told me. "We just sat in the station and cried."

I could picture the scene of a poor young couple suddenly shorn of their worldly possessions. What impressed me, however, was that he was telling me without embarrassment that he had cried in public, something that would have seemed unmanly to my forebears in Indiana. Here was a man who had been the Democratic candidate for president in 1972. He had been a World War II hero, flying 35 missions over enemy territory in Europe as a B-24 bomber pilot and winning the Distinguished Flying Cross for saving his crew in a crash landing of his shot-up bomber on a Mediterranean island. Only a man comfortable in his own skin would have confessed that he cried, moreover to an editor who had once written that he was too soft to take charge of the Vietnam War. I still puzzle at the makeup of this complex man who had lived such an eventful life.

But back to Nixon. Price controls only stalled inflation temporarily. The Federal Reserve, under the usual pressure from the White House and Congress, continued to expand the money supply, creating the false prosperity that got Nixon reelected in 1972. Bob and I went to Washington in early 1973 to interview Fed chairman Arthur Burns. Puffing on his pipe in his wood-paneled office, the former Columbia professor seemed mainly intent on telling us indirectly that he was not really to blame for the easy money policies we had criticized. He complained about the indignities he had suffered at the hands of the administration and Congress as they pressured him to keep the money spigots open. The conversation gave support to what we had always suspected—that the frequent assertions that the Fed is a politically independent body are mythical, invented by politicians to absolve themselves from blame for Fed mistakes.

The unhappy consequences of the easy money-price control combination would not be long in coming. The fuel price control lid blew off later in 1973, with a sharp rise in crude oil prices. The international market in crude oil is denominated in U.S. dollars but, of course, not subject to U.S. price controls. Price controls did, however, crimp U.S. supplies as producers shut down wells that were uneconomic at the low price levels set by federal fiat.

Naturally, Washington blamed an Arab oil embargo imposed because of U.S. support for Israel in the Yom Kippur War for this shock, asserting the implausible theory that the Arabs had somehow, overnight, acquired an enormous market power they had not had before. They had acquired market power, but it was mostly because of the sinking dollar and the price controls that were suppressing U.S. oil and gas production. Not a few economics textbooks still blame the "Arab oil embargo" for the 1973 oil shock, but in fact most of the blame should have gone to the arrogance of the Nixon administration and Congress. A good rule for governments: Markets are like Mother Nature, not to be messed with. A good reminder for voters: Governments always blame someone else when their market-rigging schemes go wrong.

In my first year as Bob's deputy, I came to accept his leadership and admire his remarkable journalistic instincts. He was guided by an uncanny intuition in separating good ideas from bad ones. We were both midwesterners, trained by our middle-class upbringing to look upon public figures with cautious reserve.

It became apparent to me that things were not going to be dull working with Bartley when the June 1969 Chappaquiddick death of Mary Jo Kopechne popped back into the news just after Bob had taken over the page. On that fateful night, Senator Edward Kennedy ostensibly was giving Mary Jo, a Senate aide, a ride from a late-night island party (I say ostensibly because her purse was still at the party) when he wandered onto a narrow lane and drove off a bridge into deep water. He survived. She drowned.

Bob was infused with a strong moral sense and was unwilling to leave unchallenged the story about this tragedy that had been given out by Senator Edward Kennedy and his entourage, that he was driving the young woman to the ferry and made a wrong turn. Bob commissioned a photograph of the corner where the senator claimed he had mistakenly turned the wrong way. The picture showed how unlikely it was that he could have accidentally turned off the main road onto the narrow lane. He would have had to negotiate an acute angle, almost doubling back. The photograph, plunked down in the middle of an editorial reminding readers of the flimsy Kennedy alibi, looked odd in a newspaper with a picture-free tradition. But it made the point—that the senator had lied about the whole sordid affair.

The knowledge that Bob was determined to have a feistier and more combative editorial page than we had had in the past gave me a sense of adventure. Bob was fond of saying that an editorial writer should have "fire in his belly," and we formed our partnership with a tacit understanding that we cared deeply about the issues we addressed. Our Cold War policy was hawkish. We were skeptical of arms control agreements with the Soviets on the solid grounds that the Soviets had demonstrated repeatedly that they couldn't be trusted.

Bob in fact told a group of Soviet editors we once entertained at a Journal luncheon, "We don't trust you." They didn't seem terribly surprised, as distrust was a healthy emotion in Russia itself in those days when you never knew whether your neighbor was your friend or a KGB informer. As someone once said, for every Russian sent to the gulag, there was another Russian who had denounced him.

The Kennedy editorial, while reflective of Bob's moral sense, was small beer compared with the other issues we were addressing in the early 1970s—Vietnam, for example. Nixon's parley with Mao Tse-tung in 1972 came about because China and the United States needed each other. Mao saw a rising threat from China's historic enemy, Russia, which had become the key patron of North Vietnam and was menacing China's western border. He wanted the United States on his side. Nixon and Secretary of State Henry Kissinger needed Mao's help for making a graceful exit from Vietnam. By the spring of 1973, that exit was well advanced.

I edited Bob's copy, not that it needed much, but I'm not sure I realized at the time, in the rush of getting out a page five days a week, how good he was as a writer. Rereading his March 30, 1973, editorial titled "Vietnam: Looking Back" 42 years later reminded me of why Warren Phillips thought I would get a lot of intellectual satisfaction working with Bob. The editorial pointed out that the war was winding down, American prisoners had been released and American soldiers now had a noncombat role assisting the South Vietnamese army. He wrote that contrary to liberal doubts, the bombing of Hanoi had brought about the Paris Peace Accords two months earlier. "For whatever reason, the world seems a safer place than it was when the war started."

And also contrary to the liberal narrative of the 1970s, liberals had not opposed America's involvement a decade earlier. "Who was it, after all, that throbbed to the rhetoric of John F. Kennedy? At the time, we heard no *sotto voce* reservations from his resident intellectuals about the pledge to 'pay any price, bear any burden, meet any hardship, support any friend, oppose any foe to assure the survival and success of liberty.'"

Indeed, Bob noted, those words reflected the perils that faced us, with Russia trying to sneak missiles into Cuba, and attempting to foment wars of national liberation. Thailand and Indonesia were under threat. But when it seemed things weren't going well, particularly after the Communists' Tet offensive of 1968 (which war opponents styled as a Communist victory when it actually was a defeat), liberal opinion turned against the war. Bob singled out New York Times Vietnam correspondent David Halberstam, who was for the war until he was against it, as having "produced the most dishonest best-seller of the year." He was referring to Halberstam's 1972 "The Best and the Brightest," in which he blamed the war on JFK's advisers but somehow sublimated the cheerleading he himself provided.

The costs of this tragic episode had been huge, but there were gains as well in "buying time for other nations to create a more stable Asia, and in contributing to the decline of Communist enthusiasm for 'wars of national liberation.' The war has been part of a process through which a calmer world has evolved.

"One can doubt that these gains justify the costs, but all the weights are not on one side of the scale. About one thing more the conventional wisdom is wrong: it has not been utterly in vain that the prisoners have suffered and the dead have died."

At the time Bob wrote this, it seemed possible that the Paris Peace Accords would hold and that South Vietnam would survive. But only three months later, Congress voted overwhelmingly to cut off all support for South Vietnam on August 15. South Vietnam held out against the Communists for another 20 months, but on April 30, 1975, it fell to the North Vietnamese army.

The most we could salvage out of the waning days of South Vietnam was reflected in an editorial on March 26, a month before the collapse, titled "Which Way Do the Refugees Flee?" It pointed out that Vietnamese were fleeing from the regions that were falling to the Communists. The lesson to be drawn from refugees fleeing Communism, "whether ballet dancers from Leningrad or peasants from the Central Highlands" [of Indochina], is that "in the world today America stands for things—a measure of personal freedom, a degree of personal prosperity—that ordinary people of the world value highly indeed. And however much American foreign policy needs to separate possible purposes from impossible ones, there is no need whatever for it to be crippled by doubt about its ultimate purpose."

The big event of 1974 was the Watergate crisis, as the Nixon administration's efforts to cover up White House involvement in a 1972 burglary of the Democratic National Committee headquarters in Washington unraveled in televised congressional hearings. We treaded carefully among the various claims of presidential culpability and demands for impeachment in this highly politicized affair, but finally on August 7, 1974, Bob felt we had heard enough to take a firm position. He wrote an editorial titled "The Nation United" that began with the words: "We believe that the new Oval Office transcripts released Monday provide ample evidence for President Nixon's impeachment, conviction and removal from office. Indeed, it seems to us, as apparently it seems to Mr. Nixon's former supporters on the House Judiciary Committee, that the evidence is now clear enough that the nation can take this momentous step in a spirit approaching unity."

It had become clear, wrote Bob, "that the President headed a conspiracy to use the powers of his office to impede no less a governmental function than the process of justice. It is a crime for an ordinary citizen to obstruct justice and surely it is an abuse of office for a President to do so for narrow political motives."

The editorial pointed out that Nixon's resignation, which the Republican leadership in Congress had called for, would be a fitting alternative to impeachment because it would allow an orderly transfer of power and because conviction was almost certain if the impeachment process ran its course. "The call for the end of his presidency is as unanimous a decision as one can expect in a free society."

The editorial argued that "the clarity of evidence and unity of opinion" would leave few doubts, even among partisans, that impeachment was appropriate. It added that "the institutional precedent about to be created will not be that a President can be easily undermined and forced from office, but that he will be removed on clear evidence of serious wrongdoing...

"There is now every reason to hope that the social and political system that has sustained us for two centuries is not faltering but renewing itself again. Somehow the Founding Fathers are prevailing once more. The outcome of Watergate is a disastrous one for Richard Nixon, but it must be a heartening one for James Madison."

The timing of the editorial was excellent. Nixon resigned the next day, turning the presidency over to Vice President Gerald Ford. In our short follow-up editorial, we wrote that Mr. Ford would inherit a "delicate and excruciating task" because of the White House disruptions the investigation had created. But we argued that he would be fortified by a "great feeling of relief in the nation" that the Watergate affair was over.

Of course, it was not quite over. On September 8, President Ford took the controversial step of issuing a pardon for Mr. Nixon to spare the country from another disruptive and drawn-out drama that would have resulted had Mr. Nixon been indicted for his crime. Mr. Ford made a strong case for putting Watergate to rest and getting on with more pressing affairs. But it may have cost him election in his own right in 1976, when he lost the presidency to former Georgia governor Jimmy Carter.

There were indeed more serious issues to deal with that could be hampered by efforts to extract the last ounce of blood from a disgraced president. The Cold War, for example, hadn't gone away just because we had put Vietnam behind us. Quite the contrary, the Soviet Union was more hubristic than ever after its proxy victory in Vietnam.

There were ongoing talks with the Soviets, based on the 1972 Strategic Arms Limitation Treaty (SALT I), to try to reduce the danger of a nuclear exchange that would mean Armageddon for both countries. After his Nixon pardon in September, President Ford was on his way to the Soviet Union for talks with Soviet general secretary Leonid Brezhnev on further nuclear missile limitations. The November talks were held in Vladivostok on Russia's Pacific coast and produced an agreement that would limit both sides to "an equal aggregate number" of nuclear missiles.

Ford and Henry Kissinger, who had remained as secretary of state after Nixon's resignation, returned home to report their achievement to Congress and the American people. Bob didn't see it as much of an achievement. Drawing on back-channel analysis slipped to him quietly by noted Cold War strategist Albert Wohlstetter, Bob wrote an editorial pointing out that the treaty didn't achieve "equality" at all but was biased in Russia's favor by "throw-weight." The Soviets had bigger missiles and could thus arm them with a larger number of multiple reentry warheads.

Bob's editorial got us a summons from Kissinger to come and visit him at New York's Plaza Hotel. He was furious with us for throwing cold water on his and the president's diplomatic success, but he didn't have a good counterargument other than that we should understand that any arms limitation treaty was better than no treaty.

We were skeptical of that claim on grounds that the Soviets were unlikely to submit to any controls that were not to their advantage and that the existence of such a treaty created a false sense of security in the United States. Bob particularly didn't like the provision in the original START I that banned ballistic missile defenses because it forced the United States to rely on the theory that a nuclear war couldn't happen because both sides knew that it would mean "mutually assured destruction," a theory that became known by the appropriate acronym, MAD. To Bob, that sounded chancy because the Soviets were likely to cheat on the Anti-Ballistic Missile (ABM) defense treaty, whereas the United States, more observant of international and domestic law, was unlikely to do so. The Soviets did in fact cheat by setting up phased-array radar stations banned under the treaty, and we would later refer frequently to that fact in our arguments for scrapping the ABM treaty.

Kissinger was a skillful diplomat, certainly. He had laid the groundwork for the famous opening to China in 1972 that culminated in the historic meeting in Beijing between Chinese dictator Mao Tse-tung and Richard Nixon. It is not clear what, if any, role the Chinese played in the United States and North Vietnam signing the Paris Peace Accords—as mentioned earlier, U.S. bombing of the North probably had more effect than any outside intercession. Our ungraceful final exit when Saigon fell in 1974 was probably more the fault of Congress than the administration. But Kissinger in 1972 had been able to negotiate a modus vivendi on a key issue, China's claims on Taiwan, and Taiwan remained free to develop into a functioning democracy.

I asked in a 1972 editorial if this new opening to a former Communist enemy would survive after the 78-year-old Mao passed from the scene. It did, but as I suggested in the editorial, Maoism itself didn't last long after his death on September 9, 1976. Deng Xiaoping abandoned it in short order and embraced a form of market capitalism. I was wrong in writing that "it is still a daring idea" to believe that the circumstance of the Mao-Nixon meeting would "benefit both Chinese and American aspirations over the long term." The relationship has lasted and provided China with massive U.S. investment and the United States with low-cost Chinese goods, thanks mainly to Deng's decision to chart a new course.

As it happened, Bob was in China on a tour with a group of American intellectuals when Mao died. He quickly mastered the skills of a foreign correspondent, wrote a piece, found his way to the main post office in Beijing and called me in New York. He dictated the piece, which was a colorful account of peasants flocking into the city on bicycles, some of them sobbing at the death of their leader, combined with shrewd analysis of what Mao's death would mean for China. We quickly provided it to the newly established Asian Wall Street Journal (AWSJ) in Hong Kong, giving them a firsthand front-page scoop they could not have gotten otherwise and, of course, it was a scoop for the stateside editorial page as well.

In the turmoil of the 1970s, Americans turned to a Washington outsider as they so often do when disillusioned by government failures. Jimmy Carter, a former governor of Georgia, was their choice. It was not a good one, at least on economic policy grounds. Carter came to lunch with Journal editors during his 1976 campaign, and we noticed how ill at ease he seemed in dealing with our questions, which were proffered in a friendly way. I concluded later that he didn't have answers because he was not really up to speed on how to deal with such crucial matters as inflation and shortages.

My suspicions were confirmed when, in his inaugural speech, he suggested that he was stepping into the presidency under conditions that resembled those of 1932, when FDR was elected. In fact, an economic recovery had been under way for months, and conditions were in no way similar to those of 1932. I think Carter was really trying to suggest, for the record, that Jerry Ford had made a terrible mess of things. In fact, Ford had begun to set right some of the things that Nixon had gotten wrong. So much for the fresh politics of a Washington outsider from Georgia.

Jody and I wrote a book about "The Carter Economy" for John Wiley & Sons, detailing his performance in his first year in office in 1977. We correctly predicted that he was heading for trouble because of his ignorance of how economic forces work. He once asked one of his advisers, for example, "Which was better, a weak or strong dollar?" The right answer would have been a stable dollar serving as a reliable store of value, something that the Carter administration and his choice for chairman of the Federal Reserve, G. William Miller, a former Textron CEO, were not capable of achieving. Mr. Carter also came under the influence of the "Limits to Growth" theorists who were asserting that America's troubles resulted from a Malthusian decline in the availability of natural resources, a message somewhat equivalent to the cries of today's "global warming" scaremongers. Thus, instead of dealing with inflation and the price controls that were causing fuel shortages, Carter put on a cardigan sweater, went on television, and told Americans, in effect, to get used to freezing in the dark. It's the "moral equivalent of war," he said.

When our 10 free copies of the book were delivered, they were stacked on the kitchen table when the gas meter reader came by. He looked at the title and said, "The Carter Economy—what's that?" We knew instantly that we had mistitled the book. Maybe we should have called it "Carter's Bitter Pills" or something equally ungenerous. Sales of the book suggested that there was no huge clamor to learn more about the Carter economy than people already knew from sad experience as shortages of price-controlled items persisted and the prices of everything else soared.

Having made positive gains after the Voting Rights Act and Supreme Court school desegregation requirements of the 1960s, many civil rights organizations turned their attention abroad, to the long-standing practice of apartheid (racial classification and separation) in South Africa. Our view was that there were fair-minded people in South Africa trying to move the country toward universal suffrage and the end of racial classification. Among them, we thought, were many U.S. and British corporations who had adopted color-blind hiring and employment policies in South Africa, sometimes defying the more radical elements of the white minority.

Hence, we opposed a political movement that was gaining momentum demanding that American companies "disinvest" from South Africa to protest "apartheid," thus putting maximum pressure on the white-dominated government. We argued that the withdrawal of American companies would cost black South Africans jobs and remove the influence of American executives who had been conditioned in the 1960s to foster better racial policies in all their plants, here and abroad. We had had visits from mixed-race groups from South Africa counseling us to take such a position while South Africans worked out their problems on their own.

I decided to go to South Africa for a firsthand look at these efforts. I found support for our arguments on the ground in the form of a great deal of movement by the new government of P.W. Botha and his Afrikaaner Nationalist Party, controlled by descendants of the Dutch settlers who had fought the English in the Boer War. I quoted Felicia Kentridge, a reformer with no love for the Afrikaaners, as saying, "Something must be happening. On one day recently I saw three stories in the paper I never expected to see. Blacks can have labor unions, the government will consider removing the ban on mixed marriages and the speed limit has been raised to 90 kilometers an hour."

But I also wrote that apartheid, designed by Prime Minister H.F.

Verwoerd after the Dutch seized control of the government in 1946, was a "social engineer's dream: a place for everyone and everyone in his place" and that a dream that was intended to foster social harmony had become a nightmare. I took with a grain of salt the assurances from Piet Koornhof, the burly minister of Cooperation and Development, that the government was moving to give the separate races better representation by establishing a mixed-race presidential council. But my visit confirmed my view that U.S. companies such as Ford and IBM were striving to follow color-blind policies to the extent possible.

Our arguments did not prevail. U.S. and European companies, to a large degree, were forced to disinvest. South Africa's black power movement that I witnessed the beginnings of in 1979 rolled on until Nelson Mandela and his African National Congress (ANC) won a national election in 1994 and gave South Africa its first black government. We had underestimated the extent to which Mr. Mandela and the ANC would take positive steps to heal past animosities, an approach that earned Mr. Mandela much deserved praise.

We were right in one sense, however. The transition was not without bloodshed, but there were forward-looking leaders of all races who helped Mr. Mandela give the country a peaceful and legal transfer of power. South Africa's later difficulties with economic growth and civil order would suggest that we at least had a point in arguing that blacks would have been better off without disinvestments. Civil rights groups in the United States were practicing transference, equating the circumstances of their own struggle with those of a country with a far different history of racial separation and racial attitudes.

In the United States, the problems that arose at the beginning of the decade did not go away easily. Price controls on some items, including gasoline, would remain until 1981, when Ronald Reagan abolished their final vestiges. Inflation got far worse in the late 1970s, under President Jimmy Carter, who won the election largely as a result of Nixon's Watergate fiasco and Nixon's subsequent pardon by

Jerry Ford. The United States suffered a combination of rising dollar prices of international commodities and shortages caused by price controls. Public confidence that Washington could rule the marketplace waned in the 1970s as Americans experienced such irritants as gasoline shortages that had many irate motorists waiting hours in line just to buy fuel to get to work. It was a harsh lesson for an American public that had been taught during the New Deal to think that Washington could solve anything just by passing a law. At the end of that decade, the failures of government dirigisme had not only become evident in the United States, but all over the world, as the problems of Communist and social democratic regimes were mounting.

Needless to say, we Wall Street Journal writers were not at all surprised by the decade-long turmoil that resulted from the futile Nixon and Carter efforts to repeal the laws of markets. The failures, damaging as they were to the well-being of the American people, had one salutary effect. They destroyed the dangerous notion that Washington could correct its own excesses by just waving a magic wand. A new and healthy skepticism about politics and government began to emerge on the gasoline queues and in the grocery stores. The way was being prepared for some new thinking about political economics.

CHAPTER 10

The Supply-Side Revolution

T he 1970s were something of a lost decade for the United States, with a lost war in Vietnam, a disgraced presidency, shortages caused by price controls, slow growth, the seizure of our embassy in Tehran by a hostile government, and ultimately, double-digit inflation. But all these troubles generated readership for the Journal editorial page as Americans sought a serious discussion and debate of the policies that were producing such dismal results.

In 1978, a readership poll showed that 60% of the Journal's readers read something on the editorial page, a high score for any newspaper considering the diverse interests of readers. Editorials are not normally a big draw, particularly those written in an equivocal way by writers fearful of offending the local elites, or more importantly, their publishers. The vigor and directness of our editorials, combined with the intelligent offerings of contributors to our feature and letters columns, created a public forum that attracted attention. The Journal also was well on its way to becoming the largest-circulation newspaper in the country.

Dow Jones management followed the tradition set by the Bancrofts and Barney Kilgore by avoiding any temptation to dictate policy to the editorial page editor. Peter R. Kann, who was CEO from 1992 to 2006, says he can't recall any instance where a Journal publisher "interfered in what the editorial page chose to say. I know from experience that there have been pressures on publishers (from directors, the news department, advertisers, etc.) to do so. But the tradition has always held."

Producing an editorial page means generating enough copy every day to "keep the column rules apart," as Bob used to say. Bob and I soon settled into a method of operation that met that basic requirement. Bob would concern himself with the lead editorial, and I would see to it that we filled the Review & Outlook column every day with other forthright, logical arguments on public policy issues. I edited Bob's editorials, and he edited mine. I would usually edit the editorials of other members of the staff. Warren had prevailed on Jack Cooper, a news department veteran known for his deft touch as a writer and an editor, to join us to acquire and edit features and letters. The Journal had some regular columnists. Washington bureau manager Alan Otten wrote a weekly column called "Politics and People," for example. But we relied more than most editorial pages on contributions from writers with special expertise, which gave our readers a variety of voices offering their views on public policy. That tradition continues.

We didn't have formal editorial meetings, but my desk was the magnet for informal morning meetings, usually starting with one or two and then attracting most of the staff. These seemed more like bull sessions than editorial meetings, but as we talked about events of the day, our thoughts were stimulated, and usually a writer would launch into a subject he or she found interesting. If it jelled, either Bob or I would say, "Why don't you write something about that for tonight." One day, after such a session, a young intern asked me when the editorial meeting would begin. I told him, "That was it."

That approach might sound overly casual, but it worked. People relaxed. Even junior members of the staff felt free to talk, and the conversation stimulated ideas. The serious part happened later, when the writing and editing process began. There was nothing casual about that. We insisted on careful and disciplined writing, often rewriting parts that needed further work and going back to the writer to clarify points. We expected the writers to do their own reporting and not rely on secondary sources, which was a departure from the approach at some editorial pages that required editorial writers to rely on news side reporting.

Rewriting was a long-standing tradition at the Journal, pioneered by Kilgore when he set up the Page One desk to turn "sows' ears into silk purses," as 1960s-era Page One editor Jim Soderlind once put it. Some stories needed very little work, but the idea was to make every piece readable and engaging. Bob would often do some heavy rewriting on lead editorials, including mine, to give them what he believed to be a stronger tone and message. I often did the same when Bob was away. For obvious reasons, I never undertook to rewrite Bob, but then I seldom found fault with his copy.

But we had good writers. Jude Wanniski bubbled with ideas, many of them good ones. James Ring Adams was capable of untangling complex subjects such as New York's debt problems. Suzanne Garment had a deft touch with social issues. Adam Meyerson was good at scouting out inanities in the federal regulatory regime. Seth Lipsky, who had been the Journal foreign editor and one of the founders of our Asian edition, was an excellent foreign policy analyst. Lawyer Ben Stein, who would later migrate to a Hollywood career, was good on legal issues.

Writing editorials is different from writing under a byline because the writer is representing an institution, not himself. Hence, he must be observant of precedents set by the editorials of the past while at the same time addressing a new set of circumstances. That's why having a philosophical foundation, in our case, "free people, free markets," is important. We never paid much attention to political labels when we were hiring writers, only to what they had written, how much writing talent it displayed and how it comported with our fundamental approach.

A socialist would not have been happy on the editorial writing team, but we did hire leftist contributors to give balance to our pages. One of the most interesting was Alexander Cockburn, a talented Scots-Irishman, who often referred with pride to his father, Claud

Cockburn, who covered the 1930s Spanish Civil War, rather one-sidedly, for the Communist Daily Worker. A distant ancestor, Admiral Sir George Cockburn, was in charge of British troops that burned down the White House during the War of 1812.

Alex specialized in burning conservatives, and sometimes even liberals, with his wicked pen. His foreign policy writings often paralleled the Soviet Union line, which I learned from occasional lunches with Soviet journalists. Alex, who often wrote anti-Israeli columns, was dismissed by New York's Village Voice in 1984 when the Boston Phoenix reported he had accepted a $10,000 grant from a pro-Arab group. Bob took a different view, writing an editorial saying in effect that we knew what we were getting when we signed up Alex as a contributor and that he would continue to write for us.

We all rather liked Alex, who had a boyish charm and seemed to regard journalism more as a game than a serious business. Although his views were diametrically opposite of ours, he wrote punchy and often amusing columns. He died at age 71 in 2012 in Bad Salzhausen, Germany, where he had gone for treatment of cancer.

Early on, in 1972, Warren had suggested that we beef up our features column by creating a board of contributors made up of prominent thinkers. Our first board included Paul McCracken, a keen-eyed economist from the University of Michigan who had been chief economic adviser to Nixon 1969 to 1971; Walter Heller of the University of Minnesota, who had guided economic policy for both JFK and LBJ; and Irving Kristol, one of the most interesting intellectuals of that era. Kristol was dubbed by leftists as a "neo-conservative" because he had gravitated from his early liberal views to an embrace of market economics. Though the description was meant to be unflattering, Kristol embraced it, and a new and influential school of politico-economic commentators, the "neo-cons," had a descriptive name. Irving's son, William, carried on the tradition as editor of the politically savvy Weekly Standard in Washington.

As Journal readership grew, the opinion section first expanded to two and then to three pages. Leisure and arts coverage was enlarged and eventually grew beyond our pages to sections of the newspaper, although the opinion columns page still carries a book review each day. Bartley once claimed that he ran the only editorial page that sold newspapers. Judging from the number of readers I've met who called the Journal editorial page their "Bible," I think there is support for that claim even if it does sound a touch boastful.

The biggest thing we did in the 1970s under Bob's leadership was to provide a springboard for what later came to be called the "supply-side revolution" in economic thought. We didn't know when we entered into this project that it would be the big deal it proved to be, transforming federal economic policy in a way that made the United States more prosperous and life better for many millions of Americans.

The early supply-siders of the 1970s advocated cutting rates in the highest income tax brackets, in what was then an even more progressive system than now. As a worker's earnings rose, he or she paid out ever-higher percentages of additional (marginal) income to the tax collector; thus, the system penalized the most productive and successful taxpayers.

Initially, I was not sure that cutting rates on the highest incomes, as the supply-siders advocated, would create greater incentives to produce. I was concerned that they were simply offering a way to make the rich even richer, an argument that has not gone away even today.

But a better understanding of what the supply-siders were driving at revealed the logic of their arguments. Men and women will work harder to improve their status in life if the work effort they expend and the investment risks they take are not burdened with excessive taxation. In other words, supply-side measures were not meant to help the rich, but to foster the work effort and investment of time and money by people who want to become rich, or at least richer. In short, they were advocating measures to promote economic growth, which improves the lot of almost everyone.

In pure mathematical terms, the willingness to risk a large investment of time and money in a career venture is improved if there is certainty that the project won't be stalled by unreasonable regulations or a large part of the returns won't be taxed away. When I realized that was the core of supply-side thought, it all made sense.

It made sense to me because of the experience of my own family. Long before I was born, my father owned a farm on the eastern outskirts of Louisville, Kentucky. It was on the south bank of the mighty Ohio River, and every spring his land was inundated by Ohio's annual flood. After the danger of flood had passed, my father cleared his land of debris and planted sweet corn. When it matured, he harvested the "roasting ears" and hauled them into Louisville to sell at the farmers' market. It was a profitable business. Eventually, he saved enough money to buy a better farm in central Indiana and enjoy a measure of prosperity of the 1920s.

My father, beginning with very little capital, was able to build a profitable business through long hours of hard physical labor. There was no farm program to support him, but on the other hand he wasn't overburdened with excessive taxes and regulation. He could use what he earned at the Louisville market to support his wife and six children (I was later to be the eighth and last) and still have savings left over for future investment in a better farm that wasn't flooded every spring. Because of his productivity, he was able to earn a surplus by supplying a marketable commodity to the townspeople of Louisville.

Men like my father questing for a better life and willing to work long, hard hours to achieve that end, supplied the productive energy that built the United States to the powerful engine it had become by the 1920s. The country's reputation as a land of opportunity where privileged elites could not keep a good man down had drawn many millions of ambitious immigrants to America's shores, and still does to this day. There, of course, had to be demand in the marketplace for what they produced, but it was their productive labor that drove the economy.

My father was demonstrating, along with millions of other Americans, the simple principles that form the foundation for supply-side economics. People produce so as to be able to consume, and they work harder and take more risks if there are few restrictions on their opportunity for gain.

American economist Bruce Bartlett, in his 1981 book "Reaganomics" (Arlington House Publishers), writes that "Supply-side economics is nothing more than classical economics rediscovered. More particularly, it is Say's law rediscovered. The essence of Say's law, named for the 18th Century French economist Jean Baptiste Say, is that goods are ultimately paid for with other goods. Thus, it is production which limits the satisfaction of human wants, not the ability to consume, which in the aggregate is unlimited. Consequently, Say argued that 'The encouragement of mere consumption is no benefit to commerce; for the difficulty lies in supplying the means, not in stimulating the desire of consumption and we have seen that production alone furnishes those means. Thus, it is the aim of good government to stimulate production, of bad government to encourage consumption.'"

This simple logic was clear enough to men like Andrew W. Mellon, who was appointed Treasury secretary by President Warren G. Harding in 1921 and whose Mellon Plan was largely incorporated in the Revenue Act of 1924, which reduced taxes by some $400 million from what was projected under previous law. The Mellon Plan is widely credited with generating the remarkable prosperity the United States enjoyed in the "Roaring Twenties." The federal budget deficit went down, not up, because revenue projections hadn't taken into account the incentive effects of the tax reduction. The economic progress of the 1920s was aborted after the 1929 crash by the taxes, tariffs and government excesses of Herbert Hoover and the Republican Congress.

The fundamental importance of encouraging production was understood as well by Ronald Reagan, a poor boy from the Illinois sticks, who minored in economics at little Eureka College in Eureka, Illinois. His professor, Alexander Clark Gray, had received his master's degree at Hiram College in 1897, so classical economics was quite likely the only economics Gray would have known. Reagan would have learned from experience as well; poor country boys find out early in life that if you want to eat, you have to work.

Reagan got his bachelor's degree in sociology and economics, both taught by Gray, in 1932. It is ironic that in that year, the old economic wisdom of Say and Mellon was being thrown overboard by a new group of theorists who had come to power in Washington. They were imbued with the idea that economic progress was driven by demand, not production. That put a new spin on government policy because government, while not apt at producing goods, could certainly generate demand through its own spending, or so they thought and proclaimed as if they had found a magic elixir.

Ironically, the idea that government could generate income and wealth was taking hold at the very time that higher taxes and tariffs concocted in Congress and a grievous error in judgment by a Federal Reserve Board that had tightened money in the mistaken fear of inflation had plunged the country into a depression. It was testimony to the political principle that government failures beget more failures, an insight contained in the essays by Journal editors I cited in the preceding chapters. In a crisis largely precipitated by government policies, Americans looked to Washington for answers, and Washington responded most willingly but not wisely.

As noted in a previous chapter, the demand-management theory was principally the brainchild of Englishman John Maynard Keynes, author in 1936 of "The General Theory of Employment, Interest and Money." Keynesian ideas caught on not only because of Professor Keynes' gift for argument. Politicians embraced them because they prescribed exactly the sort of thing they loved to do—spend public funds in ways that could win votes from their constituencies. What better theory could a congressperson ask for than one that told him it was good economics as well as good politics to spend public money to win the hearts and minds of constituents back home?

Economists teaching in colleges and universities latched onto Keynesianism because it promised them something hard to resist—the prospect of a world run by economists. In this new world of a government-managed economy, the politicians would obviously need a lot of economists to tell them what to do. They could go from the classroom to real positions of power. Keynesianism was loved, as well, by Washington journalists because if the politicians they covered were running the economy, it would make Washington coverage more important to their editors and readers and give them more prestige. Big production centers like Detroit and Chicago and financial centers like New York would henceforth take a backseat to Washington as the center of the economic universe. It thus should be no surprise that Keynesianism, despite its dubious premises, caught on like wildfire among America's opinion-shaping elites.

Keynes also was difficult to criticize because his mind was so agile that he often changed his opinions. Indeed, when Friedrich Hayek, his most formidable critic in the 1930s, published in 1944 his famous "The Road to Serfdom," a restatement of classical economic principles and a devastating attack on socialism, Keynes praised it highly, saying he agreed with it fully. When Keynes himself visited Washington in 1944 and met with professed Keynesians, he later said, "I was the only non-Keynesian in the room." And once when someone asked him why he changed his mind so often, he replied, "When I see I'm wrong, I change my mind. What do you do, sir?"

But as the comment suggests, even by the 1940s, Keynesianism had taken on a life of its own. And its enormous influence within the power structure of the United States was what the supply-siders were up against in the 1970s. Bruce Bartlett played a role in the revolution against Keynesianism as a member of the staff of the Joint Economic Committee of Congress and of other congressional staffs in the '70s. He has been a frequent contributor to Journal editorial pages. By the end of World War II, he wrote in "Reaganomics," Keynesian economics had virtually total allegiance among the younger members of the economics profession.

"By the end of the 1960s they were full professors at most universities, their influence so pervasive that Milton Friedman, the preeminent monetarist, remarked in 1965, 'We are all Keynesians now.'" Richard Nixon proclaimed himself a Keynesian at the very moment he was about to commit one of the biggest policy errors of the 20th century—the price controls he ordered in August 1971.

There was one little corner of the universe where Keynesian economics was viewed with suspicion from the very beginning of the talented Briton's fame—The Wall Street Journal's opinion pages. Thomas Woodlock, looking with great skepticism on all the grand schemes for government management of the economy in the '30s, referred sarcastically to Keynes as the "persuasive one." And Journal columnist William Henry Chamberlain, who had been sympathetic to the Soviet Union experiment before he went there in 1922 as Christian Science Monitor correspondent and saw its deep moral defects firsthand, was scornful of socialism in any form. A 1950 column scoffed at a U.N. report drafted by Keynesian disciples that, "instead of recommending freedom of international trade and a rapid all-around scrapping of controls and restrictions," prescribed "a heavy dose of the pink pills of economic statism."

It was the inimitable Vermont Royster who perceived the central problem of Keynesianism. He wrote in March 1951 that "Lord Keynes' theory had overlooked, among other things, the fact that in economics as elsewhere, narcotics are easier started than stopped." He was, of course, referring to the narcotic so popular with Congress, federal spending. Writing after several months of the Korean War, which was putting a heavy strain on the federal budget, Royster deplored the "mountainous and almost unmanageable government debt which is the heritage of Keynesian theory in practice." To assess the Keynesian legacy, he wrote, "It was only necessary to ask 'how much better prepared we would be today had we not drunk so deeply of this heady theory yesterday.'"

He further asserted: "This is the worst, but not the only consequence of Keynes. He apparently did not consider himself a socialist in the popular sense of the word but he was definitely a managed economy man. He seemed suspicious of some aspects of free enterprise with many individuals left to make economic decisions as, for instance, between 'saving' and 'investing.' He was afraid of the decisions they might make. Therefore he tended to be lenient toward monopolies and cartels if they could be controlled or managed by the government. As a corollary, he favored inter-governmental control of international trade through money management.

"So the result was that he spurred the socialist trend. Because he was a brilliant mathematical philosopher, skilled in argument, he could provide logical reasons for doing the things the socialists and statists wanted to do for political reasons. Sometimes, ironically, he provided the logic for political actions he did not believe in."

Bruce Bartlett's book observed, however, that "the heavily Keynesian economic policies of the 1960s and 1970s were sowing the seeds of their own destruction." The 1970s "stagflation" exposed the central contradiction of Keynesianism. There was nothing in Keynesian theory to explain why a country could have inflation and high unemployment at the same time, not to mention how a government that was managing the economy through extensive regulatory intervention could have gotten itself into such a fix.

"In a real sense," wrote Bartlett, "Keynesian economics died during the recession of 1974-75. In 1975 the unemployment rate hit its highest level since the Depression—8.5%—despite a $45 billion federal budget deficit (at that time the largest since World War II) and a soaring inflation rate. According to conventional Keynesian theory this could not happen. The Phillips Curve, a basic Keynesian article of faith, stated that there is an inverse relationship between inflation and unemployment—the higher the one is the lower the other should be.

"Thus, the Keynesians were completely baffled about what policy prescriptions to offer for the situation. Normally, unemployment calls for a budget deficit, while inflation calls for a budget surplus. Since they already had the largest peacetime deficit in American history, they could hardly call for more deficit spending. And a reduction in the deficit to battle inflation would exacerbate the already bad unemployment situation. The Keynesians were therefore left without anything to offer to rectify the situation. Soon, many were proclaiming the death of Keynesian economics." Bartlett was far too optimistic; Keynesianism was crippled, but not dead.

Given the background of skepticism at The Wall Street Journal about Keynesian economics, it is no accident that when Keynesianism finally began to totter on its weak foundations, we on the Wall Street Journal editorial page were there to give it a good push. The Journal revived classical economic theory at just the right moment to take advantage of the breakdown of the old order during the economic policy fumbling of Nixon, Ford, Carter and the confused congresses of the 1970s.

Jude Wanniski was one of our mainstays in the campaign to overturn Keynesianism. He was brash, colorful, bright and eccentric. When Dow Jones' National Observer weekly hired Jude from the Las Vegas Review Journal in 1965, he showed up at the Washington headquarters in a flashy convertible with a showgirl wife, his first of three. He was fond of wearing black shirts with white ties, which gave him the appearance of a Vegas high roller or, worse yet, a Chicago gangster.

In fact, he was a jolly, ebullient fellow. In Washington, he made friends with Arthur B. Laffer, chief economist at the Office of Management and Budget and a former University of Chicago professor. Laffer acquainted him with the work of another obscure economist, Robert Mundell, a Canadian-born professor at Columbia, giving Jude two economist contacts who would later gain prominence on the pages of The Wall Street Journal.

Bob, who was representing the editorial page in Washington in the late 1960s and early 1970s, was impressed with Jude's political sophistication. When he asked Jude to come to the editorial page as part of our rebuilding efforts in 1972, the veteran of the Las Vegas casinos and a stint as a reporter in Alaska protested that he had never written editorials. Bob replied, "Jude, all it takes is arrogance." Jude figured that he could muster enough of that.

Jude was born into a coal-mining family in Pottsville, Pennsylvania, in 1936, but grew up in Brooklyn. His maternal grandfather was a Communist who presented him with a copy of "Das Kapital" as a high school graduation present. Jude retained a great affection for the old man, and they remained close even after Jude had joined up with the capitalist pigs at The Wall Street Journal.

Jude, Bob and I used to amuse ourselves imagining the guesses readers might be making—particularly our adversaries—about the backgrounds of the men who were writing Wall Street Journal editorials. The class warfare barbs thrown at us by our critics on the left led us to believe that they thought we were pampered sons of New York billionaires. In fact, Bob's father taught veterinary medicine at Iowa State, I grew up in a farm village in Indiana, the son of a failed farmer, and Jude was the son of a coal miner and grandson of an ardent Communist.

We were a rather proletarian lot to be promoting capitalism, but we were not at all out of step with the special brand of populism that had been made a tradition by our predecessor Journal editorial page writers. "Free people, free markets" was in our veins for the simple reason that those principles allowed upward mobility for individuals with energy and ambition—people like us, for example. Business leaders, when they departed from those principles—as they often did—were as much fair game for our verbal arrows as statist politicians. We were not the "voice of big business," as our critics glibly called us, but exponents of free-market capitalism, an economic system that allows any individual to build a business and compete with the big boys.

The two things are definitely not the same. We didn't expect limousine liberals to love us for our proletarian origins. Distrust of self-made men is a fairly common attitude in those circles. One product of that distrust is often support for government programs that promote dependency, rather than individual enterprise. A few of us were having lunch with Barney Kilgore in Cleveland once when he offered what I thought was a particularly trenchant observation about rich liberals: "They've got theirs and they don't want anyone else to get any."

Jude was a contrarian. Indeed, he epitomized that breed. It was a very good cast of mind for a Journal editorial writer in the 1970s. There was plenty wrong with the conduct of public policy, and Jude was the ideal guy to search for alternative ideas. For that reason, he was naturally attracted to the iconoclastic views of Bob Mundell, a specialist in monetary history at Columbia, and Art Laffer of the University of Chicago.

After Jude brought these two men to our attention in 1974, Bob and I invited Mundell to lunch. He gave us our first tutorial on the practical application of supply-side policy. He told us that the government's economic policies should be exactly the opposite of what it was practicing. Beltway politics dictated easy money and steep upper-bracket tax rates. Mundell argued for tight money and big cuts in the upper-bracket rates. The monetary maneuver would stop inflation, which was seriously eroding the value of savings and capital, and the tax rate cuts would restore the incentives of the most productive Americans to work hard and take investment risks, especially the latter, which was the source of new jobs. What Mundell was espousing was what Herbert Stein, chief economic adviser to Nixon and Ford and father of our own Ben, would dub, rather disdainfully, "supply-side fiscalism," a coinage that gave supply-side economics its name.

At that time, inflation worsened the penalties of a progressive income tax code by moving the productive and enterprising Americans into higher tax brackets, thus further reducing their real income. It's hard to believe in what one would hope is today's more enlightened age that even as recently as 1980, the marginal tax on income over $108,300 was 70% for a single individual. Bartlett noted that persons with incomes in excess of $100,000 were paying an average of 48% of their income in taxes at all levels of government. Soak-the-rich taxation was in fact soaking the middle class. That seemed OK to a lot of politicians because, in the alleged words of bank robber Willie Sutton, "that's where the money is."

Given the high marginal tax rates, it should be no surprise that during the 1970s, personal savings declined steadily, to 4.5% from 7.7% of total income. Because of the low rate of capital formation, investment in plants and equipment per worker was drying up.

By historical standards, even the tax rates in 1980 looked good. At the end of World War II, the top marginal rate, on income over $200,000, had been raised to 94%. The tax plan proposed by John F. Kennedy in the early '60s and enacted in 1964 after his 1963 assassination had cut marginal rates sharply. And just as supply-siders would have predicted, they touched off a period of economic prosperity. Indeed, Kennedy economic adviser Walter Heller, who also would later join our board of contributors, claimed that a "new economics" had been established that ensured steady growth. The high hopes evaporated with the stagnation of the 1970s.

Laffer, thanks in large part to the cheerleading from Jude on our pages, would become famous for his argument that cuts in high marginal rates can sometimes yield more, not less, revenue. His now famous "Laffer Curve" was in essence the old law of diminishing returns, holding that if merchants price their products at levels above what most consumers are willing to pay, they will earn less revenue than at a lower price. That's pretty simple, as any corner grocer can attest. Laffer applied it to government. If government puts taxes at a level higher than is deemed reasonable by taxpayers, they will work less, take fewer risks and engage in tax avoidance measures, such as investing in offshore tax shelters, thus actually reducing the government's tax revenues. This concept, proclaimed by Art and Jude on the Journal's editorial page, was easily understood by the public and attracted attention to the supply-side movement.

Other supply-siders, including economist Paul Craig Roberts, complained that the Laffer Curve oversimplified supply-side economics which, of course, it did. The main goal was to increase incentives for the American people to save and invest, not to expand federal revenues. Craig said that Laffer complicated his efforts as a staffer on the House Budget Committee to explain supply-side principles to Congress. Part of Craig's strategy was to deny Congress revenues, not expand them, so as to curtail that body's profligate spending habits.

But Craig did concede that all radical political change can benefit from the capture of public interest and enthusiasm, and Art and Jude's Laffer Curve idea did that. Moreover, the Laffer Curve was soon subjected to proof. After a cut in the capital gains tax was pushed through Congress in 1978 by Republican William Steiger of Wisconsin (dubbed "Stupendous Steiger" by a Journal editorial), revenues from the tax on long-term capital gains did indeed rise, to $10.6 billion in 1979 from $8.5 billion the year before.

The political struggle to break the grip of Keynesianism on American politics was by no means easy, and in recent years this seductive philosophy has returned to guide Fed and government policy making by politicians who have forgotten the dismal lessons of the 1970s if they ever learned them in the first place. Even in the 1980s, the swing to supply-side policies required a fierce and closely fought battle in Congress, as Craig Roberts details in his 1984 book, "The Supply-Side Revolution" (Harvard University Press).

Wrote Craig: "The editorial board of the New York Times could not grasp the supply-side logic behind the personal income tax-rate reduction. All it saw was a 'murky notion' with 'no textbook or history book to support it' and the Times was not alone. I had foreseen this problem. Unlike the Keynesian policy that it was displacing, supply-side economics came out of the policy process itself and not out of the universities."

Craig's reference to the New York Times strikes a chord with me. I participated in a panel discussion in the 1980s before an Atlanta Federal Reserve Bank audience with my old friend Leonard Silk, then economics columnist for the Times. I was arguing the supply-side case. Leonard, a dedicated Keynesian, said, "That's not my church." Leonard is long gone, but apparently classical economics still finds few worshippers at the Times.

Indeed, a good many Republican stalwarts—Bob Dole, for example—couldn't grasp the principle. They were hung up on the old notion that the most important thing was to balance the budget. The supply-siders were arguing that the Republicans would never get anywhere politically just carping at the big spending habits of the Democrats and not offering a positive vision of their own for economic growth and prosperity. Tax rate cuts were something that could rally voters.

Encouraged by Bob, Jude in 1978 published a successful book, modestly titled "The Way the World Works," setting out his ideas on political economics. But his enthusiasm for politics would run him afoul of Journal policy that same year. Dow Jones president Ray Shaw spotted him passing out political literature in the Hoboken train-ferry terminal on behalf of Republican Senate candidate Jeffrey Bell and regarded it as unseemly political activity for a Journal editor.

Bob grieved over Ray's demand that he fire Jude but carried out the order, telling me that this was one time when he couldn't save Jude from his indiscretions. Jude went on to build a successful political economics consultancy, Polyconomics, but became somewhat estranged from both Bob and me in later years as, in his contrarian way, he took up some strange causes, including a defense of the Chicago black anti-Semite Louis Farrakhan. It pleases me, however, that the last email message I received from Jude was a nice note on August 29, 2005, praising a column I had written. He suffered a heart attack and died that same day at age 69.

The other half of the Mundell formula, restoring the dollar to health, was equally essential and also demanded gutsiness. Inflation was approaching 15% in the late 1970s, and Jimmy Carter finally realized that he had a political problem on his hands. Short-term interest rates had risen above 20%, further dragging down an economy still burdened with some of the price controls that Nixon had installed. The bond market was dead and the stock market gasping for air.

We had some fun with an editorial about Carter's approach to the remaining controls on fuel prices. Instead of simply removing them, he set up a shop to try to discover how the workings of the market could be replicated by regulators. Our readers howled at this ridiculous exercise.

On inflation, he did much better. He hired Paul Volcker, the tall, tough-minded president of the New York Federal Reserve Bank— also a Democrat—to take charge of the Federal Reserve Board and do whatever it took to get inflation down. Before Volcker left New York for his new assignment in Washington, he invited Bob, features editor Tom Bray and me to lunch in the elegant executive dining room at the fortress-like headquarters of the New York Fed just north of Wall Street.

It's a fortress because deep in its basement is stored much of the world's supply of gold. When a country sells gold, an attendant simply moves the required amount of gold bricks from, say, the compartment containing, say, French gold to the one labeled, say, the United Kingdom.

After a nice lunch and an exchange of pleasantries, Volcker asked the question that was his reason for inviting us: "When there's blood all over the floor, will you guys still support me?" I immediately said yes, violating protocol by not giving Bob a chance to answer first. But we were of the same mind, and Volcker, in his inimitable in-your-face style, wanted to get us on the record before the bloodletting began, a flattering recognition of the influence of the Journal's editorial page.

We knew exactly what he was talking about. During a decade of loose monetary policy and a buildup of liquidity in the banks, a great many banks and borrowers had become overextended. It was a situation not unlike the late 1920s, which C.W. Barron had analyzed so well and Herbert Hoover seemed to understand not at all. In the '70s, the buildup was attributable to wayward Fed policy conducted by Federal Reserve chairman G. William Miller, Volcker's predecessor, with Jimmy Carter's blessing.

The Fed's inflationary policies had been further aggravated by the restrictions on production that Nixon had imposed with his 1971 price controls. Price controls on oil had converted many American oil and gas wells into money losers, and the producers had shut them down. The result was that the overseas oil producers who had become major sources of supply to the American market were piling up huge numbers of "petrodollars" in American banks. When banks are rolling in dough, they have to find ways to lend it or take a loss. They started taking bigger risks, something we saw again in the 2008 subprime mortgage crisis, although in that particular round there was strong government encouragement of risky lending. The expression current in the late 1970s was that the banks had so much petrocash that they were "pushing money out the door," or in effect begging borrowers to "take our money, please."

Volcker knew that this would have to stop if he were to succeed in killing off double-digit inflation. The irresponsible borrowing and lending had been funneling credit to Latin American governments, who were seldom prudent under the best of circumstances, and certainly not when Yankee bankers were throwing money at them. He knew as well that an even more politically sensitive area was the American farm sector, where farmers were taking advantage of easy credit to buy up more land at prices inflated by the high demand. Their belief that further inflation would both increase the nominal price of land and lower the real cost of repaying their loans was digging them, along with the Latinos, into a hole that would be hard to climb out of if Volcker killed off inflation.

But that was what he was hired to do by a president who knew he had blundered into a mess where the risks to agriculture were small compared to the damage that was being inflicted on the overall populace. Personal savings were being eroded daily. The government had programs in place to bail out many of the overextended farmers. As for the Latinos, they don't vote in U.S. elections.

Volcker screwed down the spigots through which the Fed feeds money and credit to the banks, and hence to the economy. There was indeed blood all over the floor. Latin governments that had enjoyed cheap credit now found it dear. Mexico, for one, would default on external debt in 1982. Some Midwest farmers who had deeply indebted themselves to expand their land holdings were thrown into bankruptcy.

But Volcker stuck by his guns, and when Ronald Reagan defeated Jimmy Carter in 1980, partly because of the hash Carter had made of economic policy, he invited Volcker to stay on and finish the job. He also removed the remaining price controls that had played such a major role in creating the petrodollar glut.

Tight money forced the nation into a sharp but short-lived recession, which gave rise to some carping, even among some supply-siders, that Reagan had misapplied their principles. Their fear of failure after so much progress was understandable. But the downturn also gave force to the political argument for passage of the Kemp-Roth tax cuts, of which more later. Even Democrats thought tax cuts were stimulative, although they assumed in Keynesian style that the goal was to stimulate demand, not personal initiative.

Craig Roberts, who in 1978 became an editorial writer and "Political Economy" columnist for the editorial page, argued that Volcker moved too fast to shut down inflation and that the resulting recession was unnecessarily severe. I took a different view, feeling that the way to kill inflation is to do it "quick and dirty," so as to eradicate all inflation expectations. My argument was that as long as those expectations are allowed to live, consumers will engage in behavior that feeds inflation, such as overuse of credit.

Whatever the right policy mix might have been, when the recession ended in 1983, the country came out of it with a dollar rehabilitated to relative soundness and a tax system that had restored incentives to work and invest. On that basis the United States would enjoy steady economic growth, with only two brief exceptions, well into the 21st century.

Economist Brian S. Westbury wrote in The Wall Street Journal in April 2007: "During the high-tax, highly regulated years between 1969 and 1982, the economy was in recession 32% of the time. Since then, following Ronald Reagan's tax cuts and deregulation and Paul Volcker's victory over inflation, the U.S. economy has only been in recession 5% of the time."

The Mundell supply-side formula had been proved correct. Reagan had pushed aside all the old class-warfare, soak-the-rich populism that had taken hold in the 1930s and had restored the kind of free-enterprise populism that had made the United States great. It was a populism that puts its faith in the worth and ability of every individual, assuming that each will strive to create wealth for himself and the overall economy if not encumbered by excessive tax and regulatory burdens by those who govern.

Many economists and politicians ultimately contributed to the implementation of supply-side economics as a public policy that would curb, to some degree, undisciplined Keynesian politics. The supply-side "revolution" was something of a repeat of the American Revolution, which also was a revolt against excessive taxation and regulation. The main difference was that the Founding Fathers had to fight a shooting war against their oppressor, King George III of England, whereas in the late 20th century, the democratic system the founders had devised permitted a peaceful evolution away from the oppressive, meddling state that had had its beginnings with Herbert

Hoover's illusion that he could reengineer the American economy from his perch on Pennsylvania Avenue.

There were many writers and thinkers who pushed the supply-side revolution in the 1970s, among them Jude, Laffer, Mundell, Bartlett, Roberts, John Rutledge, Alan Reynolds and Norman Ture. New York congressman Jack Kemp deserves high credit for working with these advocates to design, in collaboration with Senator William V. Roth, Jr., of Delaware, the tax bill that implemented supply-side ideas. The Kemp-Roth tax act, signed by President Reagan on August 13, 1981, at his California ranch, cut the top marginal tax rate to 50% from 70% and phased in a 23% reduction in all rates over three years, reduced the still-existent World War II relic, the "windfall profits" tax, and opened the door for individual retirement accounts (IRAs). When the act became effective in January 1973, the economy began to revive, an event Bob duly noted in a triumphal editorial.

But I think of all those who could claim some credit for the revolution, the one who played the central role was Bartley. He recognized the merit of the supply-side argument early and provided a prominent platform, the Journal editorial page, for its advocates. He gave heavy play to the efforts of politicians like Kemp, Roth and Steiger. He spent many hours turning the arcane economist language of some of the advocates into highly readable copy. And in his own writing, he enlarged on their ideas and made them come to life. He won a well-deserved Pulitzer Prize as a result, but perhaps not the public recognition that was his due.

My job was to keep house. I challenged the challengers, particularly Jude, and demanded that they meet the counterarguments that the doubters would inevitably raise. Bob once told me that a friend of his had said that every organization should have both a sail and an anchor. On the editorial page, he saw Jude as the sail and me as the anchor. That metaphor didn't please me entirely because I regarded myself as more than a deadweight. But I knew what he meant, and if

Bob thought I was the one who kept order on the page, insisting that what we printed should be logical, consistent with established precedents, understandable to the readers and based on rigorous analysis, I decided to take the "anchor" metaphor as a compliment.

In November 1979, The Wall Street Journal celebrated the fact that it had become the largest newspaper in the United States in terms of paid circulation with its 2-million-plus dwarfing competitors like the New York Times and the Washington Post. Warren Phillips, by then CEO, celebrated with a big party for all employees, including mail room staff and janitors, at the City Mid-Day Club, high above Wall Street.

Warren greeted Jody as an "authoress," acknowledging her co-authorship of "The Carter Economy" with me. We sat with our old friends from our days in the Detroit news bureau, Stanley and Esther Penn. The Journal had fulfilled Barney's dream of a truly national newspaper, with printing plants in strategic locations throughout the country able to provide nearly all readers with papers on the day of publication. Too bad he wasn't there to see his dream come true.

The Journal reached that milestone at a time when the national economy was about to take a turn for the better, thanks to the supply-side revolution and what came to be known as "Reaganomics." In the preface to his 1992 book "The Seven Fat Years and How to Do It Again," Bob would write an apt description of that historic turnaround:

"In the years just before 1982, democratic capitalism was in retreat. Its economic order seemed unhinged, wracked by bewildering inflation, stagnant productivity and finally a deep recession. The diplomatic and military initiative lay with Communist totalitarianism, which proclaimed inevitable ideological victory and could send crowds into European streets to protest efforts to offset its own shiny new missiles and tanks. Economic confusions and a sense of futility sapped the morale of the Western people; leaders talked of 'malaise' in America and 'Europessimism' across the Atlantic.

"In a remarkably short time, all of this has been totally reversed. Today, mankind affirms democratic capitalism as its role model."

Indeed. It was a global revolution, led by the likes of Reagan, Margaret Thatcher and Pope John Paul II. Best of all, it was relatively bloodless.

CHAPTER 11

We Tangle with the Times

As Bob asserted, the revolution of the 1980s changed the lives not only of Americans but of all "mankind." That may sound like an exaggeration, but it was not. The economy of the entire planet took a turn for the better. As the decade began, Margaret Thatcher was already setting Great Britain on the road to recovery from socialist stagnation by privatizing moribund state industries, establishing a model that would be copied in varying degrees by other European countries. Deng Xiaoping was setting China on a new course from the horrors of Maoism by opening the door to capitalist investment.

But the Soviet empire was still presenting formidable challenges at the outset of the 1980s. Particularly worrisome were the inroads Communism was still making in our Western Hemisphere. And a certain segment of American opinion was still conducting a romance with the idea of Communist-style revolution. Bob and I were having a chat one morning in 1980 and agreed that we were both unsatisfied with the reporting coming out of the Caribbean and Central American region.

In Nicaragua, what had initially looked like a broad-based "Sandinista" movement to overthrow dictator Anastasio Somoza was showing signs of becoming a well-disguised Marxist coup. But it wasn't being reported that way in the mainstream press, most particularly the New York Times, from which a good many other reporters took their cues, most particularly the foreign correspondents in New York and Washington filing dispatches to newspapers and broadcast outlets overseas. So we decided that I should go down for a close-up look.

First, I went to Jamaica, which is not a Latin country but had been of interest to us because of signs that its premier, Michael Manley, was becoming increasingly thick with Fidel Castro, the point man for Soviet imperialist designs on the Western Hemisphere. Manley was in no way ideological, but he was probably attracted by the fundamental commitment the Communists could make to small-country politicians, help in rigging elections, or eliminating them altogether, so as to gain lifetime tenure.

An election campaign was under way in which Eddie Seaga, a Jamaican of Lebanese descent whom Bob and I had met in New York, was trying to unseat Manley. Seaga's aides, in showing me around Kingston, explained that they could tell how things were going by observing which party's graffiti dominated in the various neighborhoods. That theory sounded a bit dubious, but it reflected the rather primitive form of democracy practiced on the island.

Seaga picked me up at my hotel for dinner at a hilltop restaurant. I noticed that his driver was keeping his foot down as we sped through the streets of Kingston. It dawned on me that I was riding with a candidate who had some reason to fear an ambush. Preelection violence had already claimed several lives.

Eddie won the election and began to purge Castro's Cuban infiltrators from their camps in the hills. They were at a disadvantage because they didn't speak the Jamaican English-based patois, and locals were afraid of these strange Spanish-speaking foreigners who appeared to be up to no good.

The Jamaican economy was not doing well. At the Kingston airport on my way to Panama, I noticed a remarkable number of Jamaicans with huge suitcases arriving and leaving. Smuggling was an active industry. I wondered how much was in it for Manley's customs inspectors.

In Panama, I touched base with the U.S. Army's Southern Command, then based in the Canal Zone, to see if the generals wanted to talk about security issues arising from the more active Soviet interest in the area. That interest had manifested itself in the setting up of a Russian Lada car distributorship at Colon on the Atlantic end of the Panama Canal. It did double duty as a KGB listening post, as was manifestly evident from all the antennae on its roof, a requirement not associated with selling cars. But the Southern Command generals were rather closemouthed about what was happening in this front of the Cold War.

They had good reason to be. Had they raised an alarm, they would almost certainly have come under attack from a leftist coterie in the U.S. Congress that included, among others, Connecticut senator Chris Dodd and Massachusetts congressman Edward Patrick Boland. Some key operatives in the Carter State Department also were taking a benign view of the leftward trend in Central America. So the Socom generals were quietly going about their business, hoping for a new administration in Washington that would give them more support. They would get one with the election of Ronald Reagan later that year.

Then I flew to Managua, Nicaragua. Marxist-Leninist posters decorated lampposts, a rather obvious indication of what kind of revolution the men who now controlled the once broad-based Sandinista directorate had in mind. The strategy of Cuban-trained Marxist Thomas Borge, who now controlled the army, and his cohorts was classical Leninism.

Pedro Chamorro, son of the La Prensa editor whose mysterious assassination precipitated the Somoza overthrow and the creation of the Sandinista directorate, had visited us in New York and had been optimistic about the transition to democracy. But not long before my visit, the Marxists had pulled off the second phase of the revolution, by seizing control of the directorate and forcing the moderates out. Nicaragua had become a Castro-Soviet satellite.

In short, there were two revolutions, as the redoubtable Shirley Christian would later write in her perceptive book about the takeover. "The first was broadly based, aiming at establishing a western-style democracy; the second was narrowly based, seeking a Marxist-Leninist state." The second one succeeded as well.

I visited Pedro at his La Prensa office on the dusty main street of Managua. A thin young man, he was chain-smoking, obviously nervous. He told me why. A young Russian who had just become the Soviet ambassador to Nicaragua had visited him recently with a pointed message, to wit, "We're in charge here now." It would be only a matter of time before La Prensa was shut down. The newspaper whose editor reportedly had lost his life opposing Somoza (although the circumstances of his murder were never clearly established) would be one of the victims of the new dictatorship that succeeded Somoza.

I wrote a bylined piece about all this, scooping the reporters who were supposed to be covering Central America. I won the Daily Gleaner prize from the Inter American Press Association twice for this and other coverage of the area.

Our annoyance at the press complacency about Soviet-Cuban expansionism in Central America was heightened in 1982 when the Times printed a bylined piece by its Central American correspondent Raymond Bonner, purporting to describe a massacre in the Salvadoran village of El Mozote by Salvadoran soldiers with American advisers. It was obvious that Bonner had sources in the Cuban-sponsored insurgency.

Out of our growing annoyance at this kind of tendentious coverage, I wrote an editorial, toughened up by Bob, called "The Media's War," taking the New York Times to task for printing a story based entirely on the claims of the Marxists that other reporters had refused to credit. We reviewed past tendencies of Times reporters to swallow the Marxist line, including Walter Duranty's cover-up of Stalin's crimes in the 1930s, Herbert Matthews' glorification of Fidel Castro in the '50s and a piece by Sydney Schanberg, of "Killing Fields" movie fame, who had written before Cambodia fell to the murderous Khmer Rouge that life would be better for Cambodians after the meddlesome Americans left the area. And now we had Ray Bonner reporting as gospel what he had been told by Salvadoran guerrillas, a story other reporters had passed up as impossible to substantiate.

The editorial had immediate impact. I was invited to go on the PBS "MacNeil/Lehrer Report" to defend our position. The Times sent Schanberg, who unsurprisingly was fuming at our mention of him. His anger probably worked against him on television. I said that it is not uncommon for reporters to find revolutionary movements appealing out of a belief that the revolutionaries are fighting for the rights of "the people." But unfortunately, the people often end up with fewer, not more, rights.

I could have enlarged on this point were there time enough, noting that this concern for the people is very much in the American Populist tradition, but that Soviet-style populism was very different. It had proved to be sustainable only through harsh police state methods. The revolutions in Central America were backed by the Soviets as part of their imperial designs.

In what was perhaps a bridge too far, I added that, of course, some reporters are Marxists. Schanberg, furious, challenged me to name one such reporter, but I simply remarked that Marxist beliefs aren't uncommon: "There are college professors all over the country who call themselves Marxists." The specific reporter I had in mind wasn't Schanberg, but a young lady who had once covered Latin America for the Journal who, unadvisedly, had once told Dow Jones president Ray Shaw that she was a Marxist. She later left the Journal.

Whatever sympathies Sydney may have had before the Khmer Rouge takeover—and he was only one of many reporters critical of U.S. policy in Southeast Asia—I certainly didn't think he was a Marxist in 1982, 10 years after witnessing a genocide conducted in the name of Marxism. He had seen a living hell, and I admired him for staying in Cambodia to cover this horrible chapter of history. I had not savored an emotion-laden debate on national television with someone who had experienced what Sydney had. But it was my job to defend our position.

I felt like I had been through a wringer as I walked out of the Channel 13 studio into a cold rain, wondering if I had libeled anyone. When I got to Penn Station to catch my train, there was a woman screaming into a telephone for someone to come and get her. "I don't have any money!" she yelled. Then, in the waiting room a vagrant had attempted to slash another with a broken wine bottle. I said to myself, "My God, will this night never end?" When I finally got home, Jody assured me that I had handled things well. That was good news, even if it did come from a not altogether objective observer.

After our attack, Times executive editor Abe Rosenthal made a fact-finding trip to Central America, hosting local reporters at a dinner in San Salvador. Not long after, Ray Bonner was called back to New York and assigned to the business page. He later left the paper. We finally met as panelists at an Americas Society seminar on the Central American conflicts for New York journalists, a session where I was rather appalled at the tendency of members of the audience to indulge themselves in long speeches rather than asking intelligent questions.

Ray was remarkably amiable toward me under the circumstances, and I rather liked him. As I was leaving to catch my train, while the orators in the audience were still droning on, Ray asked me jokingly if I was going out to write another editorial. He later returned to the Times as a foreign correspondent in Asia, covering such events as attacks by environmentalists on U.S. mining companies in Indonesia. It was fairly clear that he did not sympathize with the American corporations.

An editorial I wrote in 1981 also made waves. Israel, fearing that Iraq's Saddam Hussein was shooting for a nuclear weapon by having the French build a power reactor for him at a place called Osirik, conducted a well-planned air raid and blew up the nearly completed reactor. We decided to support the Israelis, and I wrote the editorial. The State Department, of course, deplored this action, although I suspect that Reagan was secretly pleased. The Israelis who, then as today, had few friends, were denounced in the United Nations, and we were criticized for supporting this bold resort to violence.

I think our position looks better in retrospect, considering that Saddam started a war with Iran shortly afterward, used poison gas in that war and sacrificed a million young Iraqis to his megalomania during the inconclusive eight-year struggle. His attack on Kuwait a decade later had to be suppressed by an American-led coalition, and he was found to have a secret nuclear bomb project afterward. He remained a threat to his neighbors until the 2003 U.S.-led invasion that ultimately brought his death. If the Israelis feared him in 1981, they had good reason.

I spent a lot of time in the 1980s indulging my continuing interest in international affairs with full encouragement from Bob. The Journal had provided me with a membership in the club atop the World Trade Center for the purpose of entertaining VIPs. In 1981, the club sent out a letter inviting members to join a tour. Leonid Brezhnev had decided that perhaps the Soviet Union's dismal performance in international trade could be improved by hosting an international conference of World Trade Center members. The New York WTC invited club members to be part of its delegation. I thought it a good opportunity to go back to Russia without the hassle of getting a journalist visa, so I signed up as a "Dow Jones & Co. editor."

I doubt that my little subterfuge prevented the KGB from pulling out my dossier, but the Soviets were on their best behavior and raised no objection. They even invited delegations from Israel and Hong Kong. A young Hong Kong man who owned a plastics company told me that he knew they had let the bars down entirely when they welcomed Hong Kong, the citadel of private capitalism.

Capitalists from all over the world were feted at "gala dinners" well lubricated with varieties of flavored vodka and mild Russian champagne. We were bused to the old capital, Vladimir, where a diorama in city hall depicts the sacking of the city by the Mongol Golden Horde many centuries ago. Jody, who went along, was particularly amused when some fellow passenger tried to give chewing gum to little boys hanging around our bus, only to see it snatched away by angry matrons who obviously feared we foreigners were trying to corrupt their children.

In Suzdol, where we visited an ancient monastery on June 21, we could see from our hotel window large women clad only in bikinis taking advantage of the long twilight to tend their private garden plots. Back in Moscow, one of the highlights was a party given by the Moscow Soviet (city council), which gave lie to the old myth that Communists were puritanical. The female dancers were lightly clad, and because they were Russian, their dancing was far better than anything you might see in a Las Vegas nightclub.

But alas, the façade of friendliness was paper thin. A young Jewish millionaire from Manhattan named Rudy who had entertained us all with his good humor was detained and strip-searched shortly before our departure for Helsinki from Leningrad. His offense had been to visit the suburban Moscow apartment of a female conference worker one night to get some idea of how she lived. He joined us on the plane but was shaken by the experience. His parents had suffered harsh treatment at the hands of the Nazis, and his interrogation had brought back those memories.

Our Finnair plane started taxiing even before everyone had strapped in, and a cheer went up when we left the ground. A pretty young Finnish guide met us at Helsinki Airport, saying sweetly, "I will take you to your hotel so you can wash off all that Russian dirt." The Finns, who had fought the valiant Winter War against the Soviets in 1940 and had been threatened into uneasy neutrality at the outset of the Cold War, held no love for Russia.

I engaged in a bit of playfulness in the 1980s that was probably unwise. I was occupying my nightly trip home on the train by scribbling what I hoped might be a Cold War adventure novel. I found it relaxing to try to solve the problems of an unfolding plot, which involved an American involved in an effort by a Hungarian dissident group to wipe out the Soviet politburo with a bomb from a hijacked Soviet plane during a May Day flyover. One night, at a party given by the Chinese military mission to the United Nations in New York, I met a young Russian lieutenant colonel named Nicolai. I saw him as a possible source for Red Army lore for my book and perhaps a broader understanding of Russia that would aid my writing for the Journal, so I invited him to lunch at the WTC Club.

Looking around at the gleaming art deco furnishings, he muttered that I had obviously picked a place that would impress a poor Russian. But he softened up over lunch, and we had a good chat. He told me he was responsible for communications between the New York mission and the relay station in Cuba that linked New York with Moscow. I assumed that meant he was KGB.

Nicolai apparently assumed that I doubled as a CIA agent. Since Russian journalists overseas worked for the KGB, Russians ascribed the same dual role to Americans. Perhaps I was trying to open some sort of back channel. So Jody and I were invited to the next party of the Russian mission. There, I found myself the center of some interest. In what seemed like a carefully choreographed gavotte, a Russian brigadier approached and asked me about the prospects for greater trade between our two countries. I gave a polite answer citing the difficulty of extending credit lines, avoiding the real answer, that the Soviets didn't make anything Americans would want to buy.

Then, the top-ranking officer, an admiral, came up to deplore the arms race, asking why we couldn't freeze arms at the present level. Jody butted in to answer, "Because you have more than we do." I, more diplomatically, said that the terms would have to include inspection on demand. I enjoyed this brief interlude playing arms and trade negotiator, but when Nicolai came to the office one day with a present (a book) and wanted to know what I could tell him further about the problems of the Abrams tank mentioned in a Journal story, I decided to break off the contact, lest I get a visit from the FBI wondering what the hell I was up to. I would have, of course, said, "I'm just doing my job," and it would have been at least partly true.

U.S. ambassador to the United Nations Jeanne Kirkpatrick invited Jody and me to dinner at her Waldorf Tower residence in July 1983 to honor Armando Valladares, the Cuban poet who had just been released after 22 years in prison for defying Fidel Castro. He would write a best-selling book, "Against All Hope," about the brutality he suffered. We were pleased to be in the company of such luminaries as Henry Kissinger, Commentary editor Norman Podhoretz and Time magazine editor Henry Grunwald. At one point, I expressed puzzlement about why some U.S. senators were opposing U.S. efforts to combat the Soviet penetration of Central America, when surely they were "loyal Americans."

"I wouldn't assume that," the ambassador snapped back. I felt like I was being chastised for talking baby talk. She was a tough lady and good to have on our side in the Cold War.

Speaking of tough, Jody and I were in Waterville, Ireland, once for a European Union conference and were spending an evening in a pub drinking Guinness with some of our Irish hosts. After a round of "Rose of Tralee," Ted Smythe, an Irish diplomat, told us that the reason there were so many excited young lads hanging around outside was that the Waterville Gaelic football team was in the next room celebrating their victory in a national championship match. He asked if we would like to have a peek at the celebration, so we scuttled past the bar and through the small door to look in on them. These hard-looking men were sitting at a long table with their women, knocking back Irish whisky. They seemed grim. "That's the way they celebrate," Ted whispered. We decided it was best not to disturb them.

The European Union conference was about the continuing evolution of the European community toward a single market. That process would continue steadily even to the point of most members sharing a single currency. It was always gratifying to watch this process unfold on a continent that had known so much bloodshed and sorrow over the centuries. Those were hopeful times for Europe. The Cold War was creating a lot of anxieties in Europe and America, but the common threat from the Soviets was helping forward-looking leaders forge closer ties between the United States and Europe and also fostered a common goal by the Germans and French to end their long history of bloody conflict and forge a unified Europe with open borders and the free movement of people. That now is an almost-completed project, although with some continuing glitches, of major historic importance.

CHAPTER 12

The Rise of the Naderites

L ife in the 1980s involved a lot more than conferences and parties. There was also a lot of writing to be done as we tackled a broad variety of issues. On January 31, 1983, Bob wrote an editorial marking the founding of our second overseas edition, The Wall Street Journal Europe, based in Brussels, Belgium. We had started the first, The Asian Wall Street Journal (AWSJ), in Hong Kong in 1976.

Bob cited C.W. Barron's writing tours of Europe in the teens to note that we had recognized the global interconnections of business and economics for many years. Bob remarked at how the communications revolution had made those ties even more intricate and pervasive. He said this web probably had been more complex than we imagined. With a European edition, he wrote, "we hope to learn and share insights with readers in the international community, and thus help to understand and confront the problems and opportunities before us all."

We soon would have a pointed lesson in how much we were a part of the international community. In 1984, we found ourselves in a fight with Singapore's prime minister Lee Kuan Yew, whose anti-Communism we had sometimes praised in the past, over the attention we had given to one of the few opposition politicians willing to challenge the Lee regime.

When Dow Jones started the AWSJ in 1976, it carried no editorials but had a Commentary and Analysis page that published a range of signed opinion columns from the U.S. editorial page and nonstaff contributors. Melanie Kirkpatrick edited that page in the early 1980s. In 1984, a decision was made to print editorials, and Bob appointed Asian

Journal reporter Paul Gigot to be the first editor. On October 17 that year, Melanie wrote a hard-hitting editorial commenting on how the government of Singapore was using the legal system to discredit an opposition politician, J.B. Jeyaretnam, who had been disbarred:

"[Mr. Jeyaretnam] has recently suffered what many Singaporeans believe is official harassment. The problem here is government credibility. We don't know if Mr. Jeyaretnam is guilty. But even if he were, many Singaporeans wouldn't believe it because court actions, and especially libel suits have long been used in Singapore against opposition politicians."

According to a 1998 book, "The Media Enthralled," by prominent Singaporean lawyer and political dissident Francis Seow, Prime Minister Lee was furious and instructed his prosecutor to punish the offending parties. On October 30, 1984, the high court held Dow Jones Publishing Co. (Asia), Asian Journal editor and publisher Fred Zimmerman, the paper's Singapore correspondent, and the printer and distributor all in criminal contempt. Upon local legal advice, the Asian Journal apologized and pleaded guilty, receiving the U.S. dollar equivalent of a $2,822 fine, a fine of $1,411 for Zimmerman and $235 each for the printer and distributor. Paul and Melanie were also fined.

The handling of this affair was controversial within Dow Jones. Zimmerman, a former Washington bureau staffer who thought the Asian Journal should not have an editorial page, was offended at being fined for an editorial written by a writer working for Bartley. He not only wanted to accede to the Singapore demand for a "humble" apology but wanted to include in his affidavit that he sometimes didn't read the editorial page. Paul and Melanie objected to that wording and to the efforts of the Asian lawyers to go over their heads. The issue was taken up in New York, and Bob reached a compromise with executive editor Ed Cony that Zimmerman would take out his gratuitous "not responsible" claim and Bob would drop his demand that we not apologize (certainly not "humbly") for publishing the editorial, but only for offending the court.

Bob was not happy with the outcome and wrote a memo to Peter Kann, the AWSJ's first publisher and by then Dow Jones president and chief operating officer (COO), advising him that if the Journal were to succeed in Asia it would have to stand up to would-be dictators, reminding him of the precedent set by Barney Kilgore in facing down GM in 1954. He sent Melanie to Singapore to write an article about Singapore's Central Provident Fund, a compulsory savings program for Singapore workers to finance retirement and health care. We ran it on the U.S. editorial page under her byline. His point: letting Lee know he was supporting our writer.

As Bob had expected, Lee Kuan Yew, emboldened by the AWSJ backdown, continued his suppression of the press, taking aim at the foreign press in 1986. In that year, he put through amendments to the Newspaper and Printing Press Act allowing the government to "gazette" (curtail circulation) any foreign publication reporting anything about domestic politics not to the government's liking.

Reuters, the Economist and Time magazine became targets. Time had its Singapore 18,000 circulation cut in half for refusing to print in its entirety a tendentious letter from spokesman James Fu complaining of an article defending Jeyaretnam. Time finally capitulated, and its circulation was restored.

Then came the Journal's turn, with a long letter attacking Journal correspondent Stephen Duthie for an article claiming that a new Singapore securities market would be used to unload state-controlled and government-backed companies. This time, the Journal took a tough stance, with Zimmerman responding that it didn't serve our readers to print personal attacks.

The AWSJ was duly gazetted, cutting circulation in Singapore to 500, available only to libraries and government offices, from 5,100 copies a day. This time, Bob made a point to publicize the action, evoking a complaint from the American Society of Newspaper Editors, among others. Peter decided to shut down circulation altogether, denying the government access to the Journal that no one else had. We carried articles from business leaders arguing that Singapore could never hope to surpass Hong Kong as an Asian financial center so long as the government was restricting the news available to bankers and traders. Singapore hung tough for some years but finally decided it wasn't worth the candle. We settled our differences in 1994 without an apology from the Journal. Barney Kilgore was again vindicated. It just took a little longer when confronting a sovereign state.

I was among a small group of journalists cordially entertained by Lee Hsien Loong, Lee's son, when he visited Washington after he became prime minister in 2004.

Singapore, however, took another shot at Dow Jones in 2006 by banning its Hong Kong–based Far Eastern Economic Review business magazine, again for quoting an opposition politician. The Review survived that attack, but Dow Jones discontinued publication in 2009 because the magazine had become unprofitable. Lee Kuan Yew died in March 2015.

We also spent a lot of time in the 1980s trying to cope with Ralph Nader, who was then building a following among young people by proselytizing on college campuses for his particular brand of "consumerism" and "environmentalism." Ralph's was a remarkable story. As a young lawyer, he set about to demonize big business, following the lead of other Progressives who have been a part of the American political culture since the 19th century.

One particular corporate giant, General Motors, deserves Nader's thanks for unintentionally, to say the least, contributing to his rise to international prominence. Nader's 1965 book, "Unsafe at any Speed," asserted rather improbably that a young East Coast lawyer knew more about automobile engineering than the men building cars in Detroit. The title was catchy, but essentially nonsensical because no vehicle, even a cobbled-up hot rod, is intrinsically "unsafe" when moving slowly in the hands of a competent driver.

One chapter was devoted to Chevrolet's Corvair, which featured a rear-engine design that achieved a longtime Detroit goal of doing what

Volkswagen had done years before, building a car with a flat interior floor made possible by eliminating the traditional driveshaft tunnel. Like all rear-engine cars, the Corvair had some tendency to oversteer, meaning that it could turn a bit more sharply than intended with a driver at the wheel accustomed to cars with the engine mounted in front. But drivers adapt to such tendencies. Government tests later on affirmed that the Corvair was as safe as other small cars in its class. It had a loyal following among owners.

If GM executives had been wiser when this book came out, they would have ignored it. In 1956, I had written a front-page Wall Street Journal "leader," titled "Shake, Rattle and Roll," detailing customer unhappiness with automobile defects. Since I didn't play favorites, the Detroit community just rolled with the punch. But Nader had the cleverness to single out the Corvair for special attention and got what he no doubt had been praying for—a GM response. The company unwisely chose to fight back by siccing private investigators on the author, which allowed Nader to file a lawsuit for invasion of privacy and proclaim to the world that he was being victimized by the highly paid galoots running GM. He won the suit, became an instant celebrity and remained one thereafter.

GM paid a heavy price for the corporate arrogance that had grown up out of its dominance, beginning in the 1950s, among American auto producers. The company's success was well earned, resulting from its skill in making products that consumers wanted to buy. But the arrogance and touchiness about any criticism was a fault. Pride goeth before an auto crash.

There was something more to Ralph than his antibusiness bias. As the ridiculous title of his book suggested, he was a born-again fear-monger, apparently in part because of his own fears. A Midwest college administrator told me once of giving Ralph a bed for the night before he was to speak to a convocation. In the morning, my friend apologized for his husky voice, saying he had a cold. Ralph immediately demanded to know whether it was merely a cold or the flu, asking questions about the symptoms. This went on for so long that they almost missed the speaking engagement. The college provost thought Nader's preoccupation with what seemed like a minor ailment strange. But Nader's preoccupation with health and safety seemed genuine. Most likely, it contributed to his tendency to build minor hazards into dire threats. It would stimulate the creation by his acolytes of a new and dangerously pervasive public endeavor, the fear industry.

It is a testament to the beauty of the American free market-free expression culture that a crabby guy like Nader could take on one of the world's largest private corporations and win. The managers of big corporations need critics to teach them a bit of humility from time to time. Otherwise, their enjoyment of economic power can lead them astray. The Journal itself has for years made its bones by keeping readers posted on both the failures and successes of corporate leaders. There is a yin and yang in this, if honestly conducted, that serves the interest of private capitalism.

The question that came up with Nader at the very outset was whether he was an honest critic, or just hated private corporations. If the latter is true, he had plenty of company. The socialism that swept the world in the 20th century was fundamentally antithetical to private ownership of the "means of production." At any rate, Nader early on latched onto a theme that could get the attention of the public, stirring fears about health and safety. Almost always, the threats were posed, in his view, by the big private corporations. Big business was public enemy number one for the "Public Citizen" movement he set in motion.

He was an adept publicity hound. Even the smallest mention of him on our pages would win us a phone call demanding the right to reply, sometimes suggesting in a veiled way that if we didn't give him space, he would launch a political crusade to make granting the right to reply a legal obligation for newspapers, a requirement that would have meant that newspaper editors would no longer have control over their own space. Fortunately, his political influence was never quite strong enough to carry out that threat.

With something approaching organizational genius, Nader managed to turn his organization, Public Citizen, into an international movement. Some colleges and universities even collected fees from students to finance campus chapters. Today, Naderite organizations operate throughout the world, performing such chores as trying to stamp out gold mining on grounds that it exploits human labor and its mining damages the natural environment merely to serve the vanity of bejeweled rich people. Naturally, U.S. mining companies are the prime target of this campaign.

The greatest "success" of the Naderites was the stalling of nuclear power development. Translating the original Nader theme to, in effect, "unsafe at any megawatt," the Naderites conducted their campaign against nuclear power in the press and in the courts. The effectiveness puzzled utility executives and nuclear power contractors and suppliers, mainly because nuclear power had a far better safety record than any other major energy source. Coal mining, then the principal source of fuel for electricity generation, is statistically far less safe than running a nuclear plant.

The Soviet Chernobyl reactor meltdown of 1986 was caused by a faulty design and slipshod Russian management. It was the only nuclear power accident that resulted in multiple deaths, and even its effects were grossly exaggerated in the press. A U.N. report in 2006, 20 years later, said that 28 people who were directly involved died from radiation or thermal burns. By 2006, another 19 of those exposed had died, and there had been an estimated 9 deaths from thyroid cancer. The United Nations concluded that among all the others exposed to radiation, there had been no significant health effects. This tabulation is a far cry from the initial press estimates of hundreds of fatalities, even some in places as far away as Germany. "Chernobyl" would make a good synonym for "mass hysteria" generated by fearmongers.

But the Nader campaign, which resulted in legal and regulatory delays in commissioning nuclear power plants and raised investor fears of disastrous accidents, put the construction of new nuclear power plants on hold for over two decades, making the United States dependent on oil, gas and coal as major energy sources at a time when some other countries, France for one, were drawing most of their electricity from safe nuclear power plants. The Naderites pushed "renewable" energy, like solar panels and windmills, but carpeting the country with that kind of low-output technology would not begin to substitute for existing power sources. Windmills in particular are an eyesore, noisy and a hazard for wildfowl. Fear, what a powerful political tool it has become in the hands of the Naderites, not to mention political factions of other stripes.

The environmental movement began with the perfectly sensible concept that the air in some industrial areas and rivers and streams in heavily populated parts of the country had become polluted and that a cleanup was needed. Doing that job clearly needed legislation and regulation, not only of private industry but what in many areas were the worst offenders—municipal waste disposal systems.

Hardly anyone objected to the adoption of this new public policy objective. After all, if the air and water were to be cleaned up, government was best suited to ensure that the burdens were distributed appropriately to the worst polluters and that all polluters did their share in the cleanup. Clean water and air were clearly a public good just as highways and national defense are a public good. A rich society could afford a cleanup even if the benefits were mainly aesthetic. There were, of course, health benefits as well, particularly if residents of industrial centers could breathe cleaner air.

In short, nobody was in favor of dirty water or air, and there was little opposition to the environmental movement. Scientist and author Fred Hoyle theorized that the environmental movement got a big boost when earthlings in the 1960s were able to see photographs of their planet from deep space and realized that we are all dependent on the atmosphere of that pretty blue orb to sustain our lives. So it was not a bad idea to take good care of it. But the thought gave rise to the notion that the planet and its atmosphere are more fragile and vulnerable to ravages inflicted by humankind than they really are.

That rather distorted the fact that, even though the earth may look small from 25,000 miles away, it actually is a very large planet, and its atmospheric blanket is vast as well. Even if humans set out through some massive death wish to destroy all this deliberately, they would not succeed.

There were conservationists and naturists before the Space Age. But it indeed seems likely that the first pictures of a little earth had a profound impact. Who could quarrel with the idea that our only habitat must be protected and preserved? It was the nearest we could ever get to an unchallengeable principle.

But a principle on which almost everyone agrees is a powerful thing in the hands of political forces inclined toward extensive state control over human activities. It can be put to all sorts of uses, and whether the results are good or bad depends on individual interpretations of how best to save the planet, or, for that matter, the degree to which the planet is in need of "saving."

One must suspect that some of the contenders who fly the banner of environmentalism have a more selfish agenda not always defensible on its own merits. Environmentalism was immediately spotted by professional fearmongers as a handy tool for gaining political influence and power, not to mention private gain. In the half century since the first Sputnik roared into space, activists flying the banner of environmentalism have run roughshod over other important values, such as property rights, job creation or the elevation of the living standards of the world's poorest peoples.

One of the best explications of this phenomenon was presented by the late Michael Crichton in his 2004 book "State of Fear." It is actually a novel, but one with a message. It describes how fear is exploited by the press to sell newspapers, by bureaucrats and pseudoscientists vying for government grants, by politicians stirring up the pot to win votes and by elites offended by the exploitation of natural resources to make products for the masses. Lawyers built a huge multi-billion-dollar industry out of the damages extracted from corporations through product liability suits and have been very generous to politicians and elected judges who have facilitated their access to the courts and allowed them to collect a large cut of the damage awards for themselves.

Al Gore propounded his theories about the threat to the planet from "global warming" in the 1980s, and this alleged threat has become so embedded in political discourse that all evidence to the contrary, such as the sharp drop in global temperatures in the winter of 2007–08, when people in Hong Kong and other semitropical areas shivered with cold, was largely ignored by the press.

On the Journal editorial page, we battled this massive cloud of obfuscation throughout the '80s and '90s. My former Journal editorial page colleagues are still fighting it. Had the Naderites not blocked nuclear power development with their lawsuits and political actions, a larger portion of American electric power would be provided by this clean, reliable and relatively safe source.

Had the wild damage claims of plaintiff lawyers met more resistance from the judiciary, there would have been a lot fewer corrupt practices such as the illicit Milberg Weiss damage suit factory and the attempt to bribe a judge by Mississippi's billionaire Tort king, Dickie Scruggs, who drew seven years in prison for the offense. But alas, the forces arrayed against us were powerful, in large part because the monetary rewards for fearmongering are enormous.

In October 2005, I wrote a Global View column summing up my thoughts about fearmongering of the type I had seen so much of in my professional career. The headline was "I Read the News Today, Oh Boy," a line from "A Day in the Life," one of the songs of the wildly popular rock music group of the 1960s, the Beatles. John Lennon had captured, I wrote, "the sense of resignation generated by the daily diet of doom and gloom fed to us by broadcasters and newspapers. He and his Beatles collaborator Paul McCartney wrote it all off with comic inanities: 'Now we know how many holes it takes to fill the Albert Hall.'"

I wrote that some comfort can be found in sharply discounting apocalyptic theories, "including the breathless predictions of economic collapse, massive social disorder, energy shortages or pandemics. More often than not, over-the-top forecasts are the product of the innate need of all of us to get attention, a need that can now be gratified through access to microphones and TV cameras that transmit words and images instantly to a world-wide audience.

"Especially in need of attention are those of us in the news media. Our jobs and the fate of our enterprises depend on it—hence, the occasional temptation to exaggerate. For government officials, no problem means no appropriation from the legislature—so make it as big as you can. All those non-governmental organizations (NGOs) need to attract donations.

"In all cases, there's a penalty for being wrong—the loss of reputation—but tomorrow's massive news budget will blot from the collective consciousness most of the nonsense uttered today..."

In short, I learned a lot about the politics of fear over a long career in journalism. It will remain with us through thick and thin, and it will sometimes result in a governmental overreaction to a problem that could just as well have been left to work itself out, such as many of the financial crises through history. But fear, I'm told, is a healthy emotion vital to one's self-preservation, so maybe I shouldn't belabor the point. Modern social media are a means of spreading false claims but also sometimes provide an antidote when bloggers with expert knowledge use the Internet to counter exaggerated or false claims reported in the mass media.

Fortunately, some of the other things happening in the 1980s while the Naderites were growing in power were more positive. Reaganomics was restoring the health and vigor of the U.S. economy. In 1987, I launched a new op-ed column called "Business World," an initiative that grew out of our feeling on the page that we weren't devoting enough space to business. That same year, Wall Street "laid an egg," to quote the famous Variety headline of 1929. As had happened in 1929, the crash followed a sharp run-up in stock prices generated by economic optimism. The markets overshot as they so often do when investors are in an ebullient mood. But the consequences were far different.

"Black Monday," when the Dow Jones Industrial Average lost 22% of its value, just happened to be the day of one of Warren Phillips' annual parties to honor longtime Journal employees. The highlight of the evening was a special award to Joe Guilfoyle, a legendary reporter and editor, who started with the Journal as a 15-year-old copy boy and had logged 60 years of service, working his way up to editor of Dow Jones Newswires. The well-meant award was a large chunk of Dow Jones stock. But the stock Joe was handed had just lost a third of its value that day. Everybody in the room thought it was funny, except Joe. If he held it, it would come back, of course. I never asked Joe what he did with it. He might have told me, appropriately, that it was none of my business.

After the Wall Street swoon, I stuck my neck out and wrote a Business World column saying that the crash, barring some policy error in Washington, probably would not do much damage to the "real economy." The Federal Reserve chairman, Alan Greenspan, heeding the lessons of 1929, had made it clear that the Fed would supply sufficient liquidity to the financial sector to keep it afloat while it adjusted to stock portfolio losses. The Reagan tax cuts and free trade measures, as contrasted with the protectionism and tax increases of 1929, had resulted in a healthy investment climate, which was one reason for the stock run-up in the first place. And the real sector—industry and commerce—was healthy as well. As it turned out, I was right, or at least I had quoted the right analysts, who happened to be the bright folks at the Claremont Economics Institute in California. The crash was just a hiccup in a continued economic expansion.

And Greenspan didn't make the mistake he would make 14 years later, when the Fed, in response to the 2001 recession, inflated a credit bubble that collapsed in 2008 with results more serious than those of 1987. But there was a lot more to the problem than that, as I will explain later, and once again the congressional propensity for handing out goodies was at fault.

One of my Business World columns was about a very persuasive analysis of the cause of developing-country ills produced by a Peruvian think tank headed by Hernando de Soto, who had returned to Lima after some years in Europe waiting out the period when the country was ruled by a left-wing military junta. To publicize his think tank findings, De Soto wrote "The Other Path," a book whose title was meant as an alternative to the name of a murderous Maoist group in the Andes that called itself "The Shining Path." His group had studied what he called Peru's "informal sector" of entrepreneurs operating outside the protections of the law, a description that caught on internationally, and concluded that what held the poor down in most countries was government red tape.

Jody and I had dinner with Hernando and his girlfriend at a charming, torch-lit oceanside restaurant in Lima in 1983, and he described to me how college students employed by his think tank had to spend 289 days filling out forms and going through other procedures just to get government permission to start a small clothing factory. The poor people of the barrios might have the skills to start such a business, but they didn't have the time and the education to make it through the obstacle course the government had designed to protect established, politically connected firms. In other words, the poor were victims of that old devil that raises its head in politics so often, protectionism. In this case, it was measures that protected the elite establishment from competition from rising entrepreneurs.

Driven by necessity, the informal sector functioned in a sense, even to the extent of running manufacturing operations and creating its own dispute settlement processes. But its entrepreneurs could not build their businesses and become big employers without legal status. "The Other Path" became an international best seller but, because it defined government as the problem, it never made a big hit with that class of bureaucrats at the United Nations and World Bank who style themselves as economic development specialists and funnel untold billions to governments guilty of the kind of protectionist policies that Hernando exposed.

I also devoted some space in Business World to the Soviet Union, a place that had fascinated me since my days as a foreign correspondent. Mikhail Gorbachev was being lionized by the liberal press in the late 1980s as a true reformer. I took a different view in a column titled "Gorbachev Courts Capitalism, but Only Abroad." I quoted Igor Birman, an expatriate Russian economist, as saying Gorbachev's popularity in the West contrasted sharply with his unpopularity in the Soviet Union. His goal was not reform, but to save the Communist Party. All his talk about openness and reconstruction was a play for the western aid he so desperately needed. I concluded that "there is no capitalist cure for what ails the Soviet empire if the cure is to be administered solely on Mr. Gorbachev's terms." The Soviet collapse in 1991 came as no shock, but I was surprised that it came much sooner than I expected when I was writing those words.

Jody and I got in our ancient Audi, which we had bought second-hand, and went on a 5,000-mile tour of the country in June 1988. I wrote a column afterward saying that the best way to assess the health of an economy is to go out and have a firsthand look at such indicators as the amount of truck traffic, the number of new cars on the road, housing developments springing up outside the cities and whether factory parking lots are full.

I concluded that "Americans, blessed with more than five years of low inflation, tax restraint and resultant economic growth, were rebuilding the nation's economic base." The abundant evidence of that was particularly gratifying to me because it confirmed that the supply-side tax and monetary policies the Journal editorial page had promoted in the 1970s, when put into effect by Ronald Reagan, had paid off. What we saw on our jaunt through 16 states to Santa Fe and back was the real America, a place always worth a visit from anyone in the punditry business. But that was then. This is now.

CHAPTER 13

Maggie and Deng

B artley and I had similar views on most things, including the importance of property rights and the sanctity of private contracts, principles we shared with the Journal's founder, Charles Dow. We occasionally had debates over the issue of separation of church and state, which I favored and Bob was more ambivalent about. He pointed out that there's a reason "In God We Trust" is imprinted on our currency; religious belief was important to the founders. I argued that the mixing of politics and religion was more a threat to religion than politics, citing the decline of the state-subsidized churches of Germany and other parts of Europe. But we didn't disagree on the role the concept of natural "God-given" rights had played in the advancement of western civilization.

The 17th-century English philosopher John Locke is usually credited with forming the idea that men and women are born with certain "natural rights" to life, liberty and property. He argued that God would not have created mankind without providing a means for man to subsist, and thus land ownership was an inherent right. The founders of the United States were familiar with and influenced by the Lockean rationale. Thomas Jefferson drew on Locke's concepts in writing the Declaration of Independence. Although he substituted "pursuit of happiness" for "property," probably to skirt the issue of slaves being property, there is plenty of evidence in the other writings of the Founding Fathers, in the Constitution for example, that they believed that the protection of private property should be guaranteed by law.

The economic importance of the broad exercise of the natural right to own property has been demonstrated repeatedly. "How Capitalism Saved America" is an interesting little book, published in 2004 and written by Thomas J. DiLorenzo, a professor of economics at Loyola College in Maryland. He writes that the early American colonists, who actually predated Locke, were forced by necessity to recognize property rights.

The early settlers in Virginia and Massachusetts originally organized communal settlements. Many died of starvation and disease, largely due to the lack of any recognition by the investors in these enterprises or their indentured servants that they individually must do the hard labor of clearing the land and tilling the soil. The investors felt themselves to be above that, and their servants had little incentive to do so, since they had only a limited stake of their own in reaping what was sowed.

The solution, finally arrived at by the Virginia Company and later William Bradford of the Plymouth colony, was to give the colonists title to small plots of land. In 1611, men in the Jamestown colony were allotted three acres each by the English high marshal, Sir Thomas Dale. "Private property was thus put into place and the colony immediately began to prosper," writes DiLorenzo. "There was no more free riding because each individual himself bore the full consequences of any reduction in output. At the same time the individual had the incentive to increase his effort because he directly benefited from his own labor." In Massachusetts, Governor Bradford would follow this example. He is quoted by DiLorenzo as blaming the disastrous collectivism of the Plymouth colony on "that conceit of Plato" that communal property could make people "happy and flourishing."

It's interesting that the fatal flaw in the early American settlements would be rediscovered, at great cost, in the 20th century by the similarly desperate Soviet Communists after they brutally collectivized agriculture in the late 1920s and early 1930s. The Soviets quickly found out, just as the American colonists had three centuries earlier, that communes were fundamentally unproductive. But rather than give up on them, they only relented on their hidebound ideology to the extent of allowing peasants to have small private plots of about an acre each to grow food for "their own use."

In his 1976 book "The Russians," Hedrick Smith of the New York Times wrote that the tiny private plots a half century later had become a mainstay of Soviet agriculture. "Twenty-seven percent of the total value of Soviet farm output—about $32.5 billion worth a year—comes from private plots that occupy less than 1 percent of the nation's agricultural lands (about 26 million acres). At that rate, private plots are roughly 40 times as efficient as the land worked collectively."

A far more dramatic example of the power of ownership was the Chinese economic "miracle." A 1999 article in the Hong Kong magazine Asiaweek declared the creator of the miracle, Deng Xiaoping, "The Asian of the Century." It had this to say: "Those who inhabited China's vast countryside can truly appreciate Deng Xiaoping's greatness. In countless villages lived four-fifths of the hundreds of millions of Chinese, most of them in abject poverty. An entire family might share a single pair of trousers. If lucky, they might live in a small thatched roof hut with a hole at the top to let out the smoke from the open hearth fire. Peasants transported their ducks and geese to markets along rivers and ancient canals; there were few roads."

In other words, Mao Tse-tung, with his "Great Leap Forward" in his efforts to establish Communism in China, had actually succeeded in rolling the clock backward to something more closely approximating the Middle Ages in Europe, wrote Asiaweek. An estimated 40 million Chinese died of starvation and abuse. When Mao died in 1976, China was a basket case, having suffered the ravages of both the Great Leap Forward and the "Cultural Revolution" of the late 1960s in which Mao endeavored to regain control over the citizenry by turning youthful "Red Guards" loose to maim, kill and plunder. Mao invited U.S. president Richard M. Nixon to come to China in 1972, in part because he needed some big event to help him lift the broken spirits of the Chinese people, Asiaweek concluded.

When Deng took power in the late 1970s, it was clear that collectivism had failed once more, just as it had in the American colonies and the early experiments of the Bolsheviks in Russia. Deng addressed the problem with a wholesale redistribution of the government's landholdings, seized earlier from private landlords, to the peasants working the land. The farmers were free to choose what crops they would grow but required to pay in-kind taxes to the government, in the form of staples.

As Asiaweek noted: "Soon money was beginning to course through the system. Two-story brick houses rose where thatched huts used to be. Some 200 million Chinese—more people than all of Indonesia—escaped destitution. Thus, Deng lifted more people out of poverty than any other world leader, anytime, anywhere."

Signs saying "To Get Rich Is Glorious," a clear reversal of Communist "egalitarian" doctrine, were plastered in public places throughout the country. Entrepreneurship was revived. Private property ownership came back. In 2002, I visited a new apartment building in Shenzhen with my colleague Hugo Restall, editorial page editor of the AWSJ. The real estate agent showing us model apartments for sale went about her work in much the same way as would her counterparts in New York or Chicago. Private enterprise comes naturally to the Chinese as a result of their centuries-old traditions as traders. When free to do so, they had proved that spectacularly in Hong Kong and Taiwan and were setting about to prove it again on the mainland.

Of course, mainland China is not a free country in the sense of offering its people democratic choices in government. But its phenomenal growth attests to the powerful economic incentives unleashed by allowing people, as Locke would have said, to "enjoy the fruits of their own labor." If history is any guide, the rise of a Chinese middle class will be followed by public demands for more democratic government.

It is interesting that, about the time Deng Xiaoping was touching off his earth-shaking revolution in China, England's new prime minister, Margaret Thatcher, was launching one in the West. After ousting the stumbling Labour Party in 1979, she set about to carve a bloated Socialist government down to size. Mrs. Thatcher, a shopkeeper's daughter, proved to politicians around the world that seizing private property was not necessarily a route to political success, particularly when governments proved inept at managing the enterprises they seized, which was invariably the case. They seldom can compete against privately owned ventures in the world marketplace, mainly because politicians insist on turning enterprises into sources of patronage jobs and thereby robbing them of the surpluses needed for reinvestment to command resources and increase efficiency.

Thatcher conducted a wholesale privatization of Britain's moribund state industries, which were heavily featherbedded and run down through lack of investment. They were not even capable of competing in Britain's home market against private multinational enterprises.

Mrs. Thatcher's reforms set the United Kingdom, after years of socialism, onto the road to economic recovery. Hers was an experiment so successful that Tony Blair's New Labour Party, after regaining power 18 years later, made no attempt to reverse it. Indeed, it was so widely emulated elsewhere that the World Bank could report in 2005 that governments around the world had generated $410 billion in proceeds from privatizing state property in the years 1990 to 2003.

In the 20th anniversary of the Reason Foundation's annual privatization report, Mrs. Thatcher had these words to say: "All too often the state is tempted into activities to which it is ill-suited or which are beyond its capabilities. Perhaps the greatest of these temptations is government's desire to concentrate economic power into its own hands. It begins to believe that it knows how to manage business. But believe me, it doesn't, as we discovered in Britain in the 1970s when nationalization and prices and incomes policy together deprived management of the ability to manage."

We on the Journal's editorial page got a taste of Thatcher forcefulness in the late 1980s when she called on us in New York for what we assumed would be a friendly meeting because we had been among her most ardent supporters. It was friendly, except that the prime minister had one bone to pick. We had been arguing that Britain should take a tougher line in its negotiations with China over the future of Hong Kong after the British 99-year lease on the territory expired in 1997, and it reverted back to China. Mrs. Thatcher argued that she had been doing her best to ensure the rights of Hong Kong citizens, and the editorials had been "very hurtful." She wound up by leaning toward Bob across the table and asking in her best schoolmarm style, "Do I make myself cleeah?" Bob asked, "Why don't you give them British citizenship?" She replied, "You take them."

While our editorials reflected our traditional distrust of Communist promises to uphold civil rights, we may have been a bit unfair. Despite being at a bargaining disadvantage, the British were able to negotiate a basic law with substantial protections for Hong Kongers, including at least the promise of future democratic rule. That promise has not been kept and has been a source of popular protests and discontent.

But as I would point out in a column written in the 1990s closer to the event, the rulers in Beijing were smart enough to know that Hong Kong, whose freedom had made it a trade and finance center with few parallels in the world, was too valuable an asset to be destroyed by wanton authoritarianism. That has proved to be the case, and Hong Kong still ranks at the top or near the top of rankings of economic freedom. Deng revived the historic commercial traditions that Mao had suppressed, and Deng's successors know that preserving them and the rise in living standards they have provided the Chinese people is vital to the survival of a regime that is now "Communist" in name only, but still undemocratic.

Thomas Paine, in promoting the American revolution of 1776, had argued that government is a "necessary evil" to society. Ideally, it provides an umbrella of law and order and national security under which individuals can pursue honest and peaceful endeavors free of threats to life and limb or their property. Yet, as we have learned in the American experiment, people who engage in the task of governing are subject to ambitions not unlike those who involve themselves with private ventures. They find ways to promote government projects and, hence, their own careers, sometimes by dubious means.

The 1980s were a remarkable decade. In those years, the pendulum that had swung so far toward state power in the preceding decades of the 20th century swung dramatically the other way. Communism, the ultimate in state power over economic decision making, collapsed in China and would soon do so in the vast Soviet empire, granting nearly 2 billion people more economic freedom than they had ever had before. That energized the world economy in a way seldom before seen in the history of the earth.

On the Journal editorial page, we covered these events, along with the free market revival at home, with great enthusiasm. The Journal started a European edition, based in Brussels, in 1983. We put a young Rhodes Scholar named Gordon Crovitz, who had started with us as an intern while still attending the University of Chicago, in charge of the European editorial page. He would become publisher of the Journal in the years prior to the sale of Dow Jones to Rupert Murdoch in 2007. Gordon kept us up to date on the influence of Thatcherism on the European continent in the 1980s. Unfortunately, the pendulum, as with all pendulums, began swinging the other way in 2009 when the Progressives regained power in the United States, Vladimir Putin strengthened the hold of his KGB oligarchy on Russian government and a new force, Muslim absolutism, started rolling back democratic progress in the Middle East toward a style of government modeled after the caliphates of ancient times.

CHAPTER 14

On the Road Again

I n 1987, it became clear to me that I was in a tenuous position as deputy to an editor who was 10 years my junior. Bob needed a younger deputy who would be prepared to take over on Bob's retirement or in the event of some mishap. Bob wasn't saying this to me. He had always been very sensitive toward the feelings of the people who worked under him. But Peter Kann, who would eventually succeed Warren Phillips as CEO, was dropping little hints. I understood all this. Managers get paid to manage, and Peter was a skillful manager.

Bob decided that we should have a business column and that I should write it, leaving more of the day-to-day responsibilities for editorials to Dan Henninger, who had developed into an excellent editor and was clearly the choice of both Peter and Bob for the next deputy editor. He was 10 years younger than Bob and 20 years younger than me. So I started a weekly op-ed column called "Business World," which was an agreeable change in that it enabled me to get out of the office and do more face-to-face reporting, often through interviews with chief executives.

Corporate raiders were targeting many companies at the time, and CEO resentment of these buccaneers was running high. The tension made good fodder for a business column. The raiders certainly had their faults, excessive greed being one. Some of their schemes for getting control were clearly not beneficial to the companies, particularly the technique of borrowing heavily to buy out shareholders with the intent of repaying the debt out of the company's treasury. In the movie "Pretty Woman," Julia Roberts likened this strategy to stealing cars to sell the parts, to which Richard Gere replied that the difference was that his raiding was legal.

Legal or not, the raiders offended real-world CEOs just as much as Gere irked the targeted Ralph Bellamy in "Pretty Woman." They invented ways to fend off the buccaneers, including trying to get protections from Congress. An ambitious U.S. attorney named Rudy Giuliani saw a political opportunity in this resentment and launched investigations of Wall Street practices tangential to corporate raiding.

Caught in that net was a brilliant financier named Michael Milken and the trading house he represented, Drexel Burnham, which had specialized in floating issues of high-yield "junk" bonds to finance takeovers. Milken ultimately made a plea bargain for the crime of "parking," which means helping a company get some debt off its books by buying the debt temporarily. For an offense that usually brings a fine by the Securities and Exchange Commission, Milken went to jail. Drexel Burnham collapsed under a flood of lawsuits, and corporate raiders were handed a major defeat.

We at the Journal felt that Milken had been a victim of CEO payback and excessive prosecutorial zeal. Our argument was that on balance, raiders were a force for what the famous economist Joseph Schumpeter had called "creative destruction," the necessity to throw out the obsolete to get on with economic growth. Some of the most vulnerable corporations were conglomerates that had been built by overly acquisitive CEOs and that consisted of components that had nothing in common and were not well managed by the central headquarters. Breaking them up and selling off the parts often resulted in greater economic efficiency.

As to junk bonds, they today play an important role in the economy, allowing riskier ventures to get financing that allows them to grow and compete with established companies. That, of course, helps foster the product competition that keeps consumer product markets healthy. Established companies would prefer not to have that competition.

Milken completed his jail term and has used his fortune to further cancer research and finance the Milken Institute, a West Coast economics think tank. Giuliani's political ambitions were realized as mayor of New York, a role where his toughness paid off for the taxpayers, as he deployed police to high crime areas and effectively reduced street crime. He campaigned, unsuccessfully, for president in 2008.

The column allowed me to bounce around the country, sometimes with Jody, visiting old haunts like Chicago and Detroit. Big steel companies were moaning over their losses and demanding that Congress protect them from imports. But I discovered that smaller steelmakers using electric furnaces were competitive with foreign producers and were making money. The railroad industry had gone through a huge shakeout that had resulted in government creations like Conrail and Amtrak. But entrepreneurs had found they could make money picking up abandoned trackage and running short lines to serve local needs. I got a renewed appreciation for the creativity and risk-taking that has made the American economy the most dynamic in the world.

In 1989, Seth Lipsky, Brussels-based editor in charge of our editorial pages in Europe and Hong Kong, told Bob that he was planning to leave the Journal to embark on a venture of his own. He was taking charge of an English-language version of the Forward, a venerable New York Yiddish newspaper that had served its Jewish audience since 1897. It had once had a national circulation of over 275,000 but was in decline, and its owners felt that an English version would revive its fortunes.

The irony was that Seth was moving from the Journal editorial page to conduct a project for a news organization with socialist labor traditions. The Forward had once carried such anticapitalist writers as Leon Trotsky, one of the original Russian Bolsheviks and the leader of the successful military campaign against the democratic Kerensky government forces.

The marriage Seth formed with the Forward lasted 10 years, but then Seth and some of his associates parted company and founded a new version of the old New York Sun. The owner of the nameplate of the old Sun donated it to Seth so he could see it in print again a half century after it had disappeared from view. The Sun, a great little newspaper but up against competition from cable news and the Internet that was giving even big newspapers headaches, lasted six and a half years but folded in September 2008.

While Bob and I were pondering a replacement for Seth, Bob asked me, "I don't suppose you would be interested?" I replied, "I've actually been thinking about it. Let me talk it over with Jody." I knew this was my way out, a chance to give Bob what he needed, myself a way to prolong my career (I was 62), and myself and Jody a change of scenery. So I asked Jody, "How would you like to go to Europe to live for a while?" She naturally asked, "How long?" and I replied, casually, "Oh, a few months, maybe a year or so." Jody, never one to turn down a new adventure, said yes.

When I reported this to Bob the next day, he said, "That solves a lot of my problems." I knew what he meant. He added, "And you can write a column about foreign affairs." So I became "Deputy Editor, International" and author of a new column called "Global View," a title I selected because it gave me maximum scope to write about whatever I wished, including events in the United States. Jody and I, by now with three adult children who had gone their separate ways, packed up and moved to a sturdy townhouse on Rue Gachard in Brussels, Belgium.

The able Dan Henninger took over my job of writing editorials and editing those written by other members of the staff and getting out an editorial page every day. Bob began work on his book, "The Seven Fat Years," explaining how supply-side policies were translated into legislation and why, after the stagnation of the 1970s, they set the United States on a new path of vigorous economic growth.

In a bylined article on January 2, 1990, Bob took note of what he called a "national hypochondria," which he felt to be totally unjustified in view of the remarkable achievements of the 1980s.

"We are now witnessing the world-wide triumph of American values and the collapse of the empire that threatened us for two generations. A decade ago we faced the prospect of world-wide inflation and economic collapse. Over the decade this threat has been confounded and almost forgotten. Last year our per capita gross national product was 17% above 1980 in real terms, 38% above 1970 and 68% above 1945. The economy expanded for nearly the whole decade; we have now reached a peacetime record eighth year of economic expansion. Peace and prosperity."

Bob thought that part of the hypochondria might be attributable to media commentators who were not in harmony with the reforms of the 1980s, with the conventional media/academic wisdom "trying to find reasons why it was right and Ronald Reagan wrong." But he also noted that a period of change generates unease; the gloomy predictions of Thomas Malthus that world population would outrun the food supply were made in 1798, just when the Industrial Revolution was generating a widespread rise in living standards.

The new revolution that had dawned in the 1980s was the information revolution, which as Bob correctly predicted, would spell the end of the ability of totalitarian governments to keep their subjects in the dark and thus break the hold on power of authoritarian regimes in many places.

"The task before us is not to stop the new information age, but to take advantage of its vast opportunities. We will have to learn to live in a world economy. We shouldn't try to fight the marketplace but listen to what it is telling us. Clearly it is telling us to become more modern, more globally minded, more innovative, more entrepreneurial.

"An appropriate policy for the new interdependent world, indeed, would be unilateral free trade. In the long run, trade and investment barriers hurt the nation that maintains them. We should be dismantling ours, and leave it to Japanese citizens to dismantle theirs."

Bob predicted that the world of the 1990s was likely to be kind to the United States. "Our polyglot and multi-racial society has its problems but it also uniquely equips us for an interdependent world. More than other nations, we have developed the strong suit of adaptability; we can handle rapid change better than probably any other society. We certainly have the world's best entrepreneurial tradition. Barriers to starting a business are still lower here than in other nations. Risk-taking is more fashionable."

Bob wound up this remarkably prophetic essay with: "So welcome to the 1990s. From now on, let's feel free to enjoy our good fortune."

Overseeing the European and Hong Kong editorial pages from my new posting in Brussels would open up one of the most rewarding and interesting periods of my life, and Jody's as well. At a time when most people our age were thinking about retirement, we were embarking on a new phase of our careers in a world that looked much brighter, as Bob had observed, than it had in the 1960s, when we had last lived and worked abroad. I had a column and two editorial pages to look after, and Jody soon found outlets for her talents by writing for a Brussels English-language newsmagazine called "The Bulletin." She also wrote a weekly column for the Indianapolis News back "home" in Indiana. We were to make many new friends as we engaged in the social life of the "capital of Europe."

Brussels had three diplomatic communities, one associated with the North Atlantic Treaty Organization (NATO), another the European Union (EU) and the third, the Belgian government. We would form acquaintances in all three. Other major continental cities were easily accessible as well. Amsterdam was only an hour away and Paris a bit over two hours. We could pull our car out of the garage below our kitchen window and roam Europe at will. Because of my responsibility with the AWSJ editorial page, Tokyo, Delhi, Beijing, Hong Kong and Jakarta would also be among our ports of call.

Bob supplied me with a deputy who could mind the store in Brussels quite ably during my absences. David Brooks was a talented writer, as he would later demonstrate on the staff of The Weekly Standard in Washington, as a New York Times op-ed columnist, a

TV panelist and the author of several books, most notably his "Bo-Bo's in Paradise" about the young bourgeoisie in America who affected a Bohemian lifestyle.

Upon alighting in Brussels, I quickly set up a trip to my old stomping ground, the Soviet Union. I wanted to see what changes had occurred since my last visit in 1981 and, more particularly, whether the U.S.S.R. was experiencing the same kind of political ferment that had brought down the Berlin Wall and was bringing about the secession of important members of the Soviet empire, like Poland and Czechoslovakia.

As I found out when I reached Moscow, the answer was yes. The Baltic republics of the north and the Islamic republics of the south, all members of the empire that the Communists had chosen to call a "union," were more actively than ever trying to escape Russia's embrace. Azerbaijan was in rebellion, and the Lithuanian Communist Party had broken away from the Communist Party of the Soviet Union (CPSU) with the objective of making Lithuania an independent state. Even within the CPSU, a group called the Democratic Platform was demanding reforms.

Party chairman Mikhail Gorbachev had attempted to relieve these pressures with his "glasnost" or "transparency" policy, much publicized and praised in the West. But that had only created a thirst among the peoples who had been misruled by the Soviets for 70 years for more freedom and independence. Meanwhile, the Soviet economy was continuing to sludge up as the cumulative effects of the contradictions I had written about years before continued to mount. The absence of the market pricing vital to the efficient allocation of capital, materials and manpower had vitiated productivity. The party had stifled the natural creativity of the Russian people or had at least driven it underground where it was exercised mainly to find illegal ways to cope with the rigidities of a command economy.

I wrote in Global View that Mr. Gorbachev had concluded—quite correctly—"that political reform was necessary if he was to have any hope of resuscitating the dying Soviet economy." Unfortunately for Mr. Gorbachev and fortunately for Russia, his reforms, which were mostly cosmetic and intended only to save the Soviet Communist Party from impending doom, were too little too late. But I confess that, in early 1990, I didn't realize how close Gorbachev's once all-powerful political party was to the ash bin of history. I would be awakened to that by Garry Kasparov, the world-champion Russian chess master, in Prague five months later.

Gorbachev's measures provided material for several columns. I was skeptical of "perestroika," the economic restructuring also much hyped in the West, arguing that "revolutions from the throne" seldom succeed. It was interesting that, while in the West, Gorby was being praised as a great political innovator, to the Russians he was just the chairman of a party that most had hated for years and would be happy to bid adieu. For that reason, the fall of the Soviet empire, arguably one of the biggest stories of the 20th century, caught a surprising number of American "Sovietologists" napping. It is often true that experts become so wrapped up in their subject that their absorption with minutiae causes them to lose sight of a larger truth.

Of course, some of the western observers were blinded by their own left-wing ideology. In October 1989, Theo Sommer, editor in chief of the Hamburg newspaper Die Zeit, wrote in Newsweek that even though East Germany was not in good shape, it was not on the verge of collapse. Exactly one month later, the Berlin Wall was breached by Germans joyfully celebrating the collapse of their Soviet-backed Communist regime. It was a case of extremely bad timing by the pompous Mr. Sommer and, in my opinion after some brushes with his inflated ego, it couldn't have happened to a nicer guy.

My own perspective was aided by the fact that I had been kibitzing on Russian efforts to make their system work for 23 years. I had long before been cured of thinking it was a noble experiment in the creation of an egalitarian society, as some westerners still believed up until its collapse. Had it been such, the Communist Party would have put its policies and principles up for a popular vote, something they never dared to do in any serious way.

The year 1990 was to have other diversions. Jody and I flew down to Israel in March to attend a global conference of free marketers put together by my old friend Daniel Doron, who ran a free-market think tank in Israel. His goal was to try to shake the old socialists who had founded Israel, and who still were an obstacle to economic progress, out of their cherished orthodoxies. I had the pleasure of speaking from the same dais where the great economist Milton Friedman later held forth. Jody and I found Milton and his wife, Rose, to be charming dinner companions, both full of ebullience. They had for years been trying to persuade political leaders to unlock a similar ebullience in the people they govern by freeing them of government constraints and allowing them to make their own optimal economic choices.

Another charming free marketer was the estimable Trevor De Cleen, who had been revenue minister of New Zealand during its highly successful economic reform in the 1980s. He had played a key role in rolling back New Zealand socialism and adopting a supply-side course through lower taxes and reduced regulation, all of which had imparted new vigor to the New Zealand economy.

When some of the locals in an Israeli town we visited complained that it required 42 permits and took about two years just to build a house, Trevor stood up and said, in his jaunty Kiwi accent: "Let me tell you how we build a house in New Zealand. First you go to city hall and get a building permit. That costs two dollars. Then you buy the materials and a keg of beer and get all your mates together. And then you build the house!" The audience roared with laughter, not only at Trevor's delivery, but at how complicated Israeli socialism had made what, in its essentials, was a very simple project. The fact that the Israeli government owned all of the country's land was part of the problem.

From Israel, Jody returned home, and I flew to New Delhi to meet our AWSJ editorial page editor, Claudia Rosett. Claudia had distinguished herself a year before in her brilliant reporting of the Tiananmen Square massacre in Beijing. She witnessed innocent students demanding nothing more than greater freedom of expression being mowed down by the "People's Liberation" Army. The "liberation" in the title was as bitter a contradiction of reality as any of the Communists, who specialized in bizarre euphemisms, ever invented. The poor students were being liberated, all right, from life itself. The memory of that event would haunt Claudia ever after.

We made a few local calls in Delhi, including a meeting with the Indian foreign minister at his ministry, a grand old building built before air conditioning and thus ventilated with openings at the top of its outer walls that allowed birds to fly above the lobby and the heads of visiting diplomats. Then we decided to visit yet another of the world's trouble spots, Kashmir.

The Indian government had made that region off-limits to reporters to discourage stories about the grievances of the Kashmiris. But Claudia, through an adroit negotiation that kept her up most of the night, wangled tickets to Srinagar on India Airlines for a couple of American "tourists." Kashmir and its houseboats had once been a mecca for tourists, so the airline was happy to see this trade return, even if it was only two people. They didn't need to know that we were journalists writing for a major international newspaper, so we didn't tell them.

Srinagar was a tense place when we arrived. There had been a tragedy that very day in which 3 people had been killed and 20 injured by Indian troops when a crowd tried to rush past Indian troops to present a protest petition to a U.N. outpost on the edge of town. The Kashmiris, predominantly Muslim, claimed that they had been promised a plebiscite in 1947 on whether they would join India or Pakistan or be given independence. Instead, Kashmir was divided between India and Pakistan by a U.N. mandate and had been restive ever since. After the shootings, the army had issued a curfew order saying that anyone out after dark would be shot on sight.

I wrote in my column that India was blaming Pakistan for the trouble, but that Kashmiris in Srinigar were saying they wanted to be ruled by neither India nor Pakistan, but independence. "They surround my colleague Claudia Rosett and me at a neighborhood mosque, holding up two fingers in a V-for-victory sign and begging us to tell their story to the outside world."

Claudia and I found rooms at a hotel outside of town that had once done a big tourist business but was now mostly empty, except for some Italians who had come to ski in the Himalayan mountains that towered over the town. We found the leaders of the protesters in a local mosque, and they poured out their complaints about the importation into Srinagar of sexy Indian movies, alcoholic spirits and other elements of Indian culture that offended their Muslim beliefs.

This encounter with what from all appearances were sincerely devout young men dressed in white robes and skullcaps was my first look at the power of Muslim orthodoxy to inspire insurrection. Claudia received an offer from the Muslim leaders to hide us on a houseboat so we could see firsthand what happened in the mosques at night, but I nixed it because of the curfew and our lack of knowledge, after being in the city for only a few hours, of how dangerous the situation might become. Looking back, I think I should have taken the chance, but my instinct, in such situations, has always been to avoid unnecessary risks.

As it happened, we were able to experience the protest from a lakeside vantage point across the highway from our hotel. Despite the army's death threat, we thought it safe enough to be outside after nightfall at this distance from the action. Soon, the loud speakers of the mosques in town began to blare out the steady chant of "Allah Akbar!, Prepare for Holy War!" from the crowds in the mosques. I didn't stay up, but Claudia said it went on all night. It would also go on for years, with countless violent episodes, including an attack on the Indian Parliament in December 2001 that resulted in the deaths of five terrorists, six police officers and a gardener. Kashmir would be a dangerous flash point in relations between India and Pakistan until the first decade of the 21st century, when the two countries worked out a modus vivendi of sorts with U.S. encouragement.

I wrote that India's problem with its Muslims resembled that of Russia with its own large Muslim population in central Asia and the Caucasus. A sluggish economy offering limited opportunities for the poor had bred discontent. In India's case, the primary cause was the Fabian socialism India's Founding Fathers, Mahatma Gandhi and Jawaharlal Nehru, borrowed from British intellectuals after independence. When a more enlightened leadership in India in the 21st century began to emulate the Chinese swing to market economics and thereby achieved faster economic growth, India's problems with internal dissent and its relationship with Pakistan diminished.

In April, Jody and I flew to Tokyo to attend a series of briefings for the American press laid on by Nomura Securities Co., Inc., at that point the largest securities house in the world in dollar terms because its revenues had been inflated by the soaring dollar value of the yen. What I found in 1990 was a high level of anxiety, a sharp contrast to the hubris of the 1980s when Japan, Inc., had been widely touted in the United States as an economic juggernaut.

A Japanese politician named Shintaro Ishihara had in 1989 written an essay, coauthored by Sony chairman Akio Morita, with a distinctly chauvinistic tone. It urged a more independent stance toward the United States and caused some shock waves in the United States when it was reprinted in English. The strong U.S. strategic position in Asia was based heavily on its security relationship with Japan, and this seemed like a motion for breaking that tie. The essay was titled "The Japan That Can Say No." But when I arrived in April 1990, the essay was already dated. To reflect the new doubts in Japan, I titled my column "The Japan That Can Say, 'Who Knows?'"

I pointed out that the yen had been sent soaring at the behest of the central bankers and finance ministers of the seven largest industrial nations (the International Monetary Fund's [IMF's] "Group of

Seven") because of a belief that this would lower the U.S. trade deficit. The deficit was a source of political heartburn in the United States in the 1980s just as it has been since from time to time, except that China has now replaced Japan as the villain of choice. The sharp shift in the exchange rate did little to change the trade balance, confirming the argument we had made for years on the editorial page that exchange rate manipulation does not change fundamental economic circumstances known by economists as the "terms of trade." Whatever the exchange rate, 100 tons of wheat still buys a tractor, if that is the fundamental reality.

But the run-up of the yen did have a different kind of impact on Japan. The rising yen sucked foreign portfolio investment into Japan and created a huge bubble in stock prices and real estate values. Stocks were selling on the Tokyo Stock Exchange at four times what would be regarded as a normal ratio between stock prices and earnings.

We arrived just a year after Yasushi Mieno, governor of the central Bank of Japan, had pricked the bubble by raising interest rates sharply, knowing full well that the absurd level of asset prices was not sustainable over time. Mr. Mieno briefed our press group on his reasons and suggested that he would hold his ground even though the prices of stocks and real estate were falling. He did hold his ground, and the collapsing value of bank assets put the Japanese financial services sector into the tank. It would take the Japanese banks 15 years to climb out of that hole, and there would be little further talk during those years of the invincible "Japan, Inc." If that pattern sounds familiar, think of the collapse of the American real estate and stock bubble in 2008, but as I pointed out in 1990, the American and Japanese financial sectors were quite different.

The Japanese are industrious and talented people, but the country's industries, heavily dependent on banks, were exceptionally vulnerable to a banking crisis, much more vulnerable than American industry would be to a similar crisis in 2008. That's because Japan, by its own design to favor its banks, did not have a well-developed securities industry, and thus its corporations were forced to rely more heavily on banks and self-financing than American firms. Of course, the crisis might not have happened had not the IMF decided in its wisdom that monetary relationships needed reengineering by its "experts." It had been able to persuade the treasury ministers and central bankers of the seven leading industrial nations of the need for a stronger yen to curb Japanese exports, and Japan had been the victim.

Of course, Japan entered into this agreement voluntarily, so its own officials cannot be totally absolved of the mischief it caused. And as I wrote in an earlier chapter, there was an upside as well. The strong yen made it cheap for Japanese companies to build factories abroad, particularly in the United States, to better compete in foreign markets and avoid the risks of further aberrations in the rate of exchange between the yen and the dollar. The move abroad also mitigated a key problem: With an aging population and strict controls on immigration, Japan was running out of labor. Perhaps 15 years of banking malaise was not bad after all.

CHAPTER 15

Portents in Prague

But back to the collapse of Communism. In March 1990, after my trip to Russia, I wrote a column throwing cold water on the idea that had gained currency in the West that the Soviet Union had come under a more benign leadership: "Having completed his carefully-spun power web by winning the new Soviet presidency last week, Mikhail Gorbachev celebrated with an ultimatum to Lithuania: Drop that secessionist nonsense or else. Or else what? We may soon learn. But we know one thing already: this is not the kinder, gentler Soviet leader of popular myth.

"In fact, he never was. Mikhail Gorbachev is mainly a skillful, tough politician who was driven toward political liberalism by events he could not control. Even now, he may be no better able to manage the great forces that are fracturing the Russian empire. But he could choose a harder response. What the Lithuanian ultimatum suggests is that we may be seeing the end of Mikhail Gorbachev as Mr. Nice Guy...

"Already Mr. Gorbachev has used force on the party's behalf. When a popular front ousted the party in Azerbaijan, he sent in the Red Army and restored it to power, at least in a nominal sense. Because the Azerbaijanis don't have many friends outside the Muslim world, there were few objections in the west. Lithuania would be another matter. The Lithuanians do have friends. For that reason, Mr. Gorbachev may treat events there differently. So far he has had trouble making up his mind. After Lithuania's non-Communist parliament voted to secede just over a week ago, he first called the vote 'illegal and invalid,' even though the Soviet constitution has long maintained the fiction that members of the

Soviet 'union' freely chose to join and are free to leave. Then he began to sound more conciliatory. And then after winning election—although by a surprisingly small vote when you consider that he was the only candidate—he got tough again. Clearly he wants to stop the unraveling of the Russian empire where he has the means to do so."

I quoted an article in Commentary by Harvard's Richard Pipes that the U.S.S.R. had not cut back on its military buildup. A new naval facility at Tartus, Syria, would strengthen its power in the Mediterranean. It was expanding its Cam Ranh Bay base in Vietnam.

The Commentary article said: "While the military's heavy weapons do not have application for controlling internal dissent—and while troop disloyalty could be a factor in any such effort—they do have another use. They would make it very dangerous for any outside power to intervene on behalf of a threatened population. Other well-placed sources say that the world-wide espionage and political activities of the KGB have if anything been expanded, because the spy agency had lost its adjunct services in East Germany and Czechoslovakia when the Berlin Wall came down in 1989.

"The crucial element for Mr. Gorbachev remains the Soviet economy. If it continues to sink, even the use of force against popular uprisings might prove to be of little avail. Communism will have to go, and not just in name. Whether it will go with a whimper or a big and dangerous bang is a matter all of Russia's neighbors should worry about."

Amid these portents of danger in the Soviet Union, Bob and I celebrated the Fourth of July, 1990, in Prague. Bob and his wife, Edith, came over from New York, and Jody and I motored down from Brussels through an eastern Europe that was emerging from its long Communist slumber. We had last been to Prague in 1984, when it was noted for having a regime that was even more Stalinist than the home office back in Moscow. These Communist hard-liners had taken over after Soviet tanks had crushed the short-lived Prague Spring freedom movement in 1968. But now it was a very different place with a people clearly refreshed by their escape from the Soviet grip.

The occasion for our 1990 visit was a conference of "captive nations," nationalist political movements within the Soviet republics that were trying to break free of Moscow's control. Among others, there were representatives from the Baltic states, which had been grabbed by the Soviets a half century earlier, the Caucasus republics of Armenia, Azerbaijan and Georgia that had been grabbed in the early 1920s, and Ukraine.

The Ukrainians were still bitter over the vast loss of life their nation had suffered during Stalin's mass murders and deportation of Ukrainian farmers (kulaks) in the 1930s as he nationalized their land. Many of the leaders of dissident groups at the conference had spent time in Soviet gulags as political prisoners. We listened to their reports in a large hall that had been made available to them by the new government of Czechoslovakia that had emerged from the country's Velvet Revolution against Communism a year earlier. Vaclav Havel, the leader of that revolution and now president, welcomed his fellow freedom fighters from the Soviet Union with a warm and eloquent address.

Bob wrote a feature article for our pages describing a procession of 50 or so of these anti-Soviet activists to a site in Wenceslas Square where young Jan Palach had immolated himself in January 1969 to protest the Soviet invasion of the year before. The marchers carried national flags unfamiliar to anyone other than a keen student of Russia's imperial conquests.

There was even a curious flag with "a blue background with a yellow symbol looking like a horseshoe divided by a bar. It dated from the third or fourth centuries and represented the Crimean Tatars, who the early Bolsheviks had banished to central Asia. The marchers dipped their flags at the immolation site and laid red, yellow and white carnations on the spot where young Jan had killed himself."

There were western speakers at the conference, including the prominent American Cold War strategist, Albert Wohlstetter, a good friend of Bob's and also one of Bob's back-channel sources for his frequent criticisms of U.S. foreign policy. Albert gave a speech titled "The Fax Shall Make You Free," noting how the advent of modern communications had made it impossible for dictators to isolate their victims from contact with the outside world, and more importantly, with each other for the purpose of organizing opposition. It was a profound observation that would become even more true when oppressed populations began to make widespread use of the Internet. The Chinese government, for one, found that it was even harder to suppress Internet transmissions than fax messages, which is why today's Chinese are able to actively discuss the abuses of officialdom among themselves and with the outside world.

Bob, Edie, Jody and I paid a call on the American ambassador, who happened to be Shirley Temple Black. She received us with the warmth of personality and dimpled smile that had made her a darling of Americans—and the savior of her studio, 20th Century Fox, from bankruptcy during the Great Depression—when she was a child movie star in the 1930s. I didn't have the nerve to tell her that as a five-year-old I was madly in love with her. She had probably heard it before.

She asked us, in an engaging show of humility, whether we thought she should attend the conference. I replied, not waiting for Bob as was my unfortunate habit, that the conference was all about political freedom and, isn't that what America stands for? I think she was hesitant because some deep thinker in the State Department had decided that a Soviet breakup wouldn't be such a good thing because it would be "destabilizing."

In our columns, both Bob and I would ridicule this idea. As for Shirley, she did show up with an aide and sat quietly on the back row listening to the speakers. As Bob reported in his piece, Czech president Havel, a former political prisoner, told the group that freedom and justice are indivisible and, "if they are threatened anywhere they are threatened everywhere."

Bob wrote that there is a natural skepticism of the pretenders to various thrones who roam the world but that in this case, "exiles can claim some painfully won understanding of the forces in their own society. And after 1989 (when the Berlin Wall fell) there's room to wonder which is the best practitioner of Realpolitik, the State Department or the exiles."

It turned out to be no contest. The exiles were right. But the State Department persisted in its illusion that the Communist Party of the Soviet Union (CPSU) had things under control until long after it became embarrassingly evident that its view was wrong. As a result, the United States was very tardy in granting diplomatic recognition to the newly independent Soviet republics after the Soviet Union finally collapsed at the end of 1991.

My Global View column also found credible the dissident claims that the Soviet Union was disintegrating, although I was shocked into disbelief at a speech by Russian chess champion Garry Kasparov claiming that the Soviet Union would be no more by "the end of the year." (Some years later when Garry visited the Journal in New York, I congratulated him on calling the shot on the Soviet collapse. He was self-deprecating: "I missed it by a year.")

In my column from Prague, I quoted the Journal's editorial page writers David Brooks and Paul Gigot and Moscow news bureau chief Peter Gumbel on reports of turf battles between party and nonparty factions all over the U.S.S.R. I again asserted that "glasnost" (transparency) and perestroika (reconstruction) had produced nothing but expanded economic disorder in the five years since Gorbachev took power. I had written earlier that "as economic conditions worsen and western credit becomes harder to obtain, he faces further secessionist attempts. Latvia, Estonia, Georgia are lined up behind Lithuania. Even in Russia, shortages of food and other essentials are stirring civil disorder."

There was disloyalty even within the KGB, the "Sword and Shield" of the party since Lenin, with retired major general Oleg Kalugin breaking secrecy to describe "a vast KGB network of spies and agents provacateur operating within the Soviet population." I wrote of low morale within the Red Army because of low pay—even for generals—and exploitation and abuse of enlisted men by their officers. "The Soviet economy continues to spin downward," I wrote, citing railcar tie-ups generating food shortages and a government short on foreign exchange.

Jody also wrote about the conference in her column for the Indianapolis News. Rereading it not long ago, I thought it more readable and engaging than either Bob's or mine, because of her talent for evoking the drama of this gathering of men and women of widely varying ethnicities who were putting their lives on the line to fight for freedom.

Through the coverage Bob and I gave to this eye-opening event in Prague, the Journal editorial page provided readers advance warning of the historic events of 1991, when the collapse of Communism in Central Europe spread to the Soviet Union itself. Acting on Kasparov's prediction, I went to the Soviet Union again in late 1990 to have a look, entering the country by train from Helsinki. As soon as I had settled into my compartment, I could see that I was going to a place much changed from my first visit in 1967, when the CPSU, the KGB and the threat of a trip to the gulag had the populace totally cowed and afraid to utter anything approximating an independent thought. I was soon joined by five other passengers, all Russians, who were loaded with parcels from Christmas shopping in Helsinki.

I wrote in my column: "The train from Helsinki, wending its way through the snow-laden evergreen forests toward Leningrad, is a Santa Claus sleigh. Two of my Russian fellow travelers, a bearded 60-year-old music professor and a 45-year-old woman in sweat shirt and jeans, have packed all available space in our compartment with parcels. The professor alone has 11 bundles, plus suitcase. Across from me in the compartment was a small, middle-aged man in a conservative gray suit reading an autobiography of the new Russian hope for the future, Gorbachev opponent Boris Yeltsin, president of the Russian Federation. The Yeltsin fan was described to me as one of the new Russian 'bizness' men. He held forth at length about the beauties of capitalism, winning approving nods from his heterogeneous audience."

I quoted the friendly and helpful music professor. "'We have to buy our Christmas gifts outside because we have nothing at home,' he explains apologetically. And these are fortunate Russians with travel visas, hard currency and foreign friends to invite them abroad, three requirements that deny all but a tiny percentage of Soviet citizens such shopping opportunities. Leningrad isn't starving—despite what westerners have been led to believe—but a holiday dinner of cabbage, potatoes, canned fish and applesauce isn't high living either. Scarcity has become a political weapon as the old Communist elite finds ways to deny desirable goods—meat, for example—to cities such as Leningrad, controlled by anti-Communist democrats."

I drew a "Tale of Two Cities" contrast between bustling, modern Helsinki and the once beautiful but now down-at-the-heels Leningrad. In Leningrad, I visited the downtown apartment of a woman member of the city council, who lived with her husband, children and in-laws in what would have been regarded as a slum in New York. I wrote that the drinking water is polluted and medical care primitive, and that queues for needed goods, such as shoes, were growing longer. "Alcoholism and violent crime add a further sordid element to a general mood of distrust, suspicion and surliness."

In Helsinki, Finnish prime minister Harri Holkeri had told me in an interview that he was worried that there would be violence in the Baltic states as Moscow took a tough line against aspirations for independence. The prime minister had an apt railroad metaphor for the departing or soon-to-depart nation-states long held in thrall by Soviet power. The former East Germans, he said, were riding first-class with the ticket paid by their western brothers (West Germany). On the same train but in second class were Czechoslovakia, Poland and Hungary, still with national memories of parliamentary democracy and a market economy. But they have to pay the ticket themselves.

"But then there are the Russians. They are not in the same train. Their train is not moving. Their train stays in the station. They don't know what parliamentary democracy means. Russia has never been free." He said that the people are eager to talk about a better future, but do not know what to do for it. The prime minister's assessment would be brought back to me on the Santa Claus train. Another passenger in our compartment was a husky and rather disheveled young man who told me, in English, that he was a rock musician. He said that there were thousands of rock groups in Leningrad, many of them playing protest songs. But he said these songs were often incoherent, without any sense of what the composers want to replace the decaying system.

I should have paid more attention to the prime minister's metaphor and the rock musician's description of Leningrad's rock music rebels without a cause. If I had, I might have been more skeptical about the ability of Yeltsin, when he finally took charge and dissolved the Soviet Union a year later, to create a genuine democracy with this rough clay. I would have been more aware that true representative democracy would remain only a future dream as it is today. I would have been more aware that the KGB, which always held the best cards in the Soviet power structure and had once openly installed its leader, Yuri Andropov, as supreme ruler, would not be easily vanquished. The authoritarian and kleptocratic regime of another former KGB leader, Vladimir Putin, has proved that.

I also should have taken more to heart the words, dripping with Russian fatalism, of the music professor as we parted at Finland Station in Leningrad, where Lenin had arrived with yet another promise of delivery 73 years before. "Maybe it will be better for our children," said the professor, "but not for us." I concluded the column with "he's probably right."

"Better" is a relative term, and my judgment may have been a bit hasty. But if he was referring to the possibility of a society where free markets, free expression, judicial fairness and political competition exist, that is something that even his children may not enjoy. That was a quarter century prior to 2015, so by 2015 his children might be approaching middle age, still under the rule of KGB heavies. In material terms, however, his children most likely have had a better life than he had.

CHAPTER 16

'On to Baghdad,' We Urge

The big story of 1990 was Saddam Hussein's invasion of Kuwait. I wrote a column wondering why the United States has been guilty of so many mistakes in the Middle East, including this latest failure to anticipate an aggressive action that threatened vital western interests, namely, major sources of crude oil. I noted that the George H.W. Bush administration had claimed that the attack was unexpected. "In fact, few knockout punches have been better telegraphed. London's Economist, among others, had called the invasion a near-certainty a week before it happened. Columnist William Safire [of the New York Times] had been screaming at the top of his lungs about the attempt to cozy up to a man with such a long and bloody record of treachery."

A Journal editorial on August 3, the day after the invasion, noted that the attack came in a week when Congress was busy gutting the defense budget, that there was ample warning of the attack and that it would be hard to counter without greater cooperation from the Kuwaitis and Saudis.

"Basically what Saddam Hussein has conducted is a good old-fashioned caravan raid of the type his ancestors...would understand quite well...

"Years of fecklessness have left the West without a good response to Saddam Hussein. Faced with ideological conflict its leaders have forgotten the ancient threat of piracy...The need to stand up to piracy should come clear as the West finishes rubbing its eyes."

In my column, I pointed out the difficulties of responding forcefully to the invasion, including the ambivalence of Saudi Arabia and the Arab Emirates about allowing U.S. troops to operate from their soil. I mentioned that the West always calls on Turkey for help in time of trouble but doesn't want to let the Turks into the best clubs, such as the European Union. Thankfully, I was wrong in implying that the United States might allow Saddam to get by with this affront to its neighbors and the United States. I would write more favorably about the administration's resolve in January 1991, as would Bartley in New York, when the (G.H.W.) Bush administration proved that it was willing to act and would do so with massive force.

I argued before the launching of the ground phase of Desert Storm that a lasting solution to the problem of Mideast violence would require a permanent presence of western military forces in the region. Eleven days after the military effort to eject Saddam Hussein's armies from Kuwait began on January 17, 1991, I felt emboldened from past experience with Mideast conflicts to lay out a more detailed prescription for peace, pointing out that there were great numbers of Arabs who would prefer peace to the constant warfare that had taken so many Arab lives over the preceding 45 years. Huge numbers of Arab casualties had been claimed by the eight-year conflict between Iraq and Iran, in which neither the United States nor the Israelis—the usual targets of Arab propaganda—had been directly involved, although both acted with some ambivalence in supporting roles. The huge cost in Arab lives had gained nothing for the Arabs. They were mostly as poor as ever.

I wrote that, since the United States, Britain and the other Desert Storm allies had been forced into a radical solution to the Saddam problem, surely it is equally appropriate to consider "fresh and radical solutions to the problem of Middle East peace." I recommended that the western allies and Israel take this in hand, leaving known troublemakers like Syria's Hafez Assad, PLO leader Yasser Arafat, Saddam and the Russians on the sidelines. To that end, I recommended a military occupation of Iraq by the United States, Britain and France, with sufficient power to intimidate Syria and, if necessary, Iran. I recommended bringing pressure to bear on Jordan to close the Palestinian refugee camps, which under U.N. and Arab management had been breeding terrorist violence for 40 years.

Needless to say, George H.W. Bush and the Jim Baker State Department had no stomach for radical solutions, even though by the end of the war, the Iraqi army was so demoralized that the allies could have swept on to Baghdad with ease and occupied key strong points. The president wanted to cut casualties and adhere to the letter of the U.N. mandate, which called only for expelling the Iraqis from Kuwait.

Moreover, as I learned later from a Saudi military officer, the Saudis were applying pressure on the United States to forego the final defeat of Saddam Hussein. They feared the Iranians more than the Iraqis, for a complex set of reasons. They knew that, even under the pre-Khomeini shahs, Iran had always craved a hegemonic mastery over the Persian Gulf region, including the Arabian Peninsula. Moreover, the Iranians were not Arabs and, worst of all, were Shia Muslims, a branch of Islam much distrusted by the Sunnis who dominated the Arab pecking order.

Playing "what-might-have-been" is a fruitless game. We never know what might have been. But certainly the events that ensued after the allies declared that the war had ended at the Iraqi-Kuwait border are not ones to engender much confidence in the judgments that were actually made. It was discovered that Saddam had been intent on developing a nuclear weapon. At least that effort was scotched. The Iraqi Shias were encouraged by the CIA to rise up against Saddam and then were left to his tender mercies, resulting in a massacre, without further support. Later on, Saddam managed to corrupt U.N. managers of the "Oil-for-Food" program intended to relieve the hardships of the Iraqi people, creating one of the greatest international scandals of all time.

And finally, after the 9/11 attack on the World Trade Center and Pentagon in 2001 mobilized Americans against Mideast-bred terrorism and after intelligence analysts concluded that Saddam was once again developing weapons of mass destruction, it was deemed necessary by both the administration of the younger Bush and the American Congress to go back and finish the job that wasn't done a decade earlier. I claim no prescience about what happened, but I shared Bob Bartley's view that if you get into a war you should see it through to a stable peace.

The Gulf War was over by the end of February 1991 and was chalked up as a victory not only for the coalition allies but for George H.W. Bush. His administration, the State Department and the intelligence agencies may have been guilty of sleepiness before Saddam's attack on Kuwait, but he was legitimately credited with acting decisively after the attack commenced and posed a threat to the vital interests of the United States and Europe.

Saddam was on his way to getting his hands on a big share of the world's oil reserves in Kuwait, the Arab Emirates and Saudi Arabia. The State Department had recovered from its earlier embarrassment by organizing a coalition of 35 states to send troops to rescue Kuwait, although some coalition members, like Syria, were merely engaging in opportunism against a longtime rival and were not a factor in the outcome.

The American people, never in favor of prolonging a war, seemed on the whole satisfied with the Bush decision to leave Saddam in place. Democrats of 2008 argued that the invasion of Iraq in 2003 was a mistake. But that was only after it was seen that the efforts to stabilize the Middle East with a U.S. presence had proved harder than was at first expected.

Nation building is a complex business, especially if the goal is to create a liberal democracy on the ashes of a brutal tyranny. We were reminded of this truth by the retrogression of Russia into authoritarianism after the Yeltsin effort to create a constitutional federal republic. Part of the process has to be the sprouting of a civic consciousness.

America is so accustomed to having a well-functioning and vigorous civil society—individuals acting independently of government to build influential private institutions (nongovernmental organizations [NGOs])—that we sometimes forget that former dictatorships lack this kind of counterbalance to the power of government. Editorial pages of privately owned newspapers and magazines, TV commentators, lecturers and a host of other voices are a part of this civil order, ensuring that public policy issues usually will be subject to intense debate and, if that is the case, the resulting policy will have a certain legitimacy.

The first requirement for creating such a society is freedom of speech. But even with that beginning, a civil society needs time and strong legal protections to develop.

CHAPTER 17

Celebrating a Collapse

The glimmerings of a new civil order finally came to the fountainhead of Communism in December 1991 when the Soviet Union collapsed. Boris Yeltsin, using his power base as Russia's president, had seized control of the Soviet empire with the aim of dismantling it. It was a great historic event that greatly reduced the threat of nuclear war, diminished Cold War tensions, made the United States and Europe more secure and gave the millions of people under Soviet rule a measure of freedom.

My column and Journal editorials gave a lot of attention to the events leading up to the collapse. In May 1991, I wrote a column noting that Soviet paratroops were attacking Armenian villages and rounding up Armenians suspected of nationalist military activities.

I commented that this use of troops against ethnic nationalist movements in the U.S.S.R. could be seen as "the last resort of a beleaguered Communist Party trying to save itself from extinction." I noted that KGB chieftain Vladimir Kryuchkov had appeared on TV to demand law and order, an unprecedented act by the leader of the KGB, which throughout Soviet history had preferred to exercise its powerful influence from behind the scenes. What I was seeing at that time were the warning signs of what would come later, a coup by party hard-liners to force Gorbachev out and return the empire to Stalinist-style police control.

Before that happened, Gorbachev would go to Oslo to collect a Nobel Peace Prize, in yet another case of the Nobel jury being clueless about what a so-called peacemaker was really up to. I wrote that it was surely unprecedented for a Peace Prize winner to "land-mine his acceptance speech with threats against, among others, his kindly hosts." But that is what Gorby did in Oslo, threatening that if the industrial nations did not bail the Soviet Union out of its deep financial crisis, "the prospect of a new, peaceful period in history will vanish, at least for the foreseeable future."

And it would be "futile and dangerous" for the West to set conditions on this aid, which the Soviets had demanded to the tune of $250 billion over five years. I wrote that this "is not the language of peace, but the language of extortion." And if the aid was supposed to finance perestroika, or restructuring, what kind of a bet would it be to pour money into a project that had been under way for six years and had clearly failed? I wrote that no matter how many Harvard economists Gorby employed, he would not be able to restructure the economy and still preserve the Communist Party. "You can't have a free-market economy and an economy run by and for a Communist Party elite."

Of course, Gorby was desperate. Soviet GNP was in a nosedive because of strikes and crumbling factories. Its supply of foreign exchange was running out because of flagging exports of the only thing the U.S.S.R. could sell in international markets—raw materials. No doubt Gorby knew that he was in imminent danger of being overthrown, as the coup attempt only two months later proved. But the coup masters had failed to reckon with the opportunism of Boris Yeltsin, the president of the Russian Federation and perhaps the only Russian leader who was popular with the Russian people.

When he stood atop a tank in Moscow to defy the coup masters, I commented in a Journal article that, much to everyone's surprise, President Yeltsin had strong military backing, which no doubt had to do with what had become a powerful belief among the Russian people, and the officers of several key military units in the Moscow vicinity, that only he could save Russia. With several elite divisions behind him, including the Tamanskaya Guards division responsible for protecting Moscow, Yeltsin faced down the coup leaders and began the process of disassembling the Soviet empire, forming a new

Commonwealth of Independent States (CIS) out of the 12 republics that were still willing to be affiliated with Russia.

The three Baltic states, Lithuania, Latvia and Estonia, had dark memories of being seized by Stalin just before World War II and wanted no part of any official connection with Russia and chose not to join the CIS.

After the Yeltsin countercoup, I observed that "few of history's cataclysmic events have occurred with more dramatic swiftness." I wrote that "a great drama has just transpired in Russia. It will shake the world, as did the ultimately tragic drama of 1917. But the two events are opposite, the first a naked seizure of power and this one a product of democracy. If democracy's tide keeps rolling, the outcome will be different too."

Unfortunately, when I wrote those hopeful lines, I didn't reckon with the fact that the most important power center of the old Soviet Union had not been destroyed by the demise of Communism. The KGB, since its founding by the Bolsheviks, had always attracted the empire's brightest and most ambitious young people, who recognized its formidable behind-the-scenes power. After the Yeltsin takeover, these clever people quietly adapted, many taking advantage of the fall of Communism to appropriate state assets to form private ventures.

Ultimately, after the KGB had mutated into something called the FSB, a new leader, Vladimir Putin, would force Boris Yeltsin to abdicate in return for a guarantee that his family would not be prosecuted for corruption. Putin would begin rebuilding the old system, at least within the surviving Russian republic, of absolute political control from the Kremlin. The only difference would be that there would no longer be any pretense that the "people" owned the means of production. The means of production would be owned by supporters of Vladimir Putin, and it would afford them great wealth. Moscow became a city of billionaires.

Russia now had at least an approximation of a market economy and, up until the 2014 break in oil prices, the government's coffers had been swollen by the oil revenues that Putin gained partly by expropriating the giant Yukos Oil Co., from Mikhail Khodorkovsky, who had acquired it in the public auction of state properties in the 1990s. Khodorkovsky, regarded by Putin as a political rival, was sent to the new gulag, one of the first indications of how Putin would revert back to the old Soviet ways.

The Russians are better off than they were in 1990, but not as well off as they could be if freed from a kleptocracy that steals private property and thereby discourages private investment. As to free expression and the rule of law, the government has reverted to policies that, while not as harsh as in the Stalinist days, are nonetheless more attuned to the views and practices of the secret police than was the case in the Yeltsin years. Broadcasting, for all practical purposes, is under state control, and the state exercises powerful influence over court decisions when they affect the interests of the ruling party. The electoral process is so structured that Vladimir Putin has been able so far to get whatever result he has sought. Opposition parties are often harassed by agents of the state.

In 2007 and early 2008, Russian leaders, well heeled with oil money, adopted a more assertive foreign policy that centered on a renewed rivalry with the United States. After all, that's the only foreign policy KGB men ever knew. The collapse of crude oil prices has since tempered that hubris, but one should not underestimate the capacity for troublemaking by an authoritarian regime that is suffering economic adversity.

After the reunification of East and West Germany in October 1990, Jody and I decided to drive from Brussels to East Germany to see if we could look up her German ancestors. A friend specializing in genealogy had on Jody's behalf found a record at the New York Public Library showing that Ernst and Frederika Minner had arrived at the port of Philadelphia from Königsee, Thuringia, in 1851. Jody had written to the town's burgomeister and had learned that an English teacher, Eva Steinhoefel, would be happy to help us. We sought out Eva and her husband, Akim, in the village of Hirschdorf, in the hills above Königsee.

Eva had taught English in the Königsee schools, and Akim had been a Lutheran minister in Hirschdorf throughout the Communist era. When we sat down with them that evening, we found that we were the first "outsiders" they had met in 40 years. During the German retreat from the eastern front in 1945, their families had fled from the state of Silesia to escape the wrath of the Red Army and found their way to the safety of the American occupation zone. But one morning they had awakened to find that, under terms of the Yalta agreement signed by FDR, Churchill and Stalin, the Americans had withdrawn, and they were in the Russian zone. The Iron Curtain soon sealed them off from the outside world.

Eva and Akim had endured 40 years of harassment from the Communists. Akim had refused demands from the East German secret police (Stasi) that he inform on members of his congregation. Eva's dislike for Communism and her interest in America did not endear her to the Communist principal at her school. Once, when she and a few other teachers were deliberately slow in rising when the principal walked into a faculty meeting, she received a summons to report to a school in the neighboring town of Rudolstadt on a Saturday morning. The other teachers who had not shown the proper respect were there as well, all wondering what was afoot. They had worn their best clothes, assuming they were being called to a regional faculty gathering. An East German army major showed up and addressed the group with the words, "I understand you ladies need some discipline." With that, he conducted them down to the school yard and proceeded to give them close-order drill. Bystanders were treated to the spectacle of seven high school teachers in high heels marching around a school yard to the sound of "ein! zwei! drei! fier!"

Such humiliations were common. Because of their passive resistance to Communist regimentation, their three sons were denied admission to any East German university. They went to music conservatories instead, which in fact was a triumph because all three became successful professional musicians, one playing a leading role in managing the beautifully historic conservatory in Weimar.

I asked Eva what was the most important thing to her since the wall came down. She looked at me as if I might be a dunce. "We're free!" she said. But of course. Only people like us who have never been locked up would fail to understand what that means. Now free to travel, Eva and Akim later came to visit us in Brussels. They told us the story of their church bell. A fire in the belfry of the little Hirschdorf church had made the church bell unusable. They found a bell of the right tone at a foundry in Jena, but it cost 1,000 marks. Fearing that it was hopeless to raise that much in their poor village, Akim nonetheless drafted a circular asking for money, saying that "A village without a bell is a dead village." Miraculously, the next morning people were lined up at the parsonage to donate money for the bell. Even former Communists came forward, which was fortunate because they were the wealthier villagers. They raised enough, installed the bell and had a dedication ceremony in which the village brass band marched around the church playing the only religious song they knew, "Thine Is the Glory." The bell was ceremoniously rung, and Hirschdorf was not a dead village anymore.

Jody wrote this story for the International Herald Tribune in Paris, and they put it on the front page. Eva was on a bus tour of England with a group of teachers when one of her friends came up to her and said, "Eva, don't get excited, but your name is in this newspaper." In the old days in East Germany, that might have been bad news, a renunciation or some such threat. But it was Jody's story in the Herald Trib about the miracle of the bell in the village of Hirschdorf. Eva was delighted.

In Brussels, we met David McColl, who had been a World War II Royal Air Force (RAF) pilot. An electronic countermeasures expert, he told us that, during the 1940 Battle of Britain, the Air Ministry had become concerned that the Germans would cripple Britain's defense by jamming ground-to-air radio communications. He was assigned to take a squadron of Spitfires to Scotland and practice maneuvers that would defeat jamming. He succeeded, but the remedy was never needed. The Germans never thought of the idea of jamming the British radios.

I renewed acquaintance with Philip Merrill, a Maryland publisher who had attracted Bob's and my attention in the early '80s when, as the Pentagon's point man, he scuttled the first U.N. Law of the Sea Treaty. The Pentagon was mainly worried about rights of passage through the world's many narrow straits being subject to U.N. control. We were suspicious about what was obviously another U.N. effort—one of many—to get an independent source of financing to free itself from the guiding hand of the United States. The treaty would have awarded its secretariat control over deep-sea mining. Our suspicions of the U.N. secretariat's ambitions and competence were later confirmed by the Iraq Oil-for-Food scandal.

Phil, a friend of Vice President Dick Cheney, had been appointed by the first Bush administration as deputy secretary general of the North Atlantic Treaty Organization (NATO) and was kind enough to look me up when he got to Brussels. We spent a lot of time discussing the events unfolding in Europe, the Soviet collapse in particular. Phil made it a point to invite Russian military officers to his Brussels residence as a token of NATO goodwill, and I renewed my acquaintance with Russian brass at his parties. One of them gave me a private lecture about "patriotism," as if he were exhorting his troops, and I realized that he was not taking the Red Army's embarrassed circumstances with good grace.

Phil said that we should turn Russia into a big management training school to teach Russian businessmen how to function in a market economy. He had put his finger on a central problem. Russia had never had a system of free-market capitalism, and so all that would-be businessmen knew was what they had been taught by Communist theoreticians, who had preached that capitalism was, in essence, licensed theft. Russian businessmen did avail themselves of western advice, but the learning curve was aborted by Vladimir Putin and his KGB cronies when they decided to put vital industries, such as oil, back where they thought they belonged—in their own hands and indeed practice licensed theft.

Our friendship with Phil had a sad ending. In 2006, only two months after he had kindly attended my retirement party in New

York, he sailed out onto the Chesapeake Bay alone on his much-loved sloop, "Merrilly," tied an anchor to his ankle, balanced on a gunwale and shot himself with a shotgun. His body sank into the water. The Merrilly sailed on until it was intercepted by the Coast Guard. It was a week before Phil's body was found. His troubled mind was not at all evident when he stayed late after my party to regale the younger Journal editors with his stories. But I later learned that, during the time he was running the Export-Import Bank and we were out of touch, he had had open-heart surgery. Deep depression is sometimes an aftereffect of that kind of operation, so I was told.

Another tragic story touched my life when I was running the editorial page in Brussels. Alexandra Tuttle was a freelance writer who based herself in Paris and offered us feature stories mainly about art and culture. A little woman with seemingly boundless energy and nerve, she also was remarkably sophisticated in assessing the politics of out-of-the-way places. One of her pieces gave a remarkable analysis of the fighting in Somalia, one of the hot spots in the 1990s. During the Bosnian War, she had gone behind the Serbian lines to interview a sniper in the hills above Sarajevo; he was firing on civilians braving the dangerous boulevards of the city. It was a chilling story of a young man who seemed totally dispassionate about his job of murdering innocent civilians. It told better than anything I had ever read how war dehumanizes ordinary individuals.

One day in September 1993, I received a phone call from Claudia Rosett, then manager of the Journal's Moscow news bureau, asking if Alexandra was on assignment from us. She wasn't. Claudia told me that a woman journalist had been killed in a plane crash in Sukhumi in the breakaway Georgian state of Abkhazia. A secessionist war was raging there, courtesy of the KGB's efforts to punish the Georgians for leaving the Soviet Union, an effort that survives to this day.

We checked Alexandra's friends in Paris, and none knew where she was. The Georgian military plane that had crashed had been brought down by a secessionist rocket as it was landing, and there was still fighting at the airport, so it was difficult to identify the victims. But with the aid of Fred Kempe, a Journal war correspondent, we finally were able to confirm that it was Alexandra. The soldiers on the plane had made a place up front for her, telling her it would be safer. But when the plane broke in two, the soldiers in the rear survived, and the front section was engulfed with flames.

Alexandra had gone off to the war on her own, ignoring my warning that I thought she was taking too many chances. That may be why she didn't tell anyone where she was going. We had lost the contributions to our pages of a remarkably talented young woman. I wrote an editorial that concluded, "We will remember her spirit and courage and will miss her very much."

As to foreign policy, my special interest in the early 1990s, the Clinton administration was accommodationist, with the result that it presided over a relatively peaceful period of history. But that had a negative side, as I observed in my columns. The failure to take a hard line toward dedicated enemies of the United States emboldened them to expand their aggressiveness. Saddam Hussein corrupted the U.N. Oil-for-Food program, crafted under the first Bush administration to allow Iraq to sell enough oil to buy food to feed the Iraqi population. He bribed oil buyers and food suppliers to provide him with kickbacks to finance his other goals, including rebuilding his military. The U.N. official in charge of Oil-for-Food was himself corrupted, a truth exposed by two hard-digging Journal editorial writers, Therese Raphael and Claudia Rosett.

Jody and I, living in Brussels were, of course, aware of all the politicking back home, but not so distracted that we couldn't savor our life in Europe. We met Belgians who fondly remembered their liberation from the Nazis in World War II and expressed their gratitude with dinner invitations. One was Betty de Stryker, wife of a former governor of the Belgian Central Bank, who told me that she would be forever grateful to America for what it had done for the Belgian people, both when the United States relieved their famine in the aftermath of

World War I and when Americans and the British liberated them from the German occupation in 1944.

Europeans our age had lived through perilous times in the 20th century. Jody and I heard many harrowing tales from our circle of European friends. One of the most poignant was that of Liliane Smith, a Belgian woman married to Dudley Smith, an American management consultant. Born Liliane Coucke, she was engaged in her youth to marry her longtime boyfriend, Jacques Leten, heir to a sizable fortune. They were both students at the University of Brussels when, in September 1941, the gestapo took over the university and expelled the Jewish faculty. The university closed its doors in protest.

Jacques became active in the Belgian underground. In May 1942, Liliane walked to the Café de Baudet, a student's hangout just off the Rue de Namur, expecting to meet Jacques. He sent word that he was going to Ghent, and Liliane sighed with relief when five gestapo plainclothesmen showed up at the café looking for him. But a short while later, he walked into the café and told her his trip had been canceled. That cancellation sealed his doom. The gestapo agents arrested Jacques and a companion. He had been betrayed by a fellow student. Liliane never saw him again. He died in a Nazi concentration camp just north of Brussels. The cause of death, as Liliane later learned: "medical experiments."

We met German survivors as well. Dorothy Gillette, also married to an American, told us of her youth in Kiel in the between-war years, the daughter of a respected university provost. When her mother heard that Hitler had ascended to the chancellorship, she uttered three prophetic words: "We are doomed." We were less sympathetic to a former Prussian aristocrat who was angling to recover the family estate. His problem was that the land of his Junker ancestors was now part of Poland, and the authorities were not terribly friendly toward his overtures to buy back the land.

In late 1994, after nearly five years, we thought it time to come home. Bob agreed. For one thing, he needed more help in New York.

So we moved back to our house in Westfield, New Jersey, where we had had three tenants in our absence. Bob gave me the added responsibility of overseeing the Americas column, which meant that I now had the whole world outside the United States to look after, at least so far as the Journal editorial page was concerned.

David Asman, editor of the column, had left us to become a newscaster at Fox News, so as a replacement, we hired a young woman named Mary Anastasia O'Grady, who was working at a think tank in Mexico City and contributing to an English-language newspaper there. She had worked as a lower-level manager at Merrill Lynch but had grown tired of the securities business and joined the think tank to gratify her interest in Latin American economics and politics. Her grasp of economics was impressive, and she seemed to be even more of a free marketer than we were. She has proved to be an excellent addition to the cast of editorial page writers, attracting a large following for her passionate support of reformers trying to move Latino governments toward a rule of law and free-market liberalism, a task that has been made difficult by the powerful Marxist forces in the region.

Part of the fun of my job in my years as the international deputy was finding and training young talent. I have already mentioned David Brooks, David Asman, Terri Raphael, Hugo Restall, and Claudia Rosett. Cait Murphy, who was our editor in Hong Kong, later worked for the Economist, Fortune and CBS. Richard Miniter, who wrote for the Journal editorial page in Europe, has authored several popular books. Pete Keresztes returned to his native Budapest to become editor of the Hungarian Readers Digest. Bret Stephens succeeded me as Global View columnist.

Back in New York, I continued to travel around my far-flung territory. I went to Indonesia to have a firsthand look at the economic "miracle" the Suharto family had supposedly conjured up. They had had the good sense to invite in foreign investors to develop an economic infrastructure, but the flip side was that the Suhartos had insisted that they be partners in these new foreign-financed ventures. I interviewed the energy minister and soon realized that he was giving me a carefully rehearsed argument related to the Suharto partnership issue even before I asked a question about it. He said the country was building more power-generating capacity than it needed, signing "take-or-pay" contracts with foreign investors that required the state to commit hard-currency reserves for power it didn't need.

At one point, the minister's secretary opened the door to remind him that he had another visitor. He apologized and brought the interview to a quick close. As we were leaving the building, my interpreter said, "You know who the other visitor was, don't you?" I said no, and he said, "It was Titik, Suharto's daughter." Then it all became clear. Titik had the electric power concession in the family, which had divided up major industries to give each family member a cut of foreign investments. The minister had been rehearsing with me the argument he was planning to make to Titik—that it was unwise to invest in more power plants and increase the country's dollar debts that had left it so vulnerable to a decline in the Indonesia currency.

He was so right, as the later collapse of the rupiah and the Indonesian financial sector during the Asian currency crisis of 1997–98 would prove. The minister was not happy that my column told an international audience of his troubles with the boss's daughter but, of course, he was right to raise the issue. It was another case of the inherent dangers in even a relatively benign form of authoritarian rule that had at least had the benefit of fostering the nation's economic development by inviting foreign investment. Indonesia, after the debt crisis, would move toward democratic governance and would become a model of sorts for political and economic development of poor nations.

CHAPTER 18

Bob and 'Arkansas Mores'

While I had been enjoying the gypsy life of a roving foreign policy writer and editor, Bob and Dan had been dealing with domestic issues that took a surprising turn in 1992. In that election year, the Democrats had nominated as their presidential candidate a young governor of Arkansas, William (Bill) Jefferson Clinton. George H.W. Bush had alienated much of the Republican base by breaking his "read-my-lips" pledge not to raise taxes, and Texas third-party maverick Ross Perot was a Republican spoiler, siphoning off enough of the conservative popular vote to have changed the outcome. Bill Clinton became the new president-elect with a Democratic Congress.

Clinton brought with him an ardent Progressive—his wife, Hillary. Things were about to change, and not in a good way in the view of Bob and Dan.

After the climactic events of 1990 and 1991, the world had calmed down a bit. I devoted more columns to the efforts of the European states to form a more perfect union. These included fumbling efforts to stabilize currency exchange rates, efforts we at the Journal very much approved of in principle, even if we sometimes scoffed at the petty disputes and wrong turns that accompanied this endeavor. We had long argued that sound money and stable relationships between the major currencies was a boon to world trade and economic growth. The Bob Mundell principle that there is only one economy, the global one, had been part of our syllabus. And indeed, Professor Mundell had a key role in designing Europe's transition to a single currency, the euro.

But things warmed up a bit after the 1992 election. Bob became preoccupied with exposing the shady behavior of the Clintons when Bill was governor of Arkansas. Bob was offended by what he called the "Arkansas mores" the Clintons and their former associates in Little Rock brought to Washington. Over the eight-year Clinton era, the Journal editorial page gave the administration intense coverage, most of it critical. Bob and Melanie Kirkpatrick, features editor, assembled all that coverage into a six-volume set of books bearing the title "Whitewater" to commemorate the real estate scheme the Clintons had allegedly used in Arkansas to milk funds from a local savings and loan association.

There was plenty to write about. One subject was the installation of a slippery crony from Hillary's Rose Law Firm in Little Rock as de facto attorney general. This associate, Webster Hubbell, later went to jail for defrauding Rose clients out of nearly a half million dollars. There was Hillary's mysterious windfall profit of $99,000 from trading in cattle futures just after Bill was first elected governor of Arkansas in 1978. There were the various complaints from women, one of whom, Juanita Broaddrick, accused Clinton of raping her on April 15, 1978. One woman who didn't complain was the White House intern Monica Lewinsky. But when a friend leaked her account of giving the president oral sex in the Oval Office, it triggered an investigation by a special counsel, Kenneth Starr, that ultimately led to Clinton's impeachment. The Senate did not convict him.

On home leave early in the first Clinton term, I asked Bob if he might be overdoing the attack on the new president. Was there any public policy issue at stake in what he was doing, I wanted to know. He replied that yes, there was. The most important was to try to prevent Hillary from nationalizing the health care system. In that, he and other opponents, who even included some congressional Democrats, were successful. And after more and more revelations of shady doings by the Clintons hit the news, I no longer thought that Bob had overreacted to Bill's misbehavior.

Indeed, the Clintons only had two years of working with a Congress of their own party, and those were not entirely successful from their point of view. The Democrats flinched at a massive energy tax the president proposed and at the national health system cooked up by Hillary in illegally secret task force deliberations. They did pass a less destructive tax increase, and that was enough for the voters, who returned the Republicans to majority power in Congress in 1994 and kept them there for 12 years until the Republicans themselves became corrupted by the temptations to do favors for special-interest constituents.

In 1995, I ran across a Boston University commencement speech delivered by the university's acerbic, controversial and brilliant president, John Silber. It was titled "Obedience to the Unenforceable," in which he cited the importance of manners and morals to the health of a society or, in other words, the willingness of a people to adhere to certain standards of conduct without any need for compulsion. Or in still other words, morality cannot be legislated. I liked the speech so well, I quoted it in two separate columns that year. One was a column about Pope John Paul II's visit to New York during which he admonished a huge crowd in Central Park to "not be afraid." The other was a column about international crime, which had taken on a new dimension with the advent of the Russian criminal mafia that had come into being in Europe and the United States after the Soviet collapse, as former KGB agents sought remunerative employment.

In the first column, I quoted the pope as saying that the revolutions in central Europe in 1989 were inspired by "a profound and powerful vision, the vision of man as a creature of intelligence and free will, immersed in a mystery that transcends his own being." Citing the Silber lecture, I concluded the column by writing that John Paul's message was that America needs a restoration of moral authority and that "The nation will have to find that for itself. It won't be delivered by the state."

In the column about crime, after detailing examples of the breakdown of law enforcement worldwide, I again cited Silber's view that disdain for moral conduct cannot be healed by law enforcement alone. "Dealing with moral conduct on a global scale is a tall order, but that is what civilization is all about."

Very much on my mind when I wrote those words was the Journal's campaign to expose the moral failings of the Clinton administration. When Arkansas governor Bill Clinton had visited the Journal 14 years before he became president, he seemed amiable enough, but otherwise left little impression on our small group.

Bill Clinton as president was a wholly different matter. It is not necessary for a president to be a Bible thumper, and it is in fact probably not even desirable, as issues of moral behavior are best left to the church and moral philosophers, not to the nation's chief law enforcer. But that does not mean that a president should not set an example for the nation in his own personal behavior. A president who invites a young intern to administer fellatio to him as he conducts business in the Oval Office and then lies about this gross behavior is hardly setting a good example for the youth of America.

It was this kind of conduct, dating back to the financial and sexual peccadillos in Little Rock, that so offended the moral sensitivities of Bob Bartley. If Bob were alive today, he would be nonplussed at the realization that the Clintons were still with us in 2016, this time with Hillary in the limelight and Bill in the shadows.

In the introduction to a booklet of Journal opinion pieces published in 1996, Bob wrote that during the 1970s, he had written mostly about foreign and military policy, which was, of course, appropriate at the height of the Cold War. In the 1980s, he said, he had focused on economic policy, again appropriate because we were deeply engaged in the supply-side revolution and were concerned about how to restore some order to the international monetary system.

The volume he was introducing was concerned with moral issues, which had become his area of focus in the 1990s. Said his introduction: "The moral canons of the welfare state have not succeeded in building the good society, and the nation is striving for a new moral balance between compassion and individual responsibility." He was thus presenting the writings of intellectuals, such as William J. Bennett, secretary of education in the Reagan administration; Charles

Murray, author of the 1984 book "Losing Ground" arguing that the LBJ War on Poverty was actually creating perpetual poverty for the underclass; and Gertrude Himmelfarb, a historian whose 1995 book, "The De-Moralization of Society, from Victorian Virtues to Modern Values," presented a similarly gloomy view of the current trends in moral values. The booklet contained essays by other thinkers along with Journal editorials related to the morality theme.

After only two years of Democratic Party control of both the White House and Congress, Republicans led by Georgia congressman Newt Gingrich had retaken Congress by presenting a reform agenda called the "Contract with America." Thus, the governmental achievements of the second half of the 1990s, such as the welfare system reforms encapsulated in the Personal Responsibility and Work Opportunity Reconciliation Act of 1996, were in part a product of the Gingrich "contract" although mostly the result of pressure from state governors who were worried about the rising burden on their own budgets of the swelling number of people seeking a dole. Bob's wish of stalling Hillary's efforts to nationalize health care was realized, postponing that effort for 14 years, when a renewed effort by Progressives, who still could count Hillary as one of their inspirational leaders, would achieve that result with ObamaCare.

Bill Clinton had some achievements on his side of the balance sheet in his two years of one-party governance. While early in his presidency he had flirted with gratifying the wishes of a labor movement that had become increasingly protectionist in the 1990s, he pulled away from that position early on. The 1994 North American Free Trade Act (NAFTA) lowering barriers on commerce crossing the borders between the United States, Mexico and Canada passed Congress with strong Republican help, and he signed it into law. He also deserves some credit for signing onto welfare reform.

Bob's steady drumbeat of questions about the personal integrity of some of Clinton's key employees and of Clinton himself may have played a role in the 1994 Democratic rout. But it was not enough to prevent Clinton's reelection in 1996, a victory that ironically may have been partly the result of the free trade and welfare reforms that came about through the president's cooperation with the opposition Republicans.

The 1996 election pitted Clinton and Vice President Al Gore against the amiable senator Robert Dole of Kansas and his running mate, our old friend Jack Kemp, who had played such an important role in the supply-side revolution. The Republicans were again weakened by a third-party bid by Ross Perot, who siphoned off some 8 million conservative votes, although not so many, statistically, to have cost Dole the election.

While Bob adhered to our tradition of not endorsing a candidate, he left no doubt about which side he wanted defeated. Just before the election, when a Clinton win seemed likely, he filled the Review & Outlook space with a long editorial titled "Four More Years," which was a catalog of Clinton legal and ethical issues in his first term. Among them were a string of high-level resignations, most of them involving legal issues.

There also was the mysterious suicide of Deputy White House Counsel Vince Foster and testimony by a Secret Service officer that he had seen Clinton's chief of staff Maggie Williams carrying an armload of files from Foster's office just after the tragedy.

Then, there was a litigation against Hillary for allegedly conducting hearings of her Health Care Task Force in secret in violation of federal law. There were all sorts of legal issues including the May 28, 1996, conviction of James and Susan McDougal, owners of the Madison Guaranty Savings and Loan Association in Little Rock, for bank fraud and conspiracy. In the '80s, the McDougals had been partners with the Clintons in the Whitewater Development Co., which built vacation homes in the Ozarks, and investigators had found questionable dealings between Madison Guaranty and Whitewater.

Also in the long list was the charge by Paula Corbin Jones in May 1994 that she had been sexually harassed by Clinton when he was governor. The editorial was a long bill of particulars against the president, but it didn't prevent his reelection.

Perhaps most Americans were less affronted by the bad behavior of politicians than we were at the Journal editorial page. The 1990s were a freewheeling age in which standards of taste were almost nonexistent in the popular culture. But the aforementioned John Silber raised a good point in asking whether his new crop of college graduates in 1995 understood the importance to a society of obedience to the unenforceable. Dan Henninger would write in March 1993 an editorial titled "No Guardrails" that further explored the erosion of moral standards.

Dan deplored what he saw as a change from a time "when life seemed more settled, when emotions, both private and public, didn't seem to run so continuously at breakneck speed, splattering one ungodly tragedy after another across the evening news. How did this happen to the United States? How, in T.S. Eliot's phrase, did so many become undone?" Dan, stipulating that many would disagree, dated this cultural shift back to the 1968 Democratic Convention in Chicago when the party found itself "sharing Chicago with the street fighters of the anti-Vietnam War movement."

"The real blame here does not lie with the mobs who fought bloody battles with the hysterical Chicago police. The larger responsibility falls on the intellectuals—university professors, politicians and journalistic commentators—who said then that the acts committed by the protesters were justified or explainable. That was the beginning. After Chicago, the justifications never really stopped. America had a new culture, for political action and personal living.

"With great rhetorical firepower, books, magazines, opinion columns and editorials defended each succeeding act of defiance—against the war, against university presidents, against corporate practices, against behavior codes, against dress codes, against virtually all agents of established authority.

"What in the past had been simply illegal became 'civil disobedience.' If you could claim, and it was never too hard to claim, that your group was engaged in an act of civil disobedience—taking over a building, preventing a government official from speaking, bursting onto the grounds of a nuclear cooling station, destroying animal research, desecrating Communion hosts—the shapers of opinion would blow right past the broken rules to seek an understanding of the 'dissidents' (in the '60s and '70s) and 'activists' (in the '80s and now)."

Dan wrote that the intellectuals and politicians who provided the theoretical underpinnings for this shift emerged unscathed. "But for a lot of other people it hasn't been such an easy life to sustain...Everyone today seems to know someone who couldn't handle the turns and went over the side of the mountain...These weaker or more vulnerable people, who in different ways must try to live along life's margins, are among the reasons that a society erects rules. They're guardrails."

The editorial attracted a lot of attention, deservedly so. Dan had defined how even a well-ordered society, with strong institutions, can have no assurance that those institutions will survive that all-too-human tendency to smash icons and overthrow established beliefs. That is why John Silber's treatise on the enforcement of the unenforceable was worth pondering.

Clinton was impeached in December 1998 for perjury and obstruction of justice for lying to a grand jury in the Paula Jones case but not convicted by the two-thirds majority required in the Senate. After his acquittal, he was cited for contempt of court by federal judge Susan Webber Wright for his testimony in the case and had his law license suspended by the State of Arkansas the next year.

After his acquittal, Clinton went back on the offensive with: "We must stop the politics of personal destruction. We must get rid of the poisonous venom of excessive partisanship, obsessive animosity and uncontrolled anger."

Bob quoted those lines in an editorial titled "After Impeachment." Then, he suggested that we review the politics of personal destruction, such as when Clinton's aide James Carville had slandered Paula Jones with the insult, "Drag a $100 bill through a trailer park and there's no telling what you'll find," or when the Clintons fired the entire White House Travel Office staff (called "Travelgate") and caused its director, Billy Dale, to be indicted for fraud. (At his trial, a jury acquitted him in two hours.)

The editorial reminded readers that Clinton was not impeached for his sexual sins but for his "mockery of the judicial system" which, of course, referred to his lying in the Paula Jones case.

Said the editorial: "In a grave and at times moving debate on the House floor, the Democrats time and again agreed with their Republican colleagues that Mr. Clinton's behavior—not merely his appetites but his insistence on what Rep. J.C. Watts called 'the edges of truth'— was contemptible and condemnable. But while the Republicans sought impeachment, Democrats fashioned the rubber lifeboat of compromise and censure."

The editorial expressed some sympathy for the plight of the Democratic senators when the president from their party was in the dock. But it argued that in the politics of personal destruction, the first step is for Democrats and their media allies to admit that the Republicans have a point about the rule of law and the president's constitutional duty to "take Care that the Laws be faithfully executed."

The editorial concluded that "Bill Clinton has brought the presidency to the lowest repute since the impeachment of Richard Nixon."

In January 2001 when the Clintons ended their second term, Bob would write an editorial titled "Who Is Bill Clinton?", a reprise of the editorial with the same title he had written in March 1992 when the Clintons first emerged from their relative obscurity in Arkansas. Bob was no more sparing than he had been when Clinton was in power. He wrote that "Bill Clinton's flaw is that he sees everything in the whole wide world as his personal property. Mr. Clinton seems to have believed that he could use everything as he wished, not because he is an officer of the state of Arkansas or of the United States, but because he is Bill Clinton.

"And so the things he saw as belonging mainly to him included the

Presidency of the United States, the Oval Office, Monica Lewinsky, Paula Jones, the Secret Service of the United States, the lawyers of the White House counsel's office, Ron Brown's Commerce Department, the Democratic National Committee, the Department of Justice, the landing patterns at Los Angeles Airport, Madison Guaranty, the Lincoln Bedroom and, not least, the rest of the world...

"These columns have argued that this behavior is sociopathic. Psychiatrists who don't trust their profession's categories objected, but whatever the medical precision, a neurotic recklessness was clear enough. Yes, other personally reckless men have risen into the Presidency, but none were so oblivious to the need for personal or political temperance while serving as the nation's first public officer. He asked an army of federal officials and federal institutions to protect him from the consequences. His legacy is that they did so."

Bob concluded that the "great paradox of the Clinton Presidency is that even as it achieved so little, the economy flourished beginning in 1994, a breakpoint in the Clinton Presidency. In fact, bonds, as an index of economic well-being, languished midway through the first Clinton term, then rose smartly in November 1994 precisely when the GOP won control of the House."

This has a politically partisan ring to it that might be resented by Democrats, but there were indeed some important successes, including the two mentioned above, during the six years when power was split between a Democratic presidency and a Republican House. It has led a number of political theorists to argue that the republic is safest when that kind of two-party balance exists. Opinion polls have shown that the public, by and large, thinks so as well. That became an especially interesting view when the Democrats gained control of both the White House and Congress again in 2009 and loosed a new torrent of dubious Progressive policies, most particularly the widely unpopular ObamaCare.

CHAPTER 19

'We've Won!'

O n a nice June day in 1997, I walked from the Journal's World Financial Center offices the few short blocks to the City Mid-Day Club on Wall Street to sit in on a meeting British diplomats had arranged to introduce their new prime minister, Tony Blair, to the New York financial community. There was a great deal of curiosity among the denizens of Wall Street about this 43-year-old Labour Party leader who had just ended 18 years of Tory government in London by defeating the Tory Party's John Major in a national election.

The audience got a very different message from what might have been expected from the leader of a party that had been strongly socialist in the postwar era, up until its defeat by Margaret Thatcher in 1979. Quite surprisingly, his theme was a paean to private enterprise. Indeed, Mr. Blair had won the election by sounding a lot like Mrs. Thatcher, who had established a Tory dynasty of sorts in 1979 by beginning the process of dismantling Britain's moribund state-owned industries and clipping the wings of its powerful trades unions. Mr. Blair had essentially appropriated Maggie's message from under the noses of Tories, who had grown sleepy from being too long in power.

When I returned to the Journal that afternoon, I popped into Bartley's office and said, "You know, Bob, it has just dawned on me that we've won! This afternoon I heard a British Labour Party prime minister give a speech that we could print as a Wall Street Journal editorial."

Mr. Blair had outlined his "Third Way," in which he said that the function of government should be to make people employable in today's labor market, not to give them "an enormous amount of protection through traditional amounts of social legislation." On themes such as this, Mr. Blair had persuaded the British electorate that it was safe to return power to the Labour Party it had soundly rejected 18 years earlier. He had fashioned a "New Labour" party that was far more oriented toward free-market private capitalism than the "Old Labour" party of featherbedded state-owned industry, micromanagement of the private sector and a generous dole for all the people these policies left unemployed. It was a remarkable right turn for Labour and a testimony to the power of democratic elections to correct past mistakes.

If "we've won" sounds like a rather inflated claim about the role of the Journal editorial page in the bloodless political revolution that had occurred in the 1980s, I admit to an excess of exuberance. A more precise description would be that the ideas we had been promoting for many years, summed up by the words "free people, free markets," had finally regained ascendancy in world politics. We had helped that process along through our role in the public debate. The ideas that prevailed had resulted in the election of Ronald Reagan in 1980. In terms of economic philosophy, Thatcher and Reagan could have been twins.

By 1997, many of the targets of Journal criticism in years past had disappeared into oblivion. The Soviet Union had collapsed because of the inability of an inefficient state-managed economy to inspire sufficient productivity to meet the basic needs of a huge population—let alone the funding of Moscow's sweeping imperialist ambitions. The Berlin Wall had come down in 1989, and now the former Soviet satellite states of central Europe were shaping democracies. The peoples of the 15 former Soviet republics, with a few exceptions in central Asia, were enjoying greater political and economic freedom.

Communism had failed in China; the Chinese ruling party still called itself "communist" and still employed police state methods to hold onto power. But partnerships between private foreign-based companies and the state had launched a special brand of market capitalism. The party was reaping the lush fruits of its decision 18 years earlier to open China's doors to foreign investment. China had for all practical purposes abandoned Marxist-Leninist doctrine; Mao's attempt to create a new Chinese "man" through totalitarian rule had led to a massive social disruption and famine. Deng Xiaoping thought the "old" Chinese self, with its long history of engaging in commerce, was a better choice for restoring economic order, which is why he proclaimed that "to get rich is glorious." Mao Tse-tung had been denounced, indirectly at least, by Deng, and western tourists were rediscovering the sights and sounds of this formerly locked-up region of the world.

Politicians throughout the western democracies were learning a powerful lesson from Mrs. Thatcher's upending of socialism—that it is not necessarily good politics for the government to try to own and run "the means of production." When it does so badly, as it invariably does, the voters take their revenge on, who else? The politicians. In the United States, an energy tax and a national health plan pushed by the Clintons had been shot down by their own party. Newt Gingrich and his followers had seized control of Congress in 1994 on the strength of a "Contract with America" that promised voters lower burdens of taxation and regulation.

I'm sure Bob knew what I meant when I said we had won. The world had moved in our direction in the years since we first joined our thoughts together to produce Journal editorials and attract knowledgeable and interesting writers who could give our pages cogency in what Bob liked to call "the news of ideas."

Yet Bob, seldom inclined toward effusiveness, listened thoughtfully but didn't offer to break out the champagne. He and I had worked together for 27 years at that point, and we had grown fairly adept at reading each other's minds. Dan Henninger once remarked that we two taciturn midwesterners seemed to communicate through "osmosis." My guess on that occasion was that Bob was reflecting on whether Mr. Blair's conversion to Thatcherism was genuine or contrived. It was, of course, contrived in part. Mr. Blair had no intention of seriously curtailing the British welfare state to make it less of a burden on the productive sector. But I nonetheless felt it significant that the conversion, genuine or not, had won him an election, and I thought the level of sincerity was adequate by modern political standards.

Bob no doubt remembered that he himself had written an article at the outset of the 1990s proclaiming a great victory for the supply-side revolution, only to be blindsided by the 1992 electoral victory of the Democrats and the arrival of yet another left-wing ideologue, Hillary Clinton, in a position of great influence on the presidency. Still ahead was the impeachment of a concupiscent and untruthful president, adhered to by a wife who cared more about power than marital fidelity or morality.

Bob also knew, to paraphrase a sage remark of the late Princeton-based political scientist George Kennan, that there are no final solutions in politics. Even when you think you've won, there are more battles to be fought. Bob was still engaged in a fierce campaign to expose the Arkansas mores of the Clintons. Certainly there were other struggles ahead, even as we were riding on a wave of hubris. Marxist-Leninism as an economic philosophy had become the victim of its own internal contradictions, but there were new dogmas sprouting that would continue to make the world a dangerous place and raise new dangers should the U.S. government be guilty of bad policy decisions.

Bob also knew that my exuberance had more to do with the international scene than the domestic situation. The Beltway, as we had years earlier defined the multifaceted political establishment inside Washington's peripheral highways, had continued to expand its influence over domestic affairs despite the best efforts of Ronald Reagan to curb its natural expansionary tendencies. The Journal's Washington bureau had long ago gone native along with most Washington reporters for the so-called mainstream media (MSM). Our bureau manager in Washington, Al Hunt, was a likable Democrat with the kind of good looks and gift for gab that made him ideally suited for TV panel shows. A huge TV audience assumed that he was espousing

Journal editorial policy when he defended some new government restriction on the workings of the free market. We liked Al personally, but we just didn't see the world through the same lens.

In the theoretical construct of how a newspaper should operate, there should be a separation of church and state, with the church being the opinion section and the state being the department assigned to deliver news objectively. In theory, the Journal editorial page had a monopoly on opinion writing, but that principle had become largely mythical as the practice of journalism, at our newspaper and others, moved increasingly toward "interpretative" writing in its "news" columns. At least our guys and gals weren't as interpretative as the reporters for the New York Times. The difference was that the Times reporters and editorial writers were mostly on the same page philosophically.

The dichotomy between the Journal editorial page and the Washington bureau had been a source of puzzlement and amusement for our readers for years. Peter Kann, Dow Jones CEO in the '90s, brushed it off by saying that readers were getting "two papers for the price of one." Although Peter was given to tongue-in-cheek humor, it was not entirely a joke. It made business sense to publish a newspaper that had something to offer the liberal left as well as the conservative right.

It had its good side for us as well, because in a sense we were competing with our own Washington news bureau. It encouraged us to scoop the Washington reporters as frequently as we could on government failures they had overlooked, such as the ludicrous attempts by the Carter administration to invent an artificial "free market" in oil. Al wrote an excellent op-ed column for some years from a Washington perspective. Not surprisingly, he was not always in tune with readers of "the Republican Bible."

Eight years after my "we've won" effusion, I wrote a much more somber Global View column titled "There Are Always Barbarians at the Gates." In it, I remarked on how the postwar momentum toward freer world trade had been stalled in part because the farmers of developed nations had refused to give up the government subsidies that gave them a competitive advantage over farmers in poor countries. I also mentioned the flagging support in the United States for the brave and difficult U.S. effort to introduce democracy into Iraq and Afghanistan.

I wrote that these cries for disengagement, coming from both the left and the right, demonstrated a failure to understand how America had protected itself in the post–World War II era through efforts to deny demagogues the ability to exploit class warfare. I had in mind such successes as the opening up of once benighted places like China to advancing prosperity through greater freedom of trade and investment. I was also thinking of the successful resistance to Soviet imperialism and its doctrine of class struggle against western capitalism.

Part of the resistance to the promotion of economic and political freedom abroad resulted from the political mind-set of the American left, I thought, although I didn't include that argument in that particular column. The left was more focused, I thought, on expanding government's role in domestic affairs than in spreading freedom abroad.

The basic instincts of American statists had not changed significantly, as evidenced by the churning up of new regulatory programs by Washington. They were just operating under different banners. Socialism having been discredited by the Soviet collapse, their arguments for greater taxation and regulation now cited a need to ward off such dangers as "global warming," "ozone holes," "errant asteroids" or whatever other dubious scare might be employed to raise public fears.

The calls for disengagement from global politics, I wrote, "are dispiriting in light of what American engagement has accomplished in the last 65 years. They reflect not only a failure to understand U.S. history but a broader failure to understand the entirety of world history.

"That history tells us that rich nations will always be envied by the political leaders of have-not states. Rather than try to learn how America became rich and free up their own societies to follow the same road to riches, too many will do the opposite and plot to get those riches through theft. There's always a barbarian out there somewhere."

Jody and I went to Hong Kong in 1997 for the handover of that dominion by the British to the mainland government in Beijing. I wrote, correctly as it turned out, that the fears of what might happen to Hong Kong under Communist rule were exaggerated, simply because that city-state with its broad access to world trade and finance was too valuable to Beijing to be subjected to political abuse. We entertained the Asian Wall Street Journal (AWSJ) editorial page staff in a restaurant at a hotel where the Communist Chinese president, Jiang Zemin, was lodging and got a glimpse of him as he departed to attend the handover ceremonies. Interestingly enough, he traveled across Hong Kong harbor on a large yacht as the guest of one of Hong Kong's leading capitalist tycoons. The British, represented by Prince Charles, would hand over the keys to the city, so to speak, under terms of an agreement that had turned Hong Kong into a self-governing special administrative region of China.

Then, some of us repaired to the home of publishing tycoon Jimmy Lai, in Kowloon. Jimmy, who owned the Apple Daily and Next Magazine, two of the best-read Chinese-language publications in Hong Kong, had tangled at times with the mainland authorities on free-press issues. Reporters for his publications were subjected to constant harassment covering the Beijing Olympics, and the fight between Hong Kong democrats to win the rights to self-governance they were promised by China continues.

Jimmy had come to Hong Kong as a penniless refugee from the mainland and had built a large fortune with his retailing and publishing ventures. Despite his wealth, he lived in an unostentatious apartment in a middle-class Kowloon neighborhood. Among the guests that night was a woman Catholic missionary who had been working with the "home churches" on the mainland. The worship services of these churches, operated outside the protection given by the government to officially sanctioned Catholic churches, were subject to periodic crackdowns as the party endeavored to limit the influence of independent religious bodies. Of course, that mainly served to increase their popularity as a way to defy restrictions on personal freedom. Jimmy was himself a Catholic and took his religion seriously.

The party during the handover was not a particularly happy one, considering the uncertainties about the future. But Jimmy and his publications have managed quite well in the years since Hong Kong became once again a part of China. The Hong Kong people have proved to be jealous of the rights granted to them by the Sino-British treaty, turning out for large public demonstrations when they felt those rights were threatened.

The night after Jimmy's party, we witnessed the posthandover celebration with my old friend and colleague, Gordon Crovitz, who had started as an editorial page intern, was now in charge of Dow Jones operations in Asia and would eventually become publisher of The Wall Street Journal until he was replaced in 2007 when Rupert Murdoch took over Dow Jones and installed his own top executives. But that night, a decade earlier, Gordon and his charming wife, Minky, played host to us and some other guests at the Peninsula Hotel at a typical Chinese meal. The various dishes made the rounds of guests seated at a circular table on a large "lazy Susan" that we rotated as we served ourselves.

Then, we went to the parapet outside our dining room to watch the ambitious fireworks the Chinese had arranged for the watching millions, with the Roman candles and other pyrotechnics launched from ships circling Hong Kong's harbor. Despite my optimistic prediction, I felt uneasy about the gaiety among the young Chinese inhabitants of Hong Kong over the prospect of coming under a Chinese government and saying goodbye to the British who had ruled the island for almost a century. I think now that a lot of it was superficial, just the enjoyment of a good party, because the Hong Kong Chinese have certainly not been timid in asserting the special rights granted to them in the agreement the British negotiated on their behalf.

With Hugo Restall, who was on our editorial page staff at the AWSJ, we attended the last British pop concert in the city, and there was something touching when we all stood for the final rendering of "God Save the Queen." There were tears in the eyes of Brits who had made the Crown colony their home for many years.

From Hong Kong, Jody and I flew to Beijing and changed planes for a trip to Ulan Bator, Mongolia. I had written about how this former Soviet satellite had conducted free elections, with advice from America's National Endowment for Democracy, and I wanted to have a first-hand look. The rickety taxi we selected at the airport, partly because a young woman was more persuasive than the other drivers hawking rides, took us into the city while the young woman gave us a running commentary on the various sights. One was the Number Two steam and power plant, which might not sound like much of an attraction until you consider how vital it is to the city's survival during winters when the temperature sometimes hits 40 below Fahrenheit.

I wrote a column saying that this young woman and her husband, with their broken-down old Lada, were among the new class of entrepreneurs who had popped up in Mongolia since the country had shed Communism. She said she had learned English by watching television, and it occurred to me that, with her ambition and energy, surely they would get ahead.

The Mongolians were friendly and engaging. That image was not disturbed by the omnipresence of reminders of Genghis Khan, the fierce 13th-century conqueror who founded the Mongol Empire and whose statue is one of the city's most prominent landmarks. We stayed at the Genghis Khan Hotel, and I encountered the conqueror again in a beautiful mosaic as I walked up the stairs to visit the young woman, Nyamosor Tuya, who had been appointed foreign minister of the newly democratic government and who talked about her aspirations to show a friendly face to all nations.

The various edifices around town, including the hotel and foreign ministry, still retained the drab stolidity of the Marxist period in which they were built, but the Mongolians never surrendered to their big brothers in Moscow either their rugged individualism or their pride in mementoes of the long-ago time when they were a great, and greatly feared, power in the world. Interestingly, on our hotel TV in this still-primitive land we watched the landing of the U.S. Pathfinder space probe on Mars, an indication of how images of the most advanced technology now find their way to people in remote parts of the planet.

After seeing the broad and inviting open spaces of lightly populated Mongolia, we flew back across the vast Gobi Desert to spend some time in Beijing. There we found a capital city that had developed in spectacular fashion in less than 20 years. Skyscrapers with distinct Chinese characteristics lined wide boulevards. The combination of auto, motorcycle, bus and bicycle traffic was often chaotic.

James McGregor, the Dow Jones manager for China, told me that the buildings, while impressive, were underutilized and, in typical Communist fashion, represented an enormous misallocation of resources. The living quarters in the central part of the city still looked medieval. We took a rickshaw tour through the "hutongs," and even the dwelling that was open to the view of tourists, probably because it had a TV set, was substandard in western terms.

Jim assigned his secretary, a precocious 19-year-old Chinese girl named Ann, to take us on a tour of the Great Wall. Over lunch at an outdoor table, she asked Jody pointedly, "Do you believe in God?" Jody replied, "Yes. Do you?" Ann answered, "No, but I believe in the party. They do good for the people." I found it interesting that this little woman, who had employed her brains and personality to win the kind of well-paid job most Chinese could only dream about, was sounding us out on our religious beliefs. Perhaps it was her way of examining her own belief system.

With the Soviet Union now broken into 15 separate states, the rise of China as an economic power had become the biggest story in my realm of foreign affairs journalism. So in Beijing, I reported on three subjects: the absence of a reliable rule of law to match the rapid economic growth, a tentative experiment in democracy at the village level and the reluctance of Chinese authorities to make their currency, the yuan, fully convertible. All of these issues remain a work in progress, or maybe lack of progress, today.

The absence of a reliable legal system afflicts all countries emerging from periods of dictatorship, for the simple reason that dictators make up the law as they go along, and there are no set principles or precedents. I wrote that, in China, the legal system still hadn't "evolved fully from the days when mandarins acting in the name of the emperor exercised absolute and arbitrary powers, often capriciously. Communist Party cadres are today's mandarins and they, not courts, are the final arbiters of what's legal and what's not.

"But there are whiffs of reform in the air, growing out of a rising awareness in China's ruling circles that the mandarin system can't sustain a modern state. It not only is inefficient but it has bred rampant corruption as a heavy inflow of foreign capital has raised the market value of official favor." Foreign investors had been able to cope, I wrote. Many were "overseas Chinese" from Hong Kong or Taiwan with family connections to the modern mandarins and had invoked the Confucian traditions of family loyalty. Western and Japanese companies quickly learned that they could protect themselves, after a fashion, by going into partnership with local municipal authorities, who cleared the way for necessary permits to build plants and business.

China's spectacular growth put paid to another shibboleth that had gained ascendancy in the postwar era at the United Nations and associated agencies such as the World Bank. It held that income transfers to the governments of poor nations from the governments of rich nations stimulated economic development. It was pretty much the same theory as the one about expanding the welfare rolls to lift families out of poverty. Lifting nations and families out of poverty is a highly desirable goal and, pursued properly, does expand economic development. But there are better policies than welfare for that purpose. The best one is for the poor country to create an environment that encourages investment in productive ventures that provide jobs for the poor. The same principle applies to poor neighborhoods.

Foreign aid welfare usually does just the opposite, as Lord Peter Bauer of the London School of Economics discovered through his research in the 1970s and 1980s. Foreign donations of commodities, being free, often crowd out local-level production of food and fiber. Indeed, part of the justification of foreign aid spending in Washington is that the U.S. government buys with taxpayer money the surpluses of America's farmers and dumps them in Third World countries. That's a nice favor for Congress to do for wealthy American farmers, but it often puts small farmers in Africa out of business. Official aid is funneled through Third World governments, creating the conditions for corruption and bureaucratic expansion.

China and India have shown that dramatic gains in economic development and the relief of poverty can be better achieved without "foreign aid" from rich countries. It was done through policies welcoming foreign investment. Both countries offered multinational companies a vast supply of low-cost labor and more than that. It offered them vast new markets as the desperately poor of both nations moved up to jobs, even low-paying ones by western standards, in the cash economy. The World Bank and U.S. Agency for International Development are still in business (bureaucracies seldom die), but China and India have demonstrated that such agencies have very little to contribute to economic development.

Interestingly enough, post-Communist Russia never seemed to catch on to the merits of practical cooperation. An oil field equipment salesman once told me that the difference between Russia and China was that if you bribe an official in China, you are likely to get what you want, but in Russia the official you bribe "might not stay bought." This may be because the Russians, with no market economy traditions since 1917 and very little before then, were for 84 years taught by their Communist ideologues that capitalism was an evil practice conducted by plunderers and predators. No one ever told them that the modern western corporations that evolved from the age of the 19th-century "robber barons" are far different from what Lenin imagined. And no one ever told them that market economics is founded on trust; otherwise, no transactions would ever take place.

For better and for worse, modern corporations in the West are run by professional managers who at least try to enforce rigid codes of conduct to keep themselves on good terms with customers, employees and the law. The penalties when those rules are broken can be severe, as the Enrons of the world have learned. But the Russians, emerging from the long Communist darkness, had little understanding of all this. Their concept that private capitalism is a form of organized thievery has left them largely bereft of foreign investment, particularly when compared to China. Foreign investors, including such giants as British Petroleum, have learned the hard way not to put much trust in Russian partners. As a result of this and a shortage of native skills, Russia has remained a pygmy in the global market for manufactured exports while China has emerged as a giant from an even humbler beginning.

Another subject that I found interesting in Beijing was the Communist Party's flirtation with grassroots democracy. I had dinner at the Palace Hotel with an engaging young bureaucrat from the Ministry of Civil Affairs named Wang Zhenyao. He told me a story about his discussion with a local party leader in Fujian Province who was complaining that the open village elections decreed by the party in the 1980s were a lot of trouble. Mr. Wang had replied that maybe the party should do away with them.

"Oh, no," said the party leader. "Then we would really have trouble."

The party had set up the local election process in the belief that this limited amount of democracy would relieve some of the many grievances against local officials. There was talk in 1997 of gradually extending the process to the county and even provincial level, but that has not been chanced. Party cadres have not been willing to yield any real power to elected officials. That may be because local elections did not provide as much relief as the party hoped they would. Demonstrations and civil unrest are still common throughout the Chinese countryside, and the party still takes the approach that using the police to arrest ringleaders is far safer, from the point of view of party members, than expanding the scope of democratic elections. That may change gradually over time, but China remains, for the time being, a police state.

The third subject that interested me in Beijing was the Chinese banking system. In Communist countries, banks didn't function in the western sense of taking deposits and lending to promising ventures. They were mainly conduits for allocating money to state industries and were thus mere instruments of central planning. Much worse, their clients quickly became addicted to the state subsidies and used their party influence to ensure a continued flow. Thus, the banking system was captive to its clients and unable to adapt to changing economic needs. Deng Xiaoping addressed this problem by creating Special Economic Zones around China's periphery and inviting foreigners to finance ventures. China not only got foreign investment but foreign know-how as well.

In 1997, the question was how to wean the huge industrial sector composed of broken-down state-owned enterprises (SOEs) from state subsidies. They were important sources of employment for China's many millions of workers. The answer the government had come up with in 1997 was a kind of parallel banking system side by side with the old industrial banks.

At the gleaming new office building of China's central bank, the People's Bank of China (PBC), Chen Yuan, vice governor of the PBC, explained how the reform worked. Three new "policy" banks had been created to take over politically directed lending—for farmers, exporters and infrastructure builders—backed by the government treasury. The older specialist banks were directed to convert to "commercial" operations, assessing creditworthiness and risks just like free-market banks elsewhere in the world. They were also directed, said Mr. Chen, to reduce the amount of nonperforming loans (NPLs), on which no repayments are being made. Officials had admitted that such loans averaged about 20% of the bank's portfolios, but western estimates put them even higher. A western bank with 20% NPLs would be insolvent.

Well, it was a brave plan, but most recent analyses of the Chinese banking structure indicate that the reform goals are yet to be met. Converting a Communist banking structure to a capitalist one may be the hardest task in the entire realm of moving to capitalism from Communism. But China muddles along with these cumbersome creatures and their NPLs. Japan had proved in the 1990s that a government can live with banks loaded with NPLs, even if they are a drag on economic growth.

We had dinner one night at a Beijing Cantonese restaurant with Ian Johnson, a young Journal reporter who four years later would win a Pulitzer Prize for his coverage of the Chinese government's efforts to suppress the Falun Gong, a spiritual movement that claimed 70 million followers in China and was thus considered a threat to party rule. The suppression was successful in the sense that the Falun Gong at least ceased to make news. In 2004, Ian would publish an excellent book called "Wild Grass," detailing the travails of a Chinese lawyer trying to defend Chinese peasants against the arbitrary edicts of the police and courts. Ian later became Berlin bureau manager of the Journal and devoted his talents to investigating the rising influence of Islamic groups in Europe.

We flew home from Beijing with a new appreciation of the complexity of a nominally "Communist" country that was being rejuvenated by the investments of foreign capitalists and had greatly expanded its sovereignty and wealth by taking over the world capital of capitalist free enterprise, Hong Kong. We came away with a better understanding of the yin and yang, the good and the bad. It taught me to be careful about making hasty generalizations about China.

Apparently, that lesson remains unlearned by many of America's leading politicians as they put the U.S.-China relationship at risk by setting up China as a bogeyman for their fear tactics designed to win votes. To be sure, China is a U.S. rival for power and influence in Asia, and many of its activities, such as militarization of the South China Sea and cybertheft attacks on U.S. government personnel files, create dangerous tensions.

But although those problems need to be addressed, it would be dangerous and possibly damaging to world trade to put China back on America's enemies list, as it was in the days of Mao when we were in a shooting war with China in Korea. The relationship needs to be managed, and managed carefully.

CHAPTER 20

The Horror of 9/11

As the 20th century drew toward a close, Jody and I were invited to a party in Westfield hosted by our old friends Dave and Bea Greene, whom we had first met in London where Dave was working for Exxon. Bea instructed her guests to think during dinner about what they regarded as the most important event of the 20th century. The answers she received were so interesting that I wrote about them in Global View. Readers apparently found the exercise fascinating, judging from their many responses.

Surprisingly, most of the answers I cited had to do not with politics but with new inventions. "Martha Driver named the invention of the semiconductor, which opened the door to microchip technology, which gave rise to the personal computer, the moon landing, the Internet and a host of other achievements.

"David Greene cited the splitting of the atom, which led to the atom bomb and the Big Power stalemate that has given the world a half century of relative peace. My wife, Jody, thought the discovery of the DNA molecule should be tops, because it opened up wide-ranging prospects for engineering new lifesaving drugs and hardy food crops.

"Bea and I were out of step, both citing political events. She chose the collapse of the Austro-Hungarian empire, which helped touch off World War I and its sequel, World War II. My choice was the Allied victory in World War II, which, as I saw it, set the stage for the Pax Americana and the spread of democracy around the world in the 50 years that followed.

"Afterward, we all agreed that it was impossible to give primacy to any single event or invention. We hadn't even mentioned the development of the airplane, which today feeds people daily into the cultural bouillabaisses that the world's big cities have become, slowly breaking down ethnic distinctions and their attendant hostilities.

"Nor did we cite the automobile, that provider of mobility, privacy and opportunities for self-expression. Or penicillin, the early precursor to the wonder drugs that have extended human life. Or television, that other instrument of human communication that has helped dissolve cultural barriers and end political and social isolation for so many millions."

Playing Bea's game made us all realize what a remarkable century it had been, full of the usual drama of human interaction in the realms of political conflict and dispute. But more than that, it had been the greatest century ever for scientific discovery and advancement, as those of us who began life without either electric lights or running water are perhaps most aware.

But all these remarkable products of human creativity were accompanied by something else just as important, the advance of freedom of thought. Freedom House, a New York institution founded by the American labor movement, has been tracking the progress of freedom and democracy for many years now. The findings have been remarkable, enough so that in 2005, Freedom House dubbed the 20th century "Democracy's Century." At the beginning of the century, most of the world was still ruled by monarchies, either traditional or absolute, and colonial governments in most cases reporting to the monarchs. Only a tiny sliver of people enjoyed democracy. Even Americans did not have full suffrage; women wouldn't be allowed to vote until the 19th Amendment to the Constitution became law in May 1919, so the United States was classified in 1900 as practicing restricted democracy.

By 1950, thanks in part by the precedent set by U.S. advances such as women's suffrage, democracy had advanced to some 30% of the world's population, according to Freedom House records. But with the spread of Communism from the U.S.S.R. to China in particular, so had totalitarianism, which enslaved some 35% of the world's population.

But by the year 2000, with the collapse of Communism in Russia and its de facto collapse in China, the number of people living under totalitarian regimes had shrunk to a few percentage points of the world's population, although some 30% were still suffering authoritarian rule. The number with full democracy soared in the last half of the century, to almost 60%, double the percentage of a half century earlier.

So all the tumultuous events of the century that Journal opinion writers had addressed boiled down to one final verdict: Charles Dow's view of the world, in which he extolled free collective bargaining and property rights, and the free play of market forces had largely prevailed. Journal editors who succeeded Dow had focused on politics and economics as they debated the issues of the day, perhaps not paying enough attention to the marvelous technological advances that the folks at Bea's party had accorded so much importance. But of course, it was the fruits of the political-economic progress in providing a greater degree of human freedom that provided an environment for the creativity and initiative that had produced so many technological wonders. Out of all the bloody turmoil of the old century, the world entered the new century with free people and free markets in ascendancy.

It has, of course, been written that not all democracies are the same and that some are democracies in principle only with powerful political machines dominating elections and government. Well, Americans know all about political machines and that some serve the public fairly well and some don't. Nonetheless, the advance of political freedom in the 20th century was spectacular. Imagine the world of 2000 if totalitarianism had prevailed. It would be a lot like the Soviet Union and China of 1950, impoverished and repressed, just like the few remaining such states today, most notably Cuba and North Korea.

The other fascinating thing is that this century of discovery produced a counterculture, a fear of those great engines of technological development—the modern business corporations. Progress had its handmaiden in Naderism, just as the Industrial Revolution had produced the antitechnology Luddite movement in England.

But as the 1990s drew toward a close, the world was getting restless again. Middle East terrorists were escalating the attacks on Americans that had begun with the first bombing of the South Tower of the World Trade Center on February 26, 1993. I had called Dan Henninger from Brussels that afternoon to check on what the New York page was printing that night, and he told me that the office had just been shaken up by a massive bomb blast across the street. That first, unsuccessful, attempt by Arabs to bring down the twin towers killed 6 and injured 1,042 individuals.

Then, in 1996, there was the bombing of the Khobar Towers housing project in Saudi Arabia that killed 19 U.S. airmen and claimed scores more victims of other nationalities. This one was attributed to Hezbollah, a terrorist arm of Iran operating out of Lebanon, and was a continuation of the low-grade war that Iran's mullahs have been waging against the United States since the 1979 hostage crisis.

Then, on August 7, 1998, came the simultaneous bombing of U.S. embassies in Nairobi, Kenya and Dar es Salaam, Tanzania, killing 12 Americans and 200 Kenyans in Nairobi and 12 Tanzanians in Dar. The number of Africans injured in the two attacks was estimated at over 4,000. These outrages were blamed on Al Qaeda and Osama bin Laden and the government of Sudan. President Clinton launched retaliatory cruise missile attacks on a supposed Al Qaeda camp in Afghanistan and a chemical factory in Khartoum, but the U.S. response was widely regarded as ineffectual.

Then, on October 12, 2000, came the bombing of the American-guided missile destroyer, U.S.S. Cole, while it was docked in Aden, Yemen. This also was blamed on Al Qaeda. Two men in a small boat pulled alongside the Cole and set off a shaped charge that blew a large hole in the side of the American ship, killing 17 sailors. Osama had upped the ante, but again the United States offered no convincing retaliation for the outrage.

Public disquiet about the failure of the Clinton administration to deal effectively with terrorism no doubt helped George W. Bush defeat Al Gore in the 2000 presidential election. I wrote a column detailing how the U.S. military had been diminished in the Clinton years and how there was much to be done to rebuild the U.S. ability to deal with the world's villains. I mentioned that the Europeans were reducing their support for the North Atlantic alliance, that the administration's advice to Japan on how to deal with its banking crisis was mostly Keynesian nonsense, that Slobodan Milosevic was flexing his muscles in Serbia and Saddam Hussein was again emerging as a Mideast threat, that Russia and China had been thumbing their noses at U.S. demands that they stop arming Iran, and that Clinton had been double-crossed by Yasser Arafat on his promises to reach a modus vivendi with Israel. Clinton, I wrote, had followed a foreign policy of accommodation that had left his successor with a broad array of security threats to deal with.

As we would soon learn, the most important threat that had been left untended was a bearded Arab named Osama bin Laden. I would learn how important that omission was later in the first year of the Bush presidency. On that bright September day, I was on a New Jersey Transit train to Newark, where I normally changed to a Port Authority (PATH) train taking me through a tunnel under the Hudson River to the bowels of the World Trade Center. From there, it was my routine to cross West Street to the World Financial Center, where our offices were on the ninth floor of the southernmost building.

I was engrossed in my morning reading when the train conductor announced over the speaker system that PATH service had been suspended because TWO airplanes had hit the World Trade Center. I looked across the aisle at another commuter, and we both came to the same conclusion. "Two airplanes? That can't be an accident." As we turned onto the main line into Newark, I could see in the far distance the smoke billowing up from the World Trade Center.

The first bombing of the WTC in 1993 happened while I was in Brussels, and I only heard accounts relayed to me by my colleagues. After I returned in late 1994, I was given an office that looked out on Liberty Street and the WTC South Tower. Because of the earlier bombing, New

York firemen would conduct weekly drills, pulling up to the South Tower entrance and going in with their firefighting equipment, a routine that I could see from my office window. As I watched the billowing smoke in the distance on September 11, I thought this is going to be a tough one to fight, but I had no idea how tough.

I tried to call Jody on my cell phone to tell her to turn on the TV but couldn't get through. I decided to go on into New York by way of New Jersey Transit, which was still running. At Penn Station, I got through to Bob at his home in Brooklyn Heights and asked if we were evacuating. He said, "Oh, yes," and I dashed downstairs and caught the last train out of New York that day, crowded with anxious, dumbfounded commuters.

As the train crossed the New Jersey meadows, I had another view of the towers and was shocked to see that one was missing. It had already collapsed. By the time we were pulling out of Newark, the other was down. I finally was able to phone Jody, who was beside herself with anxiety. My colleague Mike Gonzalez in Brussels had phoned my home with the first news Jody had had of the disaster. He had heard about it from Nancy DeWolf Smith, another member of my international staff, who was on Liberty Street heading for the office when the first plane hit. She had called Mike on her cell phone to warn him that things would be dodgy that day and he might have to get out his pages without much help from New York.

When I finally reached home about noon, I got in touch with the page editors in Hong Kong and Brussels to fill them in on how the New York staff was endeavoring to cope with this event that had literally blown us out of our New York offices. It wasn't necessary to brief them on the unfolding tragedy. They could watch that on TV and get more details from the stories moving on the wires. The overseas editorial page editors were able to cover the tragedy partly with copy from New York and their own interpretations, the European reaction, for example.

The collapse of the second tower blew the windows out of offices in the World Financial Center and trashed the building. As the writers and editors fled along with other Dow Jones workers, many of them witnessed horrible scenes of workers trapped on the top floors of the trade center by the fire leaping to their deaths. Some of our writers crossed the Brooklyn Bridge to Bob's house to begin writing for that night's page.

Paul Gigot, who had just replaced Bob as editor of the editorial page, made his way to White Plains, rented a car and drove to the large Dow Jones printing and back-office complex near Princeton, New Jersey, where computers had been hastily plugged into the production system. Some news editors and writers also made it to Princeton and busied themselves reporting on the disaster and putting together a newspaper. A group of editorial page writers assembled at Bob's house in Brooklyn Heights and immediately began writing under Bob's direction.

Paul and managing editor Paul Steiger, who also had escaped to Princeton, supervised the production operation in Princeton, made possible by the skill of technicians in patching into the existing system. Since the Journal had not printed in New York for many years, printing was not a problem. Indeed, the editors were closer to printing presses than they ever had been—the ones in Princeton. The Journal appeared on desks and doorsteps on schedule the next morning, with full coverage of the terrorist attack that had destroyed a key part of the world's leading financial center. Editorial page writers provided eyewitness accounts for our pages. The Journal won a Pulitzer Prize for managing to put out a newspaper after its New York offices had been destroyed by the fiery collapse of the two soaring World Trade Center towers.

I got a call from Nancy DeWolf "De" Smith early in the afternoon telling me that she had walked to midtown and had managed to get on a ferry to Hoboken, where she was put through a decontamination process, no doubt unnecessarily but perhaps understandably amid all the chaos. I suggested that she come to Westfield by train. When she got off the train, she leaned against a pillar and lit a cigarette. It had been a tough day; she had seen terrible things and walked several miles through Manhattan to get to the ferry landing. But De, who had covered the Soviet-Afghan War in the 1980s for Radio Free Europe, had seen other tough days. She immediately set to work writing a piece about how this latest disaster would impact the Afghan people she had known so well. Unfortunately, it was crowded out by more urgent copy.

Also, I think features editor Max Boot, who would later become a prominent military historian, was reluctant to run anything sympathetic to the Afghans at a time when the initial evidence suggested that we had just suffered an attack orchestrated by Osama bin Laden from Afghan soil. But De had witnessed the bloody traumas the ordinary Afghan people had suffered, first at the hands of the Soviets and then from Taliban fanatics. She felt compelled to express her sympathy, not for the regime, of course, but for the people who were now certain to be subjected to America's justified retaliation.

The lead editorial on the morning of the 12th was headlined "A Terrorist Pearl Harbor." It said: "The world is a different place after the massive terrorist attacks on the United States, much as it was after the bombing of Pearl Harbor 60 years ago; a new kind of war has been declared on the world's democracies. Just as Munich led to World War II, so attempts to buy peace in the Middle East are surely behind this attack.

"The scope of the terror assault would have been unimaginable before yesterday. Multiple suicide squads conducted multiple airline hijackings, taking control of planes and diving them and their passengers into high-profile targets in New York and Washington. The nation's airports closed down, movement in and out of Manhattan impossible. Uncounted number of innocent civilians killed, grief for many American families..."

The editorial said that an attack on this scale could not have been managed without the connivance of states. At that stage, we didn't know who was complicit, but we cited the usual suspects, the Afghan Taliban (which happened to be correct) along with Saddam Hussein in Iraq and the Iranian mullahs, neither of which was directly responsible.

We argued that the evenhanded approach of both Bill Clinton and George W. Bush toward the Muslims had failed. It argued that the attack was intended to intimidate America into standing aside while the terrorists prove that "freedom and democracy are not after all the wave of the future. We can honor yesterday's dead by rallying our diplomatic, moral, financial and as necessary military resources to ensure that that purpose is convincingly defeated."

The Journal just happened to have two pieces on terrorism in the editorial page data bank, one by Rachel Ehrenfeld, director of the Center for the Study of Corruption and the Rule of Law, and the other by Daniel Pipes, director of the Middle East Forum. Both argued, in much the same vein as the Journal editorial, that past softness on Middle East terrorism had emboldened the terrorists to try something bigger. It was only necessary to contact the authors and put new lead paragraphs on these pieces to give the editorial page opinions that were on top of the news.

But the most touching pieces we carried that day were eyewitness accounts by members of our own staff. Deputy editor Dan Henninger was walking to a coffee shop in the shadow of the World Trade Center when he looked up. "Quicker than these words can convey, my mind said I think I just saw the wing of an airliner below the top of the Trade Center. Then the loud sound. I thought, my God, it hit it. But when I looked up there was no plane. There was a wide gash across the north face of the tower, very high up, and grey smoke was billowing out of the gash and there was a large fire inside the building."

Dan wrote that "A little later I saw the flames burst out of the south tower when the second airliner hit it. I saw people fall from the top of the World Trade Center."

This was part of the horror. "They were all so far away, but you always knew when people were coming off the building because they all came down the same way—spread-eagled, turning, falling fast and disappearing behind the Woolworth Building. It was awful, and one's head filled, irresistibly, with awful thoughts. Did they jump rather than be burned? Did the fire force them off the building? Just an hour before they were probably on the ground, like the rest of us. I was stooping down near a trimmed green hedge near Stuyvesant High School and I kept hearing a cricket chirp in the hedge and occasionally small birds would fly up toward the blue."

Dan, along with many other people, had fled northward toward the high school as the mighty towers collapsed. Mary O'Grady, editor of the Americas column, had come to work early, as had Paul Gigot, and they had exchanged greetings about what a beautiful day it was, crystal clear with a deep blue sky. Her office in the World Financial Center looked out across West Street to the south entrance of the South Tower. The first big boom jarred our building, and she immediately thought "earthquake." After the second plane hit the South Tower, she decided it was time to get out. She fled south through Battery Park, circling her way to the Brooklyn Bridge.

"About halfway across the bridge," she wrote, "a loud cry went up from the crowd. It was, I was sure, a plane heading right for us. But when I turned around what I saw was the total implosion of one of the towers. The foot traffic on the bridge was stopped in its tracks. I kept walking but now I had to dodge many pedestrians who were simply frozen, mouths agape as they watched the dust and smoke rise. I passed a woman walking alone with her head down mumbling. All I heard was 'Dear Lord.' I asked her if she was alright. She said yes, she was just praying for those poor people."

Dow Jones hastily arranged accommodations for key staff in the area of our Princeton plant, which became the new headquarters for the news operations of The Wall Street Journal and Barron's magazine. I could do my work, supervising the overseas pages in Brussels and Hong Kong, editing their editorials and keeping in touch with my colleagues in Princeton, from my home office. Later, Dow Jones provided the editorial page staff with quarters in the Garment District, where we remained for the year that was needed for cleaning up the World Financial Center. I fortunately had not left anything of great value in my office, which was littered with ashes and debris. So we made a hectic but seamless transition to a new way of operating.

My first column after the tragedy was a paean to the resiliency of New York City titled "Even a Wounded New York Is a 'Helluva Town.'" I quoted a 1949 essay by the former New Yorker writer E.B. White in which he said that New York was "peculiarly constructed to absorb almost anything that comes along." I wrote that it is a city of enormous energy, as was being demonstrated as construction crews worked night and day to search for survivors and begin the process of cleaning up the wreckage. Volunteers, among them Mary O'Grady, were pitching in to provide food and drinks to the rescue crews. I wrote that "it is a city of survivors and it will survive this."

In retrospect, I think I may have been too kind, not to the heroic workers who conquered that huge pile of smoking debris, but to the city and state officials who moved in afterward to take charge of the rebuilding program. In short order, they had the site so tangled up in politics that nothing was being done, and that huge hole remained for years as nothing more than a tourist attraction for the hundreds of visitors who came by every day to see the result of Osama bin Laden's handiwork. Many left bouquets of remembrance on the Cyclone fence surrounding the site.

One night, I boarded my homeward-bound train at Penn Station and sat down beside a young black woman in construction worker coveralls. Lettering on her white helmet lying on the seat between us said "Ground Zero." She said she drove a front-end loader for a Pittsburgh construction company that was called in to help with the cleanup. She was concerned about money she had sent to her daughter attending art school in Atlanta that had apparently gone astray.

While we talked, her cell phone rang. It was her boss asking her to come back and work the night shift. She agreed, telling me that the hard part would be picking up the day shift again the next morning after so little sleep. She didn't have to tell me that her job moving that still-smoking wreckage with her machine was tough and dangerous.

The worst part, she said, was the frequent discovery in that tangled mass of the body parts of Osama bin Laden's victims.

The Bush administration, to its credit, wasted no time at all, going after Osama in Afghanistan only 26 days after the attack. I wrote that the bombing that began October 7 was not a war against the people of Afghanistan or the world's Muslims, but against Osama and the Taliban elders who had sheltered him. I wrote that it was a war unlike any the United States had ever fought, with the United States subjecting the Taliban to bomb and missile attacks while at the same time dropping bundles of food and medicine to relieve hunger and disease among the Afghan population.

"This is an attempt at something that is almost a contradiction in terms, a humane war. It is an effort to win the people of a ravished land to America's side and to counter the hatreds against the West that have been fomented in so many parts of the Muslim world. It is a formula rooted in the belief that most Muslims have a normal desire for a better life, and are aware that their goal is not likely to be achieved through hatred and bloodshed. They need to be convinced that those who preach animosity toward the West are political charlatans."

As the war developed, we had some internal debates about the tactics. De Smith and I were uncertain about the wisdom of enlisting the northern tribes who had been defeated by the Taliban to again tackle them on our behalf. But Paul asked, quite sensibly as it turned out, who would we find as allies in that bleak land if we chose not to employ the warlords. We all agreed on the choice of Hamid Karzai as the Afghan best positioned to form a new government under allied protection. De had known Hamid quite well in her days of covering the Afghan War and thought very highly of him. He proved to be remarkably durable as the country's leader in the years that followed.

On my 50th anniversary with the Journal, Bob gave me a party in the Sky Club atop the MetLife Building that towers over Grand Central Station. Since my youngest daughter, Maryanne, had just moved back east after an 11-year stint writing sitcoms in Hollywood, my entire family was able to come. Jim was already in Manhattan, writing for Worth magazine, and Molly, who had become the illustrator for my column, came down from Brattleboro, Vermont. Jody and I escorted Ed Faltermayer, who was wheelchair bound with Lou Gehrig's disease, which would claim his life, and his wife, Fran. Ed, whom I first came to know in 1962 when we were both at the Journal and I reworked, under direction from my editor, a Page One piece he had written from a trip to Siberia. He was not pleased but would forgive me when we both ended up in Westfield and became close friends. He spent most of his career writing for Fortune and continued to edit pieces for Fortune almost up to the end of his life. We invited several other old friends as well, as Bob had suggested.

Peter Kann remarked on how unusual it was for someone in this day and age to stick with a single company for 50 years. I wondered if it reflected a lack of daring or imagination. Bob remembered our mid-1980s fight with the New York Times over the Ray Bonner affair, a reminder that made me a bit uncomfortable because my old friend John Lee, a former assistant managing editor of the Times, was in the room, but John later told me that he didn't mind. Dan Henninger made some funny remarks about how Bob and I, both taciturn, seemed to communicate with each other mostly through nods and "hmms," which was rather apt because we did seem to know what the other was thinking most of the time without extensive verbalization. Therese Raphael, my young protégé who succeeded me as editor of the European editorial page, remembered that when she told me she was planning to marry a Russian, Dmitri Rozanov, I said, "Well, not all those KGB men are bad guys." I was still stuck in the past when any Russian allowed an exit visa to study abroad was likely a KGB recruit, but Dmitri definitely was not KGB. After he and Terri settled in London, he became a successful banker.

In my brief remarks, I said that when ex-CEO Warren Phillips first came out from New York to manage the Midwest edition in 1954, we on the Chicago staff thought he was a teenaged messenger boy. He was in fact 27. Warren retorted in his remarks that I, as a foreign correspondent, had been an "expense account bon vivant."

I joked about how Gigot, Peter, Bob and Karen Elliot House (Peter's wife and a later Journal publisher) had won their Pulitzers. A bit of color in Peter's prize-winning entry of his coverage of the 1971–72 war between India and Pakistan over what is now Bangladesh told of war correspondents roasting marshmallows in the flames of a hibachi situated on a poker table in their badly damaged hotel in Dacca. I remarked that I had played poker with Peter and that roasting marshmallows was probably the wisest use he could make of a poker table. For all his brilliance, Peter didn't seem to have a knack for poker.

Karen had won her Pulitzer for her interviews with King Hussein of Jordan, in an effort to give Journal readers a better understanding of the Arab world. I said to Karen, "Nice try."

I twitted Paul about his easy smile when debating Mark Shields on the PBS NewsHour week-nightly TV broadcast. I said he had won his Pulitzer for congeniality. And Bob, I said, had the wisdom to submit writings on economics, knowing full well that few of the journalists who serve on Pulitzer juries know anything about economics. They probably had just said, "It sounds important," and had given him the prize. This was all in the spirit of keeping the evening light and avoiding ponderous prose. All four had, of course, won this choice prize in journalism through the high quality of their reporting and writing.

But I wound up on a serious note by saying that I had always felt extremely lucky to have landed with the Journal and to have worked with so many talented people over the years. That wasn't just blather. I really meant it.

CHAPTER 21

Cancer Claims Bob

Shortly after 9/11, Bob invited the top editorial page editors, Paul Gigot, Dan Henninger, Melanie Kirkpatrick and me, to a restaurant in Princeton, New Jersey, to plan out how we would operate while our offices were under repair. We learned that the editorial page staff would occupy space leased by Dow Jones at 38th and Seventh Avenue in the Garment District of New York. The space had formerly belonged to a Dow Jones dot-com venture that had failed. It was a modish open-plan affair that had desks cantilevered from floor-to-ceiling poles.

The mood was generally upbeat as we looked forward to getting the staff back together again. But then Bob disclosed to us that the surgeon who had performed an operation on him for prostate cancer some weeks earlier had given him an inaccurate prognosis. The cancer had not been eradicated and was still metastasizing.

This was a big shock. Bob had been turning over daily operations of the page to Paul, his chosen successor, for when he reached mandatory retirement age at 65 in October 2002. While we knew about his cancer operation, we hadn't suspected that his health was still in jeopardy. He would fight on valiantly, continuing to write the traditional editor's column, Thinking Things Over, and taking a courageous matter-of-fact attitude toward the cancer invading his bones. But finally, on the morning of December 10, 2003, we heard that he had been loaded into an ambulance at his house in Brooklyn Heights, obviously suffering great pain. He died at the Sloan Kettering Cancer Center the same day at the age of 66.

Eight days before his death, Bob received a phone call at his home from George W. Bush, telling him that he had been awarded the Presidential

Medal of Freedom, an honor conferred on only a few Americans. The citation accompanying the medal said that Bob had "helped shape the times in which we live" as "a champion of free markets, individual liberty and the values necessary for a free society."

I wrote a column recounting my 32 years of working with Bob, recalling that Warren Phillips had told me I shouldn't pass up the opportunity to work with a brilliant guy like Bartley. He had been right. It had not only been stimulating, it had been exciting. I remarked that Bob had had remarkable journalistic instincts, "a seemingly intuitive understanding of issues that mere mortals like myself could obtain only through much digging and sorting."

I also wrote that Bob's private personality contrasted sharply with his public persona. "To the outside world he was tough-minded and combative. To his close associates, he was a soft touch. He hated occasions when he had to tell someone to go find opportunities elsewhere. The messy firing years ago of a writer who had gone off the rails still haunted him in his last hours as he drifted in and out of a dream state under pain medication."

Bob's sensitivity to the feelings of his coworkers was rewarded with an intense loyalty and esprit de corps that I think contributed to the vibrancy of the editorial page copy the staff produced. Someone once said that the personality of a publication reflects the personality of its editor. That was certainly true of the Journal editorial page under Bartley. He ensured that no trees died in vain to make newsprint for the presentation of flaccid prose. Take them or leave them, our opinions were forthright and unequivocal.

As we all expected, Paul proved to be an able successor to Bob. He, like Bob and Royster before him, had won a Pulitzer Prize for commentary, in his case a Washington column called "Potomac Watch." Paul grew up in Green Bay, Wisconsin, and graduated summa cum laude from Dartmouth in 1977. He had excelled in sports as well as academics, still playing pickup basketball with a group of other ex-jocks in Washington after he was in his 40s. He had become a regular on the PBS

NewsHour and was thus well known to TV viewers. Yet he was modest enough to occasionally ask advice from an old hand like me. I had been his editor when Paul was running the Asian editorial page before Bob chose him to be our Washington columnist.

Our weekly Tuesday morning editorial meetings became more spontaneous as younger writers found Paul less intimidating than the legendary Bartley. And as Paul grew into the job, he developed a "muzzle velocity" (a favorite Bartley term) equal to the firepower Bob so often could achieve with his vigorous writing style. Moreover, as a former Washington columnist, Paul brought a knowledge of our nation's capital and its information sources that was broader and deeper than that of those of us who had only viewed Washington from a distance. We would continue to frequently scoop our Washington news bureau on important developments, much to our delight.

Departing from the antiwar positions of earlier Journal editors, we supported the controversial Bush decision to invade Iraq. I wrote in February 2003 that an attack on Iraq would simply be a new phase, albeit a more challenging one, of the War on Terror. It would be more challenging not because of a lack of military superiority—that would be established quickly—but because Saddam was a psychopath with no regard for human life. U.N. reports and other data had led us to believe that he was in possession of dangerous toxins. He had already demonstrated with poison gas attacks on the Kurds and Iranians that he had no reluctance to use this type of weapon. It was estimated that he had been responsible for the deaths of a million of his own people through wars and oppression.

I wrote that the flip side of the argument that "he is too dangerous to attack" was that is he not, then, too dangerous to leave in place? "That would allow him to proceed, using the oil money the United Nations has so generously allotted him, to perfect his weapons of mass destruction. If you think he might retaliate now, think what he could do in three or four years."

The flaw in that argument, it would be asserted later by our critics, was that no poisons or other weapons of mass destruction were ever found in Iraq after the takeover of that country by the coalition forces. That was why the more radical left would claim that Bush "lied" about the weapons of mass destruction and Saddam's affiliation with Al Qaeda.

The second point, I dealt with in the 2003 column, and it has never been refuted. "One of al Qaeda's high command, Abu Musab Zarqawi, is known to have received medical treatment in Baghdad after he was wounded in Afghanistan. Saddam funnels money to the families of suicide bombers in Palestine. Saddam himself runs a terror network to keep his own people subdued, using 'disappearances' and torture as instruments."

After Saddam's forces were quickly subdued in 2003, the war that was fought against coalition forces in the five years afterward was conducted in no small part by Al Qaeda-in-Iraq, a branch of the organization that had destroyed the New York World Trade Center. The president was correct in saying that the invasion of Iraq was an extension of the War on Terror.

The fact that no weapons of mass destruction were found was, of course, an embarrassment to the Bush administration although, as I have pointed out, key members of the Clinton administration had warned of those weapons as well. The use of the word "lie" was preposterous under the circumstances, however. It seemed to be cynical payback to the Republicans, a claim that Bush was no better than Clinton, whose impeachment document alleged that he had lied about his sexual advances. Almost everyone in 2003 thought Saddam at least had poisons, if not a nuclear weapons program. The United Nations thought so, the British thought so, the CIA thought so. And Saddam, no doubt because he hoped that the fear of his weapons would scare off the United States, did not disabuse anyone of that idea. If he had come clean, he probably would not have been attacked.

As to the idea that Bush acted unilaterally, that too doesn't bear scrutiny. A U.N. resolution had supported the use of force. Congress approved it overwhelmingly. When France and Germany raised objections, our

Mike Gonzalez in Brussels called me to tell me he had a scoop. He had called up the press aide of Silvio Berlusconi, prime minister of Italy, and asked why his boss, if he supported President Bush, didn't go public with that support. Berlusconi did better than that. He called up Jose Maria Aznar, president of Spain, and suggested a joint statement. In short order, eight heads of government in Europe had agreed to Mike's request that they sign a letter in support of Bush.

We printed the letter, causing much consternation in France, where President Jacques Chirac had thought that the classic French policy of opposing all U.S. initiatives was winning him support in Europe. The French refused to believe Mike when he told them that it was his initiative only that produced the letter and that it had not been engineered by the Bush administration.

Finally, it is still quite possible that Iraq did in fact have toxins before the invasion. They could easily have been moved out of the country, to Syria, for example, or even Russia. It should never be forgotten that the 9/11 attack was accompanied by the mysterious circulation in the United States of letters containing a deadly, weaponized anthrax powder that caused several deaths. An expert writing in the Journal on August 5, 2008, argued that poisons of that sophistication could not have been made by a scientist working in a U.S. weapons lab, as the FBI insisted. The case has never been satisfactorily resolved.

Looking back on our position on the Iraqi invasion, I see very little to regret. Saddam was a dangerous national leader with a large army and a proven capability, discovered after the first Gulf War, to make weapons of mass destruction, including an attempt at a nuclear device. Destroying him and his government gave the United States a position in an Arab country from which to rally other Arab states against yet another U.S. enemy with ambitions for weapons of mass destruction, Iran. Indeed, an Iranian facility at Natanz was, even then, producing weapons-grade uranium. The United States had been attacked and had retaliated against the governments in the region that were supporting terrorism.

The United States thereby demonstrated, as it had failed to do when it lost the Vietnam struggle during the Cold War, that it was a nation that aggressors should fear. Only that kind of respect has a chance of keeping the world a relatively peaceful place, the Journal had long argued.

There were, of course, issues other than Iraq that needed our editorial attention. As the first decade of the new century wore on, a problem that we had become quite familiar with in the 1970s, inflation, returned. We not only had a sense of déjà vu but also the impression that all the lessons of the 1970s would have to be relearned. The dollar is a fiat currency, meaning that the supply is whatever the Federal Reserve Board chooses to make it. If too many dollars are put into circulation, we get inflation, and the Fed is always under pressure from Wall Street and Congress to create a generous supply of dollars.

Unless the Fed has strong support from the president for sound money, as Paul Volcker had from Ronald Reagan in the 1980s, it often yields to those pressures. With none forthcoming from President Bush, it began to do that after the 2001 recession and didn't get stopped in time to prevent the dollar from losing purchasing power in international markets. The price of oil soared, creating a very difficult political issue for the Bush administration and the Republican Party in the election year 2004.

Things then got even worse for the Republicans in 2008. Easy money had also resulted in a relaxation of bank credit standards, and by the time the Fed belatedly began to worry about inflation, it was afraid to cut the dollar supply because the banks were awash in bad loans. That brought on a different kind of crisis. Easy credit had created a bubble in housing prices. As always, in a bubble economy, some bankers and borrowers assumed that there was no tomorrow, that the big capital gains that were resulting from the sharp rise in home prices had permanence. They went out on a limb.

But the main responsibility for the bubble should be awarded to the federal government. The Fed's dereliction was accompanied by federal policies that were even more insidious. Fannie Mae and Freddie Mac, whose loans were assumed by the market to be government backed and who were highly politicized lenders, had been key factors in the massive generation of "subprime" mortgages that were being converted into mortgage-backed securities that were polluting the global capital markets.

These vast government-sponsored enterprises (GSEs) gave lenders a wide-open secondary market for mortgage loans. As a result, banks, builders and realtors, three big political constituencies, had a field day lending money with low down payments, or none at all, with little regard for the credit status of borrowers. Fannie and Freddie stood ready to buy all the cats and dogs that resulted, with the result that these two huge enterprises that had for years claimed to be private corporations in 2008 had to be bailed out, that is, taken over, by the government.

Bob had targeted the irresponsibility inherent in the Clinton "affordable housing" policies and the slipshod mortgage guarantee practices of Fannie and Freddie in the 1990s, and Paul had kept up the drumbeat in the 2000s. But the power of the housing and banking lobbies was too great for a single editorial page to thwart. It would have helped if the Bush administration and Republican Congress had worked harder to clean up the Fannie and Freddie act, but they too bowed to the pressures of the lobbies, to their ultimate downfall.

All this was complicated by the practice of bundling mortgages into securities so that it became difficult to separate the good paper from the bad. In short, Washington politicians promoted the irresponsibility in the financial sector that finally led to the stock market and real estate crash of the fall of 2008. Even though the Democrats who regained control of Congress in 2006 were heavily responsible for the fiasco, most of the blame went to President Bush.

The voters who in 2008 elected Barack Obama and an even larger Democratic majority in Congress fulfilled the old axiom that the president usually gets the blame for government foul-ups on his watch, whatever the complicity of Congress.

Mr. Bush was, of course, not blameless. He could have applied counterpressure to the excesses of the Fed and Congress but didn't. He got caught up in the bubble mentality along with so many other movers and shakers and suffered the consequences.

Fiat money is a dangerous thing, as the world has had to learn over and over again. Most people think of money as something of substance, but it is only sound as long as the issuer protects its value. Paper money is no more than an IOU. In 1969, I interviewed a clever little man in Llandudno, Wales, who had invented, so he said, a new currency. He called it the Welsh "punt," which is Welsh for "pound." He printed "one-punt" notes displaying black sheep and an ancient harbor scene and gave each one a serial number. On each one, he wrote that the bearer was entitled to redeem his note for one British pound. He then sent his IOU through the British banking system to be redeemed by the "Chief Treasury of Wales," himself actually, and when he succeeded, he claimed he had created a Welsh currency. It was, of course, just his own private joke and never a serious attempt to create a new money.

But money can be anything that is widely accepted in payment of a debt. Over centuries, such items as cowrie shells, beads, salt and, most particularly gold and silver, have been used as money. The invention of paper money, theoretically backed by a commodity such as gold, or at least the full faith and credit of a nation-state, brought about easier portability and flexibility in denominations. The most recent innovation is electronic money moving around the world with the speed of light from account to account, revolutionizing the world of banking and commerce and contributing heavily to what we call "globalization."

Paper money led to nation-states obtaining virtual monopolies on money creation, whereas up until fairly recently in historical time, bank notes and other forms of private money were fairly common. State-issued money is called "fiat currency" because it is created by government fiat and is only as reliable as the government that issues it. In the era of fiat currencies, it is a common practice for governments to abuse their monopoly privilege by overissuing currency or, in other words, inflating the money supply with the result being a corresponding general increase in the price of goods and services: inflation.

Inflation is usually undertaken by central banks to finance an excess of government spending or for the avowed purpose of "stimulating" the economy. It was learned, or should have been, during the dollar inflation of the 1970s, that it does just the opposite, destroying investment, robbing the public of savings and in general bringing about economic stagnation.

I had witnessed this firsthand in England in the 1960s, where both Labourite Harold Wilson and his successor, Tory Ted Heath, thought inflation could lift the country out of the stagnation brought on by socialist policies. When that didn't work, they naturally blamed someone else. One of the favorite explanations was that a "wage-push" caused inflation.

Later, I would argue in editorials that labor's demands are not the primary cause of inflation, but were in fact the result of inflation. Why should working men and women be content when they were experiencing a drop in the purchasing power of their paychecks? Would you expect them to just grin and bear it, or would you expect them to take the risk of going on strike to try to maintain their living standards?

Confirmation of my argument, so I believed, came in the United States in the late 1980s, after Paul Volcker and the Reagan administration had put inflation to rest, reducing it to less than 2% from a high of nearly 15% during the Carter years. In 1989, the Labor Department was able to report that there had been the fewest work stoppages in 1988 than any of the 41 years previous. Time lost from work stoppages was at a record low. Strikes and lockouts had been on the decline since 1980. In my view, it was not coincidental that that downtrend coincided with a decline in inflation.

Fast-forward to the post-2001 inflation. Politicians, as they did in the 1970s, again railed at producers, especially the oil companies producing one of the most politically sensitive commodities that was rising in price: gasoline. But oil companies don't have the market power to arbitrarily raise prices at will, as was proved in 2008 when the banking crisis set deflationary forces in motion and the price of crude oil and gasoline plummeted. Rising prices of commodities are the flip side of a declining value of the dollar. And since the U.S. government has a monopoly on dollar creation, the culprit to be excoriated for rising prices is, and always should be, the government.

One of the arguments for devaluation, one that was promoted for a half century by the International Monetary Fund (IMF), was that it was a correction for trade imbalances. In a paper written in 1992, John Tatom of the St. Louis Federal Reserve Bank exploded the popular theory (popular at least with devaluationists in industry and academia) that reducing the relative value of a currency expands international competitiveness. He found that U.S. products were highly competitive in international markets during a period of the 1980s when the dollar was relatively strong and less so when it weakened. In Europe the same thing was true. His point was a strong currency goes hand in hand with a strong economy. He could find little evidence that debasing the currency contributes to competitiveness. I have previously cited the example of a Germany that became an exporting powerhouse in the 1960s at a time when the deutschemark was strong and stable.

A great deal of very powerful policy had been made on the erroneous assumptions that Mr. Tatom demolished. For years, the IMF's requirement for countries in balance of payments trouble was devaluation. The results in terms of inflation in the economies of those unfortunate governments were often disastrous. We would write many times, citing the United Kingdom principally as an example, that you can't devalue your way to prosperity.

The United Kingdom finally achieved the promise of renewed prosperity and a strong pound under Margaret Thatcher through privatization of state-owned industry and other policies that brought about greater productivity and new investment. Virtue can be rewarded in government just as in the private dealings of any individual, but that is not a principle that many politicians have been willing to trust.

CHAPTER 22

Two Wars, on Iraq and Drugs

A s outlined in the previous chapter, the Journal editorial page supported the 2003 invasion of Iraq, as did far more political players on both sides of the aisle than you would today imagine given the voting record revisions that took place when the going got tough in 2006. We remained unapologetic even in that dark year when the Al Qaeda-in-Iraq forces looked as if they might drive the Americans out and send Iraq tumbling into chaos.

The editorial page staff is not made up of writers with a lust for war. To the contrary, we shared the feelings of most Americans on that subject, that wars are a vast waste of blood and treasure. But we long ago concluded that the way to diminish the threat of war is for the United States, which has no extraterritorial ambitions, to maintain a high level of military preparedness and capability to deal with those states and terrorist groups that do seek gain through aggression. A good argument could be made that Osama bin Laden was emboldened to attack the United States in 2001 by the weak U.S. response to his prior bombings of U.S. embassies in Nairobi and Dar es Salaam.

In our view, there is always an Osama, or a Saddam, or Ahmadine-jad out there somewhere with dreams of the power and glory to be achieved through military means. Their ambitions know few limits, and thus they choose the most powerful country, the United States, as their favorite target. These sociopaths must be suppressed if they are not to wreak havoc. That job almost always falls on the United States. The logical conclusion is that if you hate war, always maintain the means to win a war quickly and decisively. The United States went into the Iraq War with that capability in a conventional military sense, defeating Saddam's army in a matter of days. But U.S. officials underestimated the capacity of the disparate forces of Saddam's former Sunni elite, Iran, Syria and Al Qaeda to conduct, in their own combined but separate ways, unconventional warfare. The only saving grace in this nasty struggle was that America and its allies were in fact fighting terrorists and state sponsors of terrorism on or at least near to their own turf. Quite possibly, that kept them too busy to plot further attacks on the United States or Europe.

Just as in the war in Vietnam, when the going got tough, antiwar forces emerged in the United States. Barack Obama won the most Democratic primary votes of any candidate, partly on the basis of an antiwar stance that was more credible and absolute than those of his opponents. The New York Times, which could at least honestly say that it had opposed the Iraq invasion from the outset, fed its readers a daily diet of horror stories from the front. For a while, it looked as if the United States might suffer another Vietnam-like defeat through a failure of nerve.

But meanwhile, the democratically elected government in Iraq was gathering strength, building an army with U.S. help and attracting support from powerful sheiks, whose interests were being threatened by the Al Qaeda interlopers. The combination of this process and the belated recall by a few U.S. generals of the hard-learned lessons of unconventional warfare, turned the tide. In General David Petraeus, President Bush found a commander who understood counterinsurgency warfare and had successfully employed it in Iraq. The secret was to deploy troops in Iraq's communities to win the confidence and support of Iraqis by protecting them against terrorists and terrorist threats. Bolstered by the "surge" of additional U.S. troops and the growing competence of the Iraqi forces, General Petraeus turned the tide in Iraq, and before long, even Senator Obama was backtracking on his demands for instant withdrawal, even if his reversal of his view was only rhetorical, as he would prove when he was president.

President Bush's reputation had already been damaged by attacks from Democrats and the antiwar Democrats in particular, but in surveying his record, it compares well with that of other wartime presidents. He boldly took the fight to the enemy, and when things were going badly in Iraq, he found himself a new commander who knew how to win.

During this process, he held fast against the opportunists in Congress who were trying to bring him down. He bolstered U.S. forces on the ground at a time when many were demanding a withdrawal. George W. Bush will not go down in history as an Abraham Lincoln, but one is reminded of how Lincoln in the dark days of the Civil War finally found himself a winning general in Ulysses S. Grant. Grant, by the way, was another general who believed that the best way to end the slaughter of war was to pay the heavy costs in human life of winning a decisive victory and ending the fighting.

The Iraq War was in no way equivalent to U.S. wars of the past, in particular the massive slaughter that was required to keep the country from splitting apart when the South seceded in 1861. In March 2003, I quoted the U.S. commander, General Tommy Franks, as saying this war would be unlike any ever fought in the past. I wrote that some of the ways it differed were bizarre. "The world has had access to images from T.V. cameras scanning Baghdad, the center of the enemy camp. And what do they show? Certainly the massive explosions of 'shock and awe' as the precision bombs strike military targets. But we also see street lights burning, buses running, shops and cafés open and Iraqis jamming the streets as if the war was of little concern.

"There is a reason for this. Because the allied bombing is so precise, the Iraqis on the ground know that they face little danger if they don't venture close to a presidential palace, an anti-aircraft battery or some other military installation that might be on the allied target list.

"Of course, they don't know—and Americans didn't know until it was reported in the Washington Post Sunday—that thanks to your friendly Russian arms traders, Saddam had been acquiring Russian equipment designed to defeat precision munitions. This gear jams the guidance systems of smart bombs.

"Possibly the Russian electronics gear didn't work or the Iraqis didn't succeed in deploying it, because the precision bombs found their targets. But if this ploy had worked, a lot of high explosives would have landed on Iraqi civilians. No wonder Russian President Vladimir Putin didn't want the United States to attack Saddam. He was a good customer.

"Had the U.S. attack killed large numbers of Iraqi civilians, Saddam or his survivors would have won a propaganda victory. No wars in history have been fought with such regard for world opinion. George W. Bush and Tony Blair took great pains in the effort to win United Nations Security Council support for the attack. They did in fact get a unanimous resolution last November threatening Saddam with serious consequences if he didn't disarm. Ultimately, they were able to put together a coalition of some 46 nations in the face of French, Russian, German and Chinese opposition."

I quote this column at length because of the massive revisionism that has found its way into print since the initial invasion. This has included claims that the U.S. president acted unilaterally with insufficient international backing and that the attack displayed a reckless disregard for human life. Americans might benefit from reviewing the record of how this war started and how it was fought with remarkable efforts by the coalition forces to minimize casualties among innocent civilians. That, in fact, is one reason the coalition was able to turn the tables against America's enemies, who demonstrated with their intimidation and suicide bombing attacks on crowded markets no such regard for the lives of innocents.

As the Bush versus Senator John Kerry U.S. presidential election campaigns warmed up in June 2004, Ronald Reagan died. The encomiums at his funeral from world leaders past and present were warm and grateful, as befitted the man who did so much to revive the global economy and win the Cold War with Russia. Margaret Thatcher, who had paired with Reagan to bring forth the revival of free-market capitalism in the '80s, offered a moving tribute to her good friend. Lech Walesa, the Polish labor leader who had American support in his defiance of the Soviets, was there to pay homage. And even Mikhail Gorbachev, the Soviet leader who had been Reagan's Cold War antagonist, showed up. It was a remarkable and moving scene that transpired in Washington's National Cathedral.

But I thought it fitting to point out in 2004 that when Ronald Reagan was actually in office, he saw very little of such kindness from those who surrounded him in that steaming political cauldron called Washington, D.C. I wrote that "by any objective analysis, the quotient of political conflict and vitriol in the Reagan years was equivalent to that of today.

"Indeed, some of the same people who were attacking Ronald Reagan in the 1980s are still around doing the same thing to President Bush. Teddy Kennedy was calling Ronald Reagan a warmonger in 1984, thus feeding useful nuggets to KGB propagandists; he today chortles that Iraq is President Bush's 'Vietnam.' Senator John Kerry, now on the campaign trail accusing the president of irresponsibility, was similarly scornful of President Reagan's moves to resist Soviet and Cuban efforts to grab Central America. He called the president's well-founded fears of an invasion of Honduras by the Nicaraguan Sandinistas 'ridiculous.'

"In a recent newspaper article lauding Senator Kerry, Arthur Schlesinger, Jr.—that well-known chronicler of Democratic Party triumphs and Republican failures—wanted to make sure that George W. gets the blame if things go wrong in Iraq. He wrote that the war 'was a matter of presidential choice, not of national necessity.' In 1982, Mr. Schlesinger came back from a trip to Moscow to report that there was fat chance that Ronald Reagan could push the Soviet Union into a social and economic collapse. Things were looking bright there, he said, admiringly. But of course, that is exactly what Reagan did by touching off an arms race that overtaxed the sluggish, muscle-bound communist system."

I noted that the stakes were high in those years. President-elect Reagan just before his 1981 inauguration was briefed on the procedures to be followed if the Soviets launched a nuclear attack. "Because Soviet missile submarines, called 'boomers,' were cruising in the Atlantic not far off the American coast, the president would have to decide how to respond to an attack within a space of six to eight minutes. An officer carrying the 'football,' a briefcase with the codes for launching a U.S. counterstrike, was standing nearby as Mr. Reagan took his oath of office.

"In harking back to those years, it seems clear that Ronald Reagan was no more free of political adversaries than George W. Bush today. The idea that he got along better than Mr. Bush with Europe doesn't hold up to close scrutiny either. His support for a NATO plan to deploy Pershing II rockets and cruise missiles in Germany to counter Soviet SS-20 intermediate missiles trained on Europe provoked protest riots in Rome, Bonn and Berlin. Charges that he was a wild-eyed Western 'cowboy' were similar to those leveled against President Bush today.

"Yet Reagan won in the end, and it is quite likely that George W. Bush will win in Iraq if he sticks to his program of maintaining a strong security presence in the country while turning political administration over to Iraqis. If so, he can say that he struck another blow for human freedom, not unlike those that Ronald Reagan was celebrated for before he was finally laid to rest last week."

History has treated me rather well on that prediction. Bush defeated Kerry, whose campaign was seriously damaged by charges of betrayal by his former Vietnam comrades, and did persevere in Iraq. In August 2008, Bing West, a former marine who had just published his third book based on his battlefield observations of the Iraq War, was able to write in a Journal op-ed that "The War in Iraq Is Over." Mr. West wrote that the war "had turned around in late 2006 because American troops partnered with Iraqi forces and tribal auxiliaries to protect the population. Feeling safe the population informed on the militias and terrorists living among them." He cautioned against a too-rapid withdrawal that might negate the achievements of U.S. troops.

That, of course, didn't mean that the world had suddenly become a more peaceful place. At the very time that op-ed ran, Russia was mauling a little democracy, Georgia, that had once been a part of the Soviet empire. Iran, Iraq's next-door neighbor, was actively trying to overturn the American handiwork in Iraq, meanwhile working toward a nuclear weapon with which to intimidate its neighbors. The American antiwar movement, even if it had been wrong about an impending failure in Iraq, had accomplished what such movements usually accomplish, emboldening the enemies of the United States to believe that Americans were fat, lazy, and weak and unable to sustain a strong resistance to international aggression. It's not good for the United States when foreign tyrants get that illusion.

After George W. Bush won the 2004 election over John Kerry, I wrote that few American presidents had entered a second term with better auguries. His party was in control of Congress, and he had a clear mandate from the voters. But I warned that it is very easy for a president to be blindsided by unforeseen events. The enemy in Iraq had adopted guerrilla warfare and terrorism to try to force a U.S. withdrawal and disrupt the Iraqi elections scheduled for January 30, 2005. I wrote that it would be Bush's job to make sure that the elections happen and American troops stick around long enough to ensure that the new government and other modern institutions are established. He did all that with great perseverance, much to his credit.

Mentioning Iran and a newly troublesome Russia, among others, I suggested that if Bush could keep these foreign policy threats under control, he could focus his second-term attention on domestic reforms, such as converting Social Security into a genuine insurance system and setting up a workable system for the employment of immigrant labor. What I did not foresee was the extent to which the president's own party would fail him in his efforts to achieve these ends. Some Republicans in Congress didn't have the nerve to tackle Social Security reform, and right-wing nativists emerged to scuttle immigration reforms. Worse still, the Republican leadership in Congress thought the party could consolidate its electoral gains by the liberal use of budget "earmarks" to reward useful constituencies. Federal spending and borrowing continued unchecked.

When Congress began its August recess in 2005, I wrote: "'No man's life, liberty, or property are safe while the legislature is in session.'

"Whoever uttered those rueful words—Mark Twain? Benjamin Franklin? Nineteenth-century New York Judge Gideon J. Tucker? [historians differ on their attributions]—voiced the exasperation Americans often feel toward their lawmakers. Taxpayers can rest easier now that the denizens of Capitol Hill have gone home for their August holiday. But those worthies have left behind a trail littered with the favors they've done for their special friends at the expense of the taxpaying masses. And in just a month, they'll be back doing it again."

A stronger team in the White House could have exercised more discipline over the Congress by, for one thing, urging the president to either threaten or use his most powerful tool, the veto. But instead, the White House took a permissive view and simply left the kiddies on Capitol Hill to have their play. This was the biggest mistake of the Bush presidency. When the 2006 midterm elections rolled around, the war in Iraq was going badly for Bush, and the Republicans in Congress had earned themselves a bad name with their own constituencies. They suffered a massive defeat at the polls, and the Democrats were again in charge of both houses. I had mentioned in my column the threat of unforeseen events, such as the Asian tsunami. But this was something that could have been foreseen.

When the election in Iraq succeeded in the face of terrorist threats, I wrote that the diversity in the population in that country of Kurds, Shias, Sunnis and numerous smaller tribal or ethnic groups would induce tolerance. I was really going out on a limb with that one because of the escalating strife and violence. But I was basing my assumption on the American experience, where tolerance became a necessary attribute for people thrown into the American melting pot. Democracy, which had now come to Iraq, ensured that each individual would have his vote and could not claim that his ethnic origins had denied him participation. It turned out I was dead wrong, as later events would prove.

During this period of nation building in Iraq, I dwelt at some length on the importance of economic freedom to unleash the creative energies of a population. In one column, I dwelt on what a tragedy it was that so many young Arab men who in a normal world would be working at jobs and starting families, were jobless and footloose, making prime candidates for recruitment by ambitious power seekers.

In another, I recalled that in my days of covering Africa, I had done a story about a Nigerian man who had built a successful business selling bread that was sliced and wrapped, thereby gaining a competitive advantage over bakers still selling bare, unwrapped loaves. "My Nigerian friend didn't need a World Bank consultant to advise him," I wrote. "He had heard of wrapped bread being sold in London and thought it would go well in Lagos, a place where sanitation leaves much to be desired."

The column argued that "economies are built from the ground up, by entrepreneurs who have ideas and are willing to take some risks to start a business and make it grow. If the business is legal, governments can contribute mainly by staying out of the way, something they are not inclined to do in many poor countries.

"The rap against multilateral development banks and national efforts like USAID is that they are set up by governments and thus, by convention, work through governments. The aid is only as effective as the government it passes through."

I noted that Bush's appointment of free marketer Paul Wolfowitz to be president of the World Bank was met with fear and loathing by the bank's staffers. That fear and loathing intensified when Wolfowitz attempted to root out corruption in the bank's dealings with Third World governments and to obtain greater accountability of whether the bank's loans ever achieved positive results. A bureaucracy provoked to defend itself is a dangerous animal, and it took less than two years for the World Bank bureaucrats to figure out a way to get rid of

Wolfowitz on a trumped-up charge of favoritism to a girlfriend who had worked at the bank. The bank then settled down again to its old ways, using the backing of the taxpayers of the industrial nations to give support to some of the world's most odious regimes.

When Jody and I lived in Brussels, we went one afternoon to a garden party at the estate of one of the Solvays, the family that draws its wealth from the huge multinational Solvay chemical and pharmaceutical enterprise. I happened to be chatting with Mr. Solvay and a tall, rather cadaverous man that I knew to be a displaced Polish count. The count said that he had been down to Rome and had had an audience with his fellow Pole, Pope John Paul II.

"He used to work for us, you know," said Solvay. I blinked but later checked and found it was true. Karol Wojtyla had worked in a Solvay factory in Krakow when the Germans were occupying Poland in the 1940s. He was a pope who had risen from humble beginnings as a factory worker, which is perhaps why he was so much admired by the ordinary people of the world.

I thought of this incident when the pope died in April 2005. His proletarian background may have endeared him to the peoples of the free world, but not to the Communists who claimed to represent the proletarian class. They regarded him as a dangerous man precisely because of his common touch and tried to assassinate him. I wrote:

"The Bulgarian KGB, an adjunct of KGB Moscow, was implicated in the attempt on the pope's life in May 1981. No link to Moscow was proved, but clearly the Kremlin was well aware of the threat the former Karol Wojtyla posed with his popularity among freedom-loving Poles and other millions living under the Communist yoke. He later visited his would-be assassin, Mehmet Ali Agca, in jail and forgave him, a magnanimous gesture that many of the pope's admirers will never forget."

I concluded that column by recalling the belief by America's Founding Fathers that each individual possesses certain "inalienable" God-given rights. "A basic assumption of Christian belief is that God cares for every person, no matter how lowly his status. It has been argued that this theological assertion has been an important force in the creation of institutions in the Western world for the protection of the individual's rights. A corollary is that those political protections have fostered human creativity and economic advance. No wonder John Paul II was on such good terms with U.S. presidents and that his last words to [U.S.] Ambassador [to the Vatican Jim] Nicholson were 'God Bless America.'"

In late January 2006, I was playing some winter golf when Jody showed up to tell me that I had a message from the Pentagon asking if I wanted to accompany the secretary of defense on a trip to Munich. I, of course, said yes, and on February 2 found myself on Don Rumsfeld's plane on my way to the Wehrkunde Conference, an annual gathering of government officials and national security specialists initiated in 1962 by the North Atlantic Treaty Organization.

The air force plane was a Boeing 737 converted to a command center capable of long-distance flight. Its electronics communications system allowed messages from anywhere in the world to be patched into the laptops of the secretary's personal staff, which included his senior military aide, Vice Admiral James Stavridis; Special Assistant Lawrence Di Rita; along with three assistant secretaries and various other officers dealing with such matters as communications, travel arrangements, and security. In a brief chat with Rummy after boarding at Andrews Air Force Base outside Washington, I mentioned that I had once lived in his old congressional district in north Chicago, but that was while he was still at Princeton. He seemed to take pleasure in talking about his days as an elected official, something I've often noticed in talking with former congressmen who've gone on to high appointive posts. There's something about having won the votes of a large number of citizens that instills pride.

We landed at the Munich Airport at early morning, traveled into town in a motorcade protected by German police blocking access to our route and police helicopters monitoring us from above. I went to my room to catch a brief snooze. The secretary, who had taken an Ambien and caught some sleep on his office couch in the rear of the plane, went right to work, meeting with officials and holding forth at a televised press conference. Special pains were taken to give Georgian president Mikhail Saakashvili a prominent place on the agenda, no doubt as a signal to Vladimir Putin that the Georgian was a friend of the United States, a message that would go unheeded two years later.

Angela Merkel, who had succeeded the unlamented Gerhard Schroeder as chancellor of Germany, demonstrated that Germany was very much back in the U.S. camp again by giving a tough message to the Iranians about their nuclear ambitions. "When Abbas Araghchi, Iran's deputy foreign minister, spoke up from the floor denying such intentions," I wrote in my column the following week, "she replied tartly that she hadn't heard him deny the threat by Iranian president Mahmoud Ahmadinejad to wipe Israel off the map. 'I assume a president speaks for his country,' she remarked acidly."

After Rummy had given his own Saturday morning speech, also a warning to Iran, it was back to motorcade to the plane and into the air. He granted me an hour's interview in his flying office high above the Atlantic in which he picked up on his remark to the conference that Iran was the world's leading supporter of terrorism. He was obviously pleased that Germany was back in the western fold after the troublesome Schroeder period when it had allied itself with France to try to block the Iraq invasion. Schroeder had gone to work for Russia's big energy enterprise, Gazprom, which suggests that he was being rewarded by Putin for serving for a time as a fly in America's soup.

Rumsfeld had made a significant contribution to the U.S. ability to project power into remote places like Afghanistan and Iraq by reorganizing the military to put greater stress on Special Operations Forces, while at the same time preserving the capability to fight a conventional war if necessary. I wrote that the just-published Quadrennial Defense Review had said that "the military is shifting 'from an emphasis on ships, tanks and planes to focus on information, knowledge and timely, actionable intelligence.'"

Shaking up the Pentagon had not made the secretary popular with some of the uniformed brass. It's a cliché that military men often are mentally geared to fight the last war rather than the next one, and there is some truth to that in that there is always resistance to changes in war-fighting doctrine. But the Special Operations Command had been elevated despite the resistance and had acquired components from all three services, each with special skills.

I noted that "Navy Seals are adept at underwater stealth and airborne commandos can descend on the enemy from above. They all have the same mission statement: 'To be the premier team of special warriors, thoroughly prepared, properly equipped, and highly motivated: at the right place, at the right time, facing the right adversary, leading the Global War on Terrorism, accomplishing the strategic objectives of the United States.'" They are prepared to go anywhere on unconventional missions, sometimes working with friendly armies, to provide medical services and win the confidence of villagers, a key component of unconventional warfare that played an important role in turning the tide of the war in Iraq.

I mentioned that "One of the classic stories was the special ops soldier who four years ago rode out on horseback with northern tribesmen in Afghanistan, spotted the Taliban army and used his GPS to call in a devastating U.S. air strike on the enemy troops."

Clearly Rummy had the right idea in reorganizing the military to more effectively fight terrorists and insurgents. That didn't save him from being cashiered by President Bush when the Iraq War was going badly, and it may well be that he was not dedicated enough to the principles for fighting an unconventional war. But there is no doubt that the U.S. military would be far less effective today if Rummy had not run roughshod over the bureaucratic resistance in the Pentagon and adapted the military to this new kind of threat that faces the United States and its allies today.

In February 2006, I started a Global View column by citing Milton Friedman's 1972 prediction that President Nixon's "global war against drugs" would be a failure. "Much evidence today suggests that he was right. But the war rages on with little mainstream challenge of its basic weapon, prohibition."

That mainstream included the Journal editorial page, of which I had been a deputy editor for 33 years. Therein lies a tale. Bob and I had both taken note of the Friedman article in 1972. I agreed with it, and Bob did not. I took a Libertarian view. Bob believed that it is important to the health of a democracy to have a set of agreed-upon standards that covered human behavior. A ban on potentially harmful drugs was one such standard.

We debated this issue, but I was well aware that my Libertarian view had little chance of prevailing in the broader political debate. Jody had sat on a grand jury at the Union County (New Jersey) courthouse, which had examined the question of decriminalizing marijuana, and they had all, including Jody, voted against such a measure. I had my own doubts, frankly, about how exactly decriminalization should or could be accomplished in a practical sense. So I let the matter drop and merely smiled when Bob would sometimes say, "Melloan doesn't think any drugs should be banned," implying that mine was a radical position—which in fact it was.

But over the years, my position began to look better and better. William Buckley and the National Review, both with impeccable right-wing credentials, declared the war on drugs a failure in the mid-1990s. Our Americas columnist, Mary O'Grady, was writing about how a peasant backlash against heavy-handed U.S.-backed efforts to shut down coca growing in Bolivia had resulted in the election of Evo Morales, an admirer of Fidel Castro, as president.

I wrote that "The drug war has become costly, with some $50 billion in direct outlays by all levels of government, and much higher indirect costs, such as the expanded prison system to house half a million drug-law offenders and the burdens on the court system. Civil rights sometimes are infringed. One sharply rising expense is for efforts to interdict illegal drug shipments into the U.S., which is budgeted at $1.4 billion this fiscal year, up 41% from two years ago. That reflects government's tendency to throw more money at a program that isn't working."

I cited how the vast sums gained from sales of illicit drugs—tax-free, by the way—have fed corruption of public officials. That problem would become particularly acute in Mexico, where the war against drugs ultimately turned into a shooting war that endangered fragile institutions and human life. Mexico took on the look of Chicago in the 1920s era of alcohol prohibition as drug gangs and the police fought it out on the streets.

I concluded the piece by writing that American politics had not yet swung toward decriminalization and that a large percentage of Americans opposed it "mainly because they are law-abiding people who maintain high moral and ethical standards and don't want to surrender to a small minority that flouts the laws, whether in the ghettos of Washington D.C. or Beverly Hills salons."

In deference to Bob's memory, I wrote that "The concern about damaging society's fabric is legitimate." But I concluded by asking, "Is that fabric being damaged now?" Clearly, I thought it had been and, interestingly enough, a surprising number of readers agreed with me, judging from the letters we got. One reader, David H. Padden in Chicago, wrote: "Finally, a conservative newspaper acknowledges what everybody knows: The drug war is an abject failure. But George Melloan points out it is more than a failure of its objectives ("Musings About the War on Drugs," Global View, Feb. 21). Its collateral damage is fostering anti-Americanism throughout the globe, particularly in South America, and at home it has trashed the Fourth Amendment and is filling our jails with people whose only crime is to find pleasure in ways that other people don't like. Our nation once had the courage to right a wrong (alcohol prohibition) and put the problem right back where it belongs: with individuals and families."

But the most interesting letters were from law enforcement officers. Howard J. Wooldridge of a group called "Law Enforcement Against Prohibition" wrote that "As a police officer, I worked the trenches of the war on drugs for 18 years. Mr. Melloan's comments were right on. I would add that as we chase pot smokers, etc., we have less time to arrest DUIs, pedophiles and people who fly airplanes into buildings. As a detective, 75% of my case load was generated by drug prohibition. Drug gangs now plague medium and even small towns. What part of this policy is benefiting America? None of it."

For the Journal editorial board, my column was a minority opinion. The prevailing sentiment was, and remains, consistent with Bob's long-standing belief that prohibition of certain mind- or mood-altering drugs was a proper function of the state in the interest of maintaining community standards and protecting health and safety. Although we were "Friedmanite" free marketers on most other issues and frequently argued that individuals should be responsible for their own well-being, drug prohibition was an exception.

As 2006 wore on, I began preparing for retirement. I had mentioned to Paul in 2005 that I was thinking about that step, but I stayed on to help see the overseas pages through changeovers to a tabloid-style format. Even after 54 years at the Journal, I still loved the stimulation that derives from being part of an intellectual debate about politics, economics and social mores. Although some of my editorial page colleagues were young enough to be my grandchildren, they didn't seem to mind having me around. But all things must end, and so on April 25 I wrote my last Global View column, bidding "sayonara" to readers.

I recalled the optimism implicit in my first columns in early 1990. The United States had made a remarkable economic recovery through the application by Ronald Reagan of the classical economics the Journal had played a role in promoting. Something-for-nothing Keynesianism had been banished, or at least so it seemed. The Soviet empire was beginning to collapse for the simple reason that captive peoples had finally mustered the will to topple a system that had promised utopia but had only delivered poverty and tyranny.

Japan, Inc., much feared as a U.S. rival in the '70s and '80s, had proved to be a bit too overorganized to adapt to the stresses of a financial meltdown. So there would no longer be any talk in the United States about emulating the "Japan model." China was demonstrating that the surest way to achieve economic development was to throw open the door to private investment, or in other words, abandoning Communism for capitalism.

Europe, for its part, was perfecting one of history's greatest experiments in free-market economics, the single European market. The crowning achievement of this effort would be a common currency, the euro, which would contribute enormously to economic efficiency by eliminating exchange risks and transaction costs throughout a huge population area. Welfare state costs would continue to burden Europe's economy, but it's not pleasant to think about how poor the European states would be today if they had not removed trade barriers and adopted a common currency. Europe's bloody past of wars and rivalries was being laid to rest, a truly great historic achievement. It was also a victory that owed much to the backing European unity received from the United States in the postwar years when the continent lay shattered by the second great war in a quarter century.

The transition to a common currency, the euro, by continental Europe had been planned by our old colleague in the supply-side wars, Bob Mundell. Bob Bartley supported the single currency because it eliminated troublesome exchange rate fluctuations for an area inhabited by 375 million people, a large chunk of the developed world's population. It partly solved a problem Bob and I had often debated: how to move back to the relative monetary stability that existed under the Bretton Woods system.

But I mentioned in my closing column that history has its ups and downs. Russia was tending back toward authoritarian rule. A new dangerous virus, international terrorism, had been hatched in the Middle East petri dish. In short, there were still enough problems to keep my successor busy.

Then, I thanked my readers and said goodbye. Many responded in letters to the Journal and me with heartwarming farewells of their own. Paul wrote a nice, lighthearted editorial seeing me off, and he and Dow Jones CEO Peter Kann threw a party at the Ritz-Carlton in lower Manhattan for Jody and me. It was a great ending to what had been a highly satisfying and rewarding career working with some of the best journalists in the business to produce a first-class newspaper. What better life could an Indiana farm kid who dreamed of becoming a newspaperman have asked?

CHAPTER 23

Murdoch Keeps the Faith

A few months after my retirement, Dow Jones underwent big changes. In December, Peter Kann stepped down as CEO and was replaced by COO Richard Zannino, who, with a background in finance, was the first nonjournalist to head Dow Jones.

Less than a month later, members of the Bancroft family, whose control of the company stretched back to 1902, were given an offer they couldn't refuse. The Bancrofts, descended from Hugh Bancroft and the stepdaughter of Clarence Barron, in modern times had controlled Dow Jones through a two-tier voting system, with the Class B shares held by them and a few others worth 10 votes versus 1 vote for the Class A shares held by the public. Throughout the history of the company after the death of Clarence Barron in 1928, they had exercised their ownership rights with a light hand, letting talented managers like Hogate and Kilgore run the company and simply collecting the dividends and capital gains, which had made them extremely wealthy.

But in January 2007, Australia-born press tycoon Rupert Murdoch offered to buy Dow Jones stock for $60 a share, a 67% premium over the then-market price. Financial advisers and trustees for the Bancrofts, some of whom in the younger generation had little sentimental attachment for the company, advised them to sell. Some of the more senior members of the family opposed the offer, but by August 1, Murdoch had enough votes from the Bancrofts and public shareholders to gain control. The Wall Street Journal became part of the Murdoch empire, which included such properties as 20th Century Fox (now 21st

Century Fox), Fox Broadcasting, the London Times, the New York Post and various other holdings.

Its acquisition had cost Murdoch $5 billion, which some analysts thought excessive in view of the problem that Internet giants like Google were snatching away newspaper advertising revenues. But the fact that he was willing to pay that much showed that he himself placed a very high value on the journalistic enterprise Dow Jones had become and thought it could compete in the new media environment. Also, according to people who knew Murdoch well, he had a special love for newspapers, which had been the family business since his father, Keith Murdoch, had covered World War I and later built a press empire in Australia after taking charge of the Melbourne Herald in 1921.

Rupert Murdoch brought in his own team of managers and editors, and big changes began at the Journal in late 2007. The traditional gray and stolid front page designed by Barney Kilgore was converted further into a more conventional newspaper format, with important breaking news featured in the right column. The popular news summary was slimmed down to one column. Most significantly, a newspaper that seldom had printed pictures over its history blossomed out with full-color art throughout its several sections. Foreign affairs coverage was expanded, as was hard news coverage of Washington.

The senior Bancrofts sought to obtain guarantees for the newspaper's reputation for integrity, which had been so hard won by the newspaper's editors down through the ages. Gordon Crovitz, whom I had given his first writing assignment when he was an editorial page intern from the University of Chicago in 1980, had risen rapidly and was publisher of the Journal when it became clear that Murdoch had gained control. On August 1, 2007, the Journal published a "Publisher's Letter" explaining what the Murdoch takeover would mean for readers.

"You will make the ultimate judgment," he wrote, "but the talented and committed journalists who produce the Journal have a simple plan. They will aim to do what they have done for more than a century.

Earn and keep the trust of the world's most demanding readers by delivering the most essential news and analysis."

He wrote that the Journal's nearly 2,000 reporters and editors had attracted a record number of paying subscribers to the print and online Journals. "The Journal franchise remains the leading outlet for business advertisers; and people now get our news from many new media outlets. In a digital world where best brands have the best opportunities, the sizable offer by News Corp. is a reminder that value goes to those who apply the great brands to changing technologies for the benefit of consumers."

Gordon reported that the first thing Murdoch and the Bancrofts discussed in their negotiations had been the importance of accurate and independent journalism. Murdoch had said that "any interference—or even hint of interference—would break the trust that exists between the paper and its readers..."

The results of this meeting of minds was a set of standards that News Corp. agreed to abide by. Among them was one applying to the opinion pages. "Opinions represent only the applicable publication's own editorial philosophies centered around the core principle of 'free markets and free people.'"

Paul's lead editorial on August 1 addressed predictions by critics of the deal that Murdoch's ownership would destroy the Journal, or in one hopeful opinion, move it leftward. "The critics insult the standards and culture of our reporters and editors. They aren't potted plants who will abandon the habits of a lifetime because someone else owns Dow Jones," he wrote.

But the editorial said that the "editorial independence" agreement isn't intended to be some "heat shield protecting Journal editors from their new owner. We know enough about capitalism to know there is no separating ownership and control. We see the editorial agreement as an expression of Mr. Murdoch's intention to maintain the values and integrity of the Journal."

The most important guarantee of the future quality of the Journal was simple self-interest. "No sane businessman pays a premium of 67% over the market price for an asset he plans to ruin."

The editorial concluded with: "The ultimate verdict on the new Journal will, of course, be rendered by you, our readers. We realize that skepticism about media today is rampant, and rightly so. For our part today, we can only say that we intend to stand for the same beliefs tomorrow and into the future as we have for a century."

Years have passed. Paul Gigot, a holdover from the Bancroft era, still runs the editorial pages and associated leisure and arts operations. In my opinion, the quality of the writing and editing has never been better. The Journal remains a lively forum of opinion, with well-written letters responding to and often challenging editorials, columns, or articles written by contributors. Editorials are a combination of opinion and high-quality interpretative reporting, often dealing with complex issues, for example, Federal Reserve policies and their impact on economic growth.

Michael Gartner, a Journal alumnus who went on to run newspapers in Des Moines and Louisville and was, at one point, president of NBC News, in 2005 published a charming book about editorial pages in collaboration with the Newseum in Washington. He wrote that the Journal "probably has the best editorial page in America." That was before Murdoch, but not before Gigot.

The year 2008 brought the first economic crisis of the new 21st century. It had familiar origins, a credit bubble inflated by cheap borrowing that resulted from a Federal Reserve low-interest rate policy. Paul had anticipated this problem on December 9, 2003, in an editorial titled "Speed Demons at the Fed." He wrote: "If Federal Reserve Board members were Nascar drivers, their motto might be, 'Look, Ma, no hands.' The economy has begun to speed along, and some key price signals are raising the yellow flag, but the Federal Open Market Committee, which meets today, refuses to put its hands on the steering wheel, much less its foot on the monetary brake. The governors have leaked that they aren't likely to tighten what may be the most accommodative monetary policy since Arthur Burns roamed Fed hallways in the 1970s. The fed funds rate will apparently remain at 1% 'for a considerable period,' as the Fed language of recent months puts it."

Paul was spot on. Easy credit pumped up housing prices in the late 1990s and early 2000s. Federal affordable-housing policies meanwhile were encouraging banks to make subprime loans—even forcing them to in some cases—to many home buyers whose abilities to make mortgage payments were marginal at best. Banks thought, incorrectly, that they were spared most of the risk because Fannie Mae and Freddie Mac stood ready to buy the mortgages generated by banks with few questions asked. As mentioned earlier, Fannie and Freddie, along with other finance houses, bundled mortgage holdings to create mortgage-backed securities, which sold internationally in great quantities with Triple-A investment-grade bond ratings that took no account of the huge number of subprime mortgages backing them.

But when air began to leak out of the housing bubble in 2006 and housing prices began to drop, more and more mortgages came to be underwater, meaning the mortgages were higher in nominal value than the houses that secured them. Many of the marginal buyers who had signed mortgages they couldn't afford had little or no equity in their homes after home prices dropped. So rather than continuing to make payments, they simply walked away or stayed put but stopped paying on their mortgages. Fannie and Freddie, which had taken over most of the secondary market for home mortgages, were left holding the bag. But then so were the purchasers of mortgage-backed securities. It began to dawn on them that their supposedly investment-grade holdings were not really well secured at all but were backed by mortgage bundles riddled with obligations secured by a housing market that was melting away and on many of which no payments were being made. The mortgage-backed securities market froze up, and banks and securities houses began to topple. By the fall of 2008, the country was in full crisis mode.

The Journal editorial page had seen this coming. As early as the late 1990s, Bartley had run editorials warning of the rapid expansion of Fannie and Freddie. The two had private shareholders and raised money in the open market, but the Journal never bought their pretense that they were like other private financial institutions. The markets believed they had federal backing, and thus, they were able to raise funds at favorable rates to buy or guarantee mortgages.

By the time the crisis occurred in 2008, Fannie and Freddie were acquiring 80% of all new home mortgages and owned over half the nation's mortgages. Sure enough, the market expectations were correct, or at least partly so. When these two giants became insolvent in 2008, the U.S. government bailed them out to the tune of $189.5 billion and put them into conservatorship under the management of the Federal Housing Finance Agency (FHFA). Their creditors were protected, which meant that U.S. taxpayers became responsible for $5 trillion in government-sponsored enterprise (GSE) debts, but owners of their common and preferred stock took a beating as market values plummeted, dividends were suspended and their stock was subordinated to an issue of preferred stock to the U.S. Treasury in partial compensation for the bailout. The Fed also stepped in with massive purchases of distressed mortgage-backed securities.

The Journal's editors treaded cautiously in commenting on the emergency measures quickly devised by Treasury secretary Henry Paulson, Federal Reserve chairman Ben Bernanke and New York Fed president Timothy Geithner. This was, after all, a genuine crisis in the financial system. Eight days after the GSE bailouts, the giant, 164-year-old financial house Lehman Brothers, with $600 billion in assets, filed for Chapter 11 bankruptcy after piling up huge losses on the falling market value of its large store of mortgage-backed securities. Lehman, unlike the smaller Bear Stearns, which earlier in the year had been effectively donated to J.P. Morgan, was deemed too big to save by the crisis management triumvirate. Its stock crashed on the bankruptcy news, and with it so did the Dow Jones Industrial Average, which lost 500 points that day.

The triumvirate quickly devised a bailout plan for banks called the Troubled Assets Relief Program, or TARP, and it was quickly legislated by Congress, although not without some objections from Republicans. It set aside $700 billion in public funds to buy up toxic securities from banks, but Secretary Paulson soon found that this was easier said than done, so without bothering to consult Congress, he simply used the money to prop up shaky banks. The Journal, conscious of the fragile financial structure, supported TARP, although not all members of the staff agreed with Paul's decision.

In an editorial, Paul argued that "We are told this is a 'bailout for Wall Street.' But if Americans are honest with themselves, they will admit that bankers are far from the only cause of our current predicament. The U.S. is living through the aftermath of a classic credit mania, one that all of us enjoyed while it lasted. We don't remember many protests when home prices were rising by 15% a year, or when interest rates stayed at 1% for a year and real interest rates were negative for far longer. Some of the loudest voices now invoking 'free markets' to denounce the Paulson plan were most opposed to tighter money. We know because their complaints were often aimed at us.

"Our point isn't to absolve Wall Street or Washington—far from it. The point is that credit manias are by their very nature societal, which is why the panics that follow can do so much damage to Americans outside the financial arena. They are part of a larger psychology that sweeps everyone up in euphoria for a time, only to send everyone into a defensive crouch when the credit stops.

"The challenge at such a moment is to prevent a panic from becoming a crash that does far more extensive damage. This is where we are now, and this is why the House should pass the bill that passed the Senate last night, even with its flaws. The government needs the power to use public capital to defend and stabilize the financial system. In that sense, we are really bailing out ourselves."

Even though it was controversial at the time, Paul's editorial looks sound with the benefit of hindsight. No one knows what would have happened if Secretary Paulson had not provided public funding to the banks during the crisis. But we do know that it worked out OK for the taxpayers because the banks that were funded by TARP repaid the money that had been advanced to them.

Of course, right in the middle of the financial crisis came a presidential election pitting a relative newcomer to the national scene, Barack Obama, against Vietnam War hero Republican John McCain. Both were senators. The Democrats had already captured Congress, in 2006, thanks in part to the spending excesses of the Republican House led by majority leader Thomas DeLay of Texas. The 2008 election of Obama would give them full control of the government. Moreover, the balance of power would belong to the party's Progressive, or leftmost, wing, of which Obama was a part.

A sharp recession followed the crash, and Fed chairman Ben Bernanke, a former Princeton economics professor and student of the monetary policy the United States followed before and after the 1929 crash, was determined that the 2009 Fed would not allow prices to deflate in the way that the 1929 Fed had done. During the financial crisis, he began an extraordinary experiment in Federal Reserve monetary management that would have widespread consequences. The Fed drove its target for the federal funds rate, the rate at which banks lend among themselves to balance out the reserves they are required to hold, down to a range between zero and one-quarter of a percentage point. There it would stay for many years, damping down interest rates throughout the economy.

The policy provided liquidity to the financial sector, forestalling, as Mr. Bernanke intended, any repeat of the banking chaos that resulted from erratic Fed policies from 1928 to 1933. But some of the other consequences were less praiseworthy. Savers and pension funds were robbed of normal returns on their investments. Cheap credit touched off a federal borrowing boom of epic proportions, with annual deficits rising above $1 trillion. And the monetary "stimulus" that low rates were supposed to engender didn't happen, as the economy made one of the feeblest recoveries from a recession that had ever been recorded. Journal editorials, which had been critical of the Fed for inflating the credit bubble with low rates in the early 2000s, remained critical of the 2009 effort at monetary "stimulus." Paul wrote an editorial on January 6, 2009, titled "Feel Like a Trillion Bucks," which harked back to the memorable 1960s remark by Illinois senator Everett Dirksen that a billion here and a billion there pretty soon adds up to real money. "How quaint," wrote Paul. "In modern Washington, trillion is the new billion." He noted that the postcrash "fiscal stimulus" bill offered up by President Obama would probably cost close to $1 trillion.

He observed that $1 trillion would be about one-third of total U.S. government spending and 13% of the U.S. economy. "The all-but-certain minimum deficit in the federal fisc in 2009" could be as much as a trillion and a half, a forecast that proved to be prophetic.

But Keynesianism was back in the saddle. President Barack Obama not only fully endorsed monetary "stimulus," but added in the profligacy of "fiscal stimulus" as well.

On February 1, Paul wrote another editorial noting that the new president had chosen to let House Democrats write the "stimulus" bill. "They cleaned out their intellectual cupboards and wrote a bill that is 90% social policy and 10% economic policy. It is designed to support incomes with transfer payments, rather than grow incomes through job creation."

The long-ago discredited economic management ideas of the New Deal were being revived, and the Journal once more had a battle to fight similar to those it had waged in the 1970s and 1930s. The fight was not made any easier by the fact that the stimulus didn't actually stimulate the American economy. Beneficiaries of government largesse became a powerful political constituency that was little concerned about how the rest of the population fared. That constituency was little moved by Journal editorials pointing out the pointlessness of this mass effusion of taxpayer money.

I was reminded of this by one of Bob Bartley's favorite poems. He asked me one day if I had ever read Rudyard Kipling's "The Gods of the

Copybook Headings." I said no, and he said, "You should. I think you'd like it." And so I did and could quickly see what Bob was driving at. The poem was written in 1919 when Kipling was mourning the death of a son in World War I and, more recently, a daughter. It has a bitter, biting tone. The theme was that the ancient aphorisms topping the pages of the books used by schoolchildren to practice handwriting, the copybook headings, contained greater truths than whatever happened to be the conventional wisdom of the day, or as Kipling put it, the current "marketplace" of ideas.

Thus, Kipling wrote of the Gods of the copybook headings: "With the Hopes that our World is built on they were utterly out of touch; They denied that the moon was Stilton; they denied it was even Dutch; they denied that wishes were horses: they denied that a pig had wings; so we worshipped the Gods of the Market Who promised these beautiful things."

And further down: "In the Carboniferous Epoch we were promised abundance for all, By robbing selected Peter to pay for collective Paul; But, though we had plenty of money, there was nothing our money could buy; And the Gods of the Copybook Headings said: 'If you don't work, you die.'"

Bob was equating Kipling's poem with our traditional warnings about political promises that go unfilled simply because politicians, with all their power, can't alter the iron rule, so exquisitely stated by Milton Friedman, that there is no such thing as a free lunch. Somebody has to pay for it, even if it isn't the diner. And the French economist Jean-Baptiste Say in 1803 codified the ancient wisdom that goods are paid for by other goods, which have to be produced by someone's work effort.

Money is only an intermediary unit of exchange. Politicians fulfill their promises by transferring wealth or income. The politicians themselves produce nothing. In the modern welfare state, this is believed to have social merit, but it should always be clear that government is not a provider, but a distributor. And the supply-side economics that we fostered in the 1970s and 1980s attempted to make it clear that good economic policy fosters work and investment, or as the "Gods of the Copybook Headings" reminded little English schoolchildren in dire terms, "If you don't work, you die." So it is with nation-states.

Of course, the Progressives who came to power in 2009 won elections with promises. They were upholders of the fine old tradition of wealth and income redistribution, and there was no mention in their eloquent speeches that someone would have to pay for what they delivered. The default answer to that question had always been the same answer: rich people. That always sounds good because only a few Americans consider themselves to be rich and thus potential carriers of a huge tax burden, and even some who are quite rich have guilt feelings about the disparity between their wealth and that of the hoi polloi.

In good Keynesian tradition, the focus of the Obama administration was on stimulating "consumption," which is the favorite economic justification for redistributionist policies. Most people don't need to be "stimulated" to consume; all they need is the money. And the Progressives promised to get them the money, in the words of Rudyard Kipling, by "robbing selective Peter to pay collective Paul." The main trouble with this theory, as a good many excellent economists have pointed out over the years, is that you may get more spending out of Paul, who gets the money, but you get less out of Peter, who gives it up. And if Peter feels he is being robbed, he is less likely to do the hard work to earn the money.

After only two years of Progressive rule, it became clear to the voters that the promised "stimulation" wasn't happening. So they cashiered the Democratic House majority in 2010 and replaced it with a Republican majority, meanwhile purging many state houses throughout the country of Democrats.

The flaws of President Obama's massive 2009 "stimulus" bill were evident from the beginning, as Journal editorials pointed out. For one thing, a large chunk of money, about $144 billion, would go to bail out states that were in financial difficulty, which just happened to be mostly states that the Democrats controlled, like Illinois and California. Another important part of the stimulus was a temporary cut in payroll taxes and the extension of the term in which a worker can draw unemployment benefits. But these types of benefits have little incentive effects, and unemployment benefits may actually have the opposite effect of encouraging longer periods of idleness. Journal editorials doubted that these measures would afford much stimulus, and that proved to be the case.

But the stimulus bill was only the beginning of the Progressive earthquake. In 2010, the Progressives rolled out two major pieces of legislation, the Affordable Care Act (ACA) (ObamaCare) and the Wall Street Reform and Consumer Protection Act (Dodd-Frank). As might be expected, neither of these bills received a warm welcome from the Journal editorial page.

A Journal editorial on March 10, 2010, on the eve of the House vote on ObamaCare, said that "Democrats are on the cusp of a profound and historic mistake, comparable in our view to the Smoot-Hawley tariff and FDR's National Industrial Recovery Act" in that it "vastly accelerates the country's march toward a totally state-driven [medical] system." It said that the ugliness of the bill, which attracted no Republican votes in the Senate and was passed through political bribery and intimidation, meant that some or all of it might be repealable, "but better not to make the tragic mistake in the first place."

The two massive bills were rushed through Congress with little heed for what was in them. Speaker Nancy Pelosi was quoted as saying that Congress had to pass the ACA to find out what was in it. The Progressives were in a rush because they were afraid their window of opportunity might close with the 2010 elections. They were right. The Republicans regained control of the House.

Congress having failed to do so, editorial page writers and contributors set out to find out what was in the two bills. Paul assigned one of his brightest young editorial writers, Joseph Rago, to make himself a specialist on health care and health insurance, which he did with sufficient skill to earn himself a Pulitzer Prize for his work in 2010.

Three months after ObamaCare passed, Joe wrote that President

Obama had claimed that the law was essentially identical to the "RomneyCare" law that Massachusetts had passed in 2006. "As events are now unfolding, the Massachusetts plan couldn't be a more damning indictment of ObamaCare," he wrote. "The state's universal health-care prototype is growing more dysfunctional by the day, which is the inevitable result of a health system dominated by politics."

He pointed out that Massachusetts governor Deval Patrick was trying to prevent health insurers from raising rates but that the net effect was that they were being asked to write insurance at a loss, as underlying health costs were rising on average at 8% a year. The state's insurance commissioner was predicting a train wreck, or possibly several train wrecks. Sure enough, as Joe's article predicted, ObamaCare raised insurance costs, contrary to White House predictions.

The Journal was particularly critical of the role the big health insurers and pharmaceutical companies had played in supporting ObamaCare in Congress. An editorial titled "Big Pharma Loves Harry Reid" pointed out that pharmaceutical and health insurance trade associations were running a TV ad in Nevada supporting the Progressive Senate majority leader's reelection.

"It seems odd that the drug makers are working to reelect the Senator who passed legislation to rule the health-care industry; welcome to post-ObamaCare politics. Big Pharma and the health insurance companies are betting on short-term rent-seeking from legislation that subsidizes Americans to use more of their products—so the ad is partly a thank-you for new customers. But it's also political protection. With their business model in the hands of the government, the drug makers have to make sure the government doesn't squeeze them in the bottom line."

As if the editorial wasn't a harsh enough indictment of corporate rent-seeking, Peter J. Wallison of the American Enterprise Institute observed in a letter to the editor that the Journal was missing the real significance of the TV ad: "The most disturbing element of both ObamaCare and the financial regulatory legislation now before the

Senate is that they set up, in different ways, a partnership between the government and the largest companies in a particular industry.

"In ObamaCare, the private insurers and pharmaceutical manufacturers have become, through regulation, both a tool of the government and perennial seekers of both more government support and more government leniency—hence the Nevada ad; while in the financial legislation [Dodd-Frank] the largest non-bank financial institutions will be both protected by the government and controlled through Federal Reserve regulation and the threat of a break-up.

"It's vital to recognize the pattern: The Obama administration is gradually changing the nature of our economy and society by putting government at the center."

Mr. Wallison was echoing the warning issued to business by Barney Kilgore in 1933 when big corporations merrily signed on to the fascistic National Industrial Recovery Act that organized them into cartels. Wrote Barney: "In any partnership between business and government, government will always be the senior partner."

Mr. Wallison, in his op-ed articles in the Journal, indeed hearkened back to the New Deal in further criticizing the Dodd-Frank financial regulation bill that would be signed into law on September 2, 2010. He wrote in May 2010:

"In the rapturous days after Barack Obama's victory and the Democratic congressional sweep that accompanied it, House Financial Services Committee chairman Barney Frank declared that the new Congress would enact a 'new New Deal.' Few people really thought at the time that he or his party meant this seriously. After all, the original New Deal—as anyone who has read history knows—failed to revive the economy.

"Indeed, the modern era of rapid economic growth commenced after both Democratic and Republican presidents undertook to lift costly and stultifying New Deal regulations. The deregulation of trucking, railroad and airline rates produced lower prices for travelers and lower costs for consumers. The deregulation of interstate voice and data communication fostered the growth of the Internet and the cell phones that are ubiquitous today. The deregulation of oil and gas prices eliminated shortages and gas lines; and the deregulation of fixed commissions for securities trading led to markets where shares can be traded literally for pennies.

"But Barney Frank was right. The signature initiatives of the Obama administration were very much in the mold of the old New Deal—the heedless spending, a stimulus plan focused on government employment, a health-care program that brought one-sixth of the economy under government control, and now the financial regulatory bill that would control another sixth. It will be years before the damage can be undone."

It seems that American voters agreed with the Journal and contributors like Peter Wallison. The November 2010 midterm election swept the Democrats out of control of the House and brought an even bigger bloodbath of Democratic candidates for state legislatures and governorships, shifting power at the state level heavily to the Republican side.

But the Republicans hadn't won the title of being the "stupid party" for nothing. In the lead-up to the 2012 presidential election, the Republicans somehow managed to nominate a candidate who was weakest on the issue that most troubled voters, ObamaCare. The Democrats also flayed him for his background as a businessman and for having committed the sin of making himself personally rich.

My successor writing the Global View column, Bret Stephens, was prophetic on January 24, 2012, when he wrote that the Republicans deserved to lose the presidential election in November because of the likely poor choice of a candidate. The Republicans chose Mitt Romney, who had signed a state law that was the model for ObamaCare in Massachusetts when he was governor of that state. So he was not in a good position to attack the issue on which the Progressives were most vulnerable. Bret would win a Pulitzer Prize for his columns in 2012.

The Journal editorial page was still not endorsing candidates in 2012, but it clearly favored Romney, despite his weaknesses, over Obama. Romney lost, of course, and the Journal had to accept four more years of progressivism in the White House. A Journal editorial just before the election addressed what it believed was a misunderstanding about Obama:

"Many of our friends who saw genius in the crease of Barack Obama's trousers four years ago lament that he might be cruising to re-election had he only focused first on the economy and postponed his liberal social priorities. This may be true, but it also misjudges the man and his Presidency.

"Mr. Obama has governed from the left not because he miscalculated his priorities but because these are his priorities. His first term is best understood as a race to put himself in the pantheon of the great Progressive presidents—Wilson, FDR, LBJ—who expanded the state's control over the private economy and over the wants and needs of the American middle class.

"The price of this governing choice includes a weak recovery, achievements like ObamaCare that are unpopular, the loss of the House in 2010, and a polarized electorate. Unable to run on his record, he has conducted a low-down re-election campaign based on destroying his opponent's character. If the polls are right, even if he wins re-election, he will do so as the first president since Wilson to win with a smaller margin than he did the first time. But for Mr. Obama, this won't matter. His great progressive gamble will have paid off. His second term will be about preserving the government gains of his first term, especially ObamaCare, and using regulation to press government control wherever else he can."

The editorial proved to be correct. Obama did win, and his second term demonstrated an even greater reluctance than his first term to seek compromise with his Republican opposition. He made more use of presidential memoranda to guide more pervasive regulation by the "independent" agencies, particularly at the Environmental Protection Agency (EPA) and the National Labor Relations Board, than any president in history. The most egregious example, of course, was the 2015 agreement that gave Iran a green light to become a nuclear power, deliberately negotiated as a nontreaty that would not require Senate approval, which would not have been forthcoming.

In 2014, the Republicans expanded their control over the Congress, winning control of the Senate as well as the House. The rallying cry for Republicans was repeal and replace ObamaCare. Chief Justice John Roberts, in two major Supreme Court decisions, made it clear that he was not going to solve the political dispute, even though he had to rewrite the law to make it constitutional, which he did on one occasion, when he chose to describe the unconstitutional "mandate" exacting a penalty for noncoverage as a constitutional "tax" even though the administration had earlier denied that it was a tax.

In some ways, his stance helped the Republicans because it became clear to voters that if ObamaCare was to be reformed, they would have to elect a Republican president, since no Democratic successor to Obama was likely to do so. So with ObamaCare as the central issue and a flock of Republicans seeking their party's nomination, the campaigns for the 2016 presidential election got under way.

In 2015, as the campaigning picked up steam, confounding developments muddled American politics. A multibillionaire developer, brand merchandiser and TV personality named Donald Trump entered politics. In short order, rich demagogue Donald Trump moved into an opinion poll lead as the most favored Republican candidate. An avowed Socialist, Congressman Bernie Sanders of Vermont, was making a strong showing among Democrats. Hillary Clinton, assumed to be a shoo-in for that party's nomination because of the powerful Clinton machine, encountered trouble with revelations that she had conducted classified government business on her own email server, an act that from recent precedents seemed to be illegal. But she remained the likely Democratic candidate for the 2016 presidential election.

Clearly, the voters were in an angry mood and, at least when they answered the opinion pollsters, expressing their protests against Washington by showing favor to the most unlikely candidates. As Journal editorials pointed out, it was a disturbing climate. Bret Stephens wrote another column in late 2015 similar to the one in early 2012 saying that the Republicans might as well concede the 2016 election to Hillary Clinton if they couldn't come up with better candidates than those leading in the opinion polls.

But there were plenty of other issues to write about as a new election year approached. One was the discovery in 2013 that the Internal Revenue Service (IRS) was harassing conservative public policy groups through long delays in giving them tax-exempt status and other means. Kimberly Strassel, who had inherited the Potomac Watch Washington column when Paul moved up to the editor's spot, wrote a tough piece challenging liberals who were arguing that the IRS political partisanship was merely staff-level misbehavior.

Wrote Kim: "Was the White House involved in the IRS's targeting of conservatives? No investigation needed to answer that one. Of course it was.

"President Obama and Co. are in full deniability mode, noting that the IRS is an 'independent' agency and that they knew nothing about its abuse. The media and Congress are sleuthing for some hint that Mr. Obama picked up the phone and sicced the tax dogs on his enemies.

"But that's not how things work in post-Watergate Washington. Mr. Obama didn't need to pick up the phone. All he needed to do was exactly what he did do, in full view, for three years: Publicly suggest that conservative political groups were engaged in nefarious deeds; publicly call out by name political opponents whom he'd like to see harassed; and publicly have his party pressure the IRS to take action."

Yet another egregious case of the abuse of government power for political purposes was uncovered by editorial page writer Collin Levy. Collin, who grew up in the Chicago area, got wind of the hijinks emanating from the office of Milwaukee County district attorney John Chisholm. Democrats had launched a campaign in 2013 to recall reformist Wisconsin governor Scott Walker, who had offended unions by restricting public employee bargaining power and pushing for a right-to-work law, eventually enacted in 2015, requiring that union membership could not be a condition of employment. The recall failed, but during Walker's campaign for reelection in 2014, an assistant district attorney and special prosecutor working from Chisholm's office had tried to muzzle Walker supporters by issuing subpoenas charging them with violation of the state's campaign finance laws. Collin's editorials put Chisholm under a national spotlight.

On January 10, 2014, Wisconsin judge Gregory A. Peterson quashed the subpoenas on a lack of any evidence that a crime had been committed. Federal courts later that year ruled that Wisconsin's campaign finance law violated the First Amendment. Collin cautioned that these legal victories didn't mean the war had been won, and Wisconsin Democrats continued the fight. But she and Paul had exposed a prima facie case of prosecutorial abuse. Both the IRS and Wisconsin power plays were issues that Obama's Justice Department chose to sweep under the rug.

Events abroad were also becoming more menacing. The Journal editorial page was well equipped to cover the drama in Ukraine that began with the fall of the corrupt government of President Viktor Yanukovych in February of 2014 and mutated into an armed struggle between Ukraine and Yanukovych's patron, Vladimir Putin's Russia. A Journal editorial writer, Matthew Kaminski, was born in Poland and learned Russian at the behest of the country's Russian overlords. Paul dispatched him to Ukraine, where Russian was also a second language, to cover the crisis. In March 2014, he reported from Donetsk in a by-lined piece that Russia's grab of Crimea was only an appetizer. "The real prize for Vladimir Putin is likely to be Eastern Ukraine. Without this vast region of coal mines and factories, the Kremlin strongman won't be able to achieve his goal of either controlling, destabilizing Ukraine or splitting Ukraine."

Matt was right. Before long, the "little green men," Russian soldiers in a not very convincing disguise, were pouring across the Ukrainian border, and Putin's campaign to bring back Ukraine into the Russian empire was under way. Matt, with his lifetime of knowledge about the methods of Russian imperialism, provided some of the best coverage of the developing and continuing conflict as it threatened to ignite a new Cold War between Russia and the West, reporting from Ukraine, Crimea and Russia itself.

The editorial page also was well equipped to cover the rise of Jihadist terrorists (Islamic State, Al Qaeda and their offshoots). Sohrab Ahmari, who was born in Tehran, had come to the page through the summer internship program titled "Bartley Fellows," established in memory of Bob Bartley. Sohrab's knowledge of the area and its languages, plus his writing skills, have been particularly valuable to Journal readers for understanding the complex issues surrounding U.S. policy in the region.

When the Kerry State Department, during its nuclear arms negotiations with Iran, hailed the new president of Iran, Hassam Rouhani, as being far more friendly toward the United States than his predecessor, Mahmoud Ahmadinejad, Sohrab wrote a piece pointing out that Rouhani had played a key role in crushing the 1999 student uprising in Tehran and that, when he is speaking to Iranians in Farsi, he sounds just about as anti-American as Ahmadinejad. His writings offered special knowledge as to why Americans should put little trust in the nuclear agreement the Obama administration struck with Tehran. The flimsiness of the agreement was reflected in the fact that the administration refused to call it a treaty. It thus escaped Senate "advise and consent" scrutiny.

CHAPTER 24

Modern Times

Gigot's editorial pages waded into the 2016 presidential campaign debate with firmly established public policy positions and forthright opinions about the qualifications of the candidates and the merits of their views. Along with many other commentators, some editorial page writers were surprised and uncomfortable with the early opinion poll successes of the bombastic real estate tycoon Donald Trump. Nor did Journal writers display admiration for another Republican front-runner, the opportunistic Texas senator Ted Cruz.

Particularly off-putting was the hostility of both toward immigrants, which the Journal felt was damaging to the chances for serious reform of the nation's broken set of immigration policies. Trump's talk of building "walls" and applying other draconian measures against immigrants, in the Journal view, merely worsened the worst features of current policy, which had made illegal immigration across America's southern border inevitable by damaging the old policy of allowing "guest" workers to move back and forth across the border in response to the availability of jobs.

This flexibility had suited the needs of both the migrants and their employers, particularly growers who needed seasonal labor at planting and harvest time. But it didn't suit labor unions who complained to their congressmen that the law allowed cheap foreign labor to undercut the pay levels and job opportunities of American workers. The Simpson-Mazzoli Act of 1986 responded to union pressures with the effect that the flexibility of the immigration laws was sharply reduced. Immigrants kept coming because jobs that Americans didn't want were available, but they were coming by illegal rather than legal means. And no longer able to move freely, they stayed. The population of illegals rose steadily, roughly tripling in the 30 years after Simpson-Mazzoli.

Trump, in particular, displayed such negative, nativist attitudes that if his rants were to be taken seriously, it was easy to believe he would make matters far worse, damaging U.S. relations with an important and friendly neighbor, Mexico. The problem went beyond seasonal and menial labor. American companies were complaining that the difficulties in obtaining H-2B visas were preventing them from hiring foreign nationals with special skills, in science, for example, graduating from American universities, even though those skills would clearly benefit high-tech industries and the American economy.

Some Journal writers saw Trump, who also sounded like a threat to free trade agreements, as a one-man wrecking crew with little regard for constitutional limits on presidential power. Washington columnist Kimberly Strassel wrote a telling op-ed in February of 2016 in which she quoted Ben Sasse, a conservative Republican senator from Nebraska, thusly: "We have a President who does not believe in executive restraint; we do not need another."

Senator Sasse was referring to Obama's habit of legislating from the White House through the issuance of executive orders and signing "agreements" instead of treaties with foreign powers. His clear intent had been to shut Congress out of its rightful constitutional lawmaking role and to deny the Senate its power to review treaties and withhold its consent from any deemed contrary to America's national interests. Senator Sasse, recognizing the danger that any Obama successor, Republican or Democrat, might continue these willful practices, wanted Republican candidates to pledge to observe the constitutional limits on executive power. He no doubt feared that Trump, with his contempt for "the establishment," might be even worse than Obama.

Kim had another question for Republican candidates: "Do you

promise to reject dark power?" She was referring to the increasing tendency of federal bureaucrats—the "permanent government"—to expand their power by making rules that they justified through some vague or loosely drafted provision of existing law but not bothering to ask Congress what the law actually meant. Along with his other transgressions against the Constitution's separation of powers requirements, Obama had encouraged administrative lawmaking to fulfill his goal of creating a more powerful executive branch.

Kim cited the case of the IRS targeting conservative nonprofits by slow-walking their legitimate applications for tax exemptions. Kim had written in an earlier column that this political maneuver had been directed from the White House. Her claim was never successfully challenged.

As the initial primary contests began in 2016, the angry mood of the voters became manifest with Cruz winning the Iowa caucus and Trump claiming the New Hampshire primary with "anti-establishment" screeds. The Democrats fared even worse, with Socialist Bernie Sanders upsetting Hillary Clinton, who had been presumed to be the party's anointed candidate, in New Hampshire. This mood of anger and protest suggested that the 2016 election might prove to be unlike any that had gone before, with a significant danger that both parties would pick candidates unequal to the task of wielding the vast powers of the modern American presidency and conducting a foreign policy that would protect the country's security.

Amazingly, only 25 years after the collapse of socialism in Europe and Asia because of its failure to deliver decent living standards, Sanders seemed to have a strong following, particularly among young people with abiding attachments to cell phones but little acquaintanceship with history books. The costs and chaos deriving from Obama's Progressive policies to expand government control of health care, energy and banking had somehow persuaded many Democrats that what was needed was more of the same. The ignorance of college students was a particular shock to those of us who thought the battle against socialist authoritarianism had been fought and won years ago. It seemed to be a manifestation of the old story that bad government policies often beget policies that are even worse as politicians meddle further to try to fix what went wrong.

The Journal editorial page tasked itself, as ever, with explaining why so many things went wrong in the Obama years and why so many voters were displaying extreme unhappiness with the status quo, an anger that had opened the doors to the likes of the bombastic Donald Trump and an ancient red, Bernie Sanders.

Some of the problems were quite obvious. ObamaCare's irrationalities were manifesting themselves in higher health insurance premiums, in direct contradiction of the president's promises of lower costs. For one thing, the law demanded that insurers accept applicants without regard to their existing health problems. This created an incentive for people to remain uninsured, paying a relatively small penalty (and sometimes not because of lax enforcement) until they got sick. Insurance is based on the principle that the premiums of the many pay for the problems of the few. When that equation was disturbed by the "existing conditions" rule, premiums for the unsubsidized middle class had to go up.

Adding new burdens onto the public at a time when the economy was already saddled with excessive taxation and regulation is a recipe for discontent. Years after the 2008 crash, the U.S. workforce remained stuck where it had been 30 years earlier. Household incomes also had remained stagnant. Thanks in part to the Fed zero-bound interest rate policy and Washington's ravenous spending appetite, the federal government had piled up far more debt in the Obama years than it had in all its past history.

Dodd-Frank had forced banks to improve their capital bases and had subjected them to some 20,000 pages of new regulations. But little had been done to address the failures of public policy responsible for the 2008 crash.

Fannie Mae and Freddie Mac were still around as the year 2016 began, still enjoying the advantage over private lenders that comes from Uncle Sam's backing. The Journal had been raising alarms about the unsound, politicized lending and borrowing practices of the two government-backed mortgage giants for almost 20 years. There had been talk of liquidating them, but it went nowhere. The Fed had stepped in to buy up the toxic mortgage-backed securities they and others had issued. And so there we were in 2016 with the federal government for all practical purposes holding half the nation's mortgage debt and continuing the old practice of using much of it as collateral for mortgage-backed securities sold on world markets. It was assumed that this collateral contained fewer nonperforming "toxic" mortgages than in 2008, but who knew what would turn sour in another housing slump?

Paul ran an editorial on the last day of the year 2015 titled "Fannie and Freddie Forever" that began with, "Washington is the place where bad ideas go to live forever. How else to explain the latest innovation from federal regulators to keep Fannie Mae and Freddie Mac dominating the market for mortgage finance?"

The editorial noted that the Federal Housing Finance Agency (FHFA), the "conservator" of the toxic twins after their taxpayer bailout in 2008, was now using another artifact of the 2008 debacle, synthetic collateralized debt obligations (CDOs), to off-load some of their risks. In simplest terms, CDOs are insurance policies for investors against defaults. Wall Street provides CDOs at hefty costs. Asked the editorial: "But how about simply not holding these risks in the first place? Then taxpayers would have no need for insurance."

Good question, of course. The answer, recited earlier in this book's discussion of the toxic twins, is that builders, bankers and real estate interests are a powerful lobby in Washington and like nothing better than shifting mortgage risks to taxpayers. The editorial ended with, "And the Beltway crowd wonders why Donald Trump is winning."

Another macroeconomic issue still with us in 2016 was the 15-year-old departure from monetary policy orthodoxy. The Federal Reserve was continuing its long experiment in providing cheap borrowing for the government and low returns on prudent investments for savers, with very little evidence that its policies had provided the kind of economic "stimulation" that neo-Keynesians persist in promising.

Because of low return on investments, many state public employee pension funds, to cite one example, were wallowing in red ink and in need of more support from hard-pressed taxpayers. Late in 2015, the Fed decided to try to climb out of the box it had put itself in by raising short-term interest rates by a quarter of a point from the zero-bound level.

Since a huge buildup of the excess reserves held by banks on account with the Fed, the traditional means for raising rates, tightened up the reserves banks trade among themselves, the Fed had to adopt a more cumbersome method using overnight borrowing in the broad financial services market to set higher rates. Some monetary economists were optimistic that the Fed was finally on the right track toward rates more balanced between borrowers and savers, but this form of rate setting, requiring huge trading volumes, was experimental. It raised new questions about the Fed's ability to conduct a monetary policy that would give the dollar sufficient stability to engender business confidence in the United States and foster international trade and investment.

By killing off a decent return on bank deposits, Federal Reserve policy had forced small investors seeking a higher return to venture into an increasingly volatile stock market. This flow into financial assets had ballooned the fortunes of the very rich, like the conservative Koch brothers of Wichita, giving Hillary and Bernie Sanders an excuse to deplore the rise of "income inequality" as a political issue, which, as always, had resonance with striving lower- and middle-income families. Progressives, of course, had been fully supportive of the Fed policy because it afforded the government with cheap borrowing to support the entitlement freebies with which the Progressives win votes. What Hillary and Bernie were really deploring was not so much income inequality but wealth inequality, which is not the same but close enough for government work.

The credit market distortions created by the Fed's experiments were far reaching. A Journal editorial in August 2015 was titled "Emerging Market Rip Tide." It explained that Fed direct massive purchases of government bonds and mortgage-backed securities, known as "quantitative easing" (QE), had brought such an outpouring of newly created dollars that it had driven their value down. "Investors borrowed dollars at low rates, converted them into other currencies and bought assets with a higher return, a phenomenon known as the carry trade." Emerging market economies, particularly exporters of commodities like Brazil, boomed. But when the Fed started "tapering" its asset buying, the process reversed itself. The dollar strengthened, and the hot money that had flowed into emerging markets flowed out again. The strong dollar lowered the dollar price of commodities, an emerging market export staple. Places like Brazil and Malaysia were left in the lurch.

Said a Journal editorial: "The destabilizing effect of QE threatens global growth at a moment when none of the major economies is firing on all cylinders. By encouraging over-investment in developing countries, it may have created new deflationary pressures. China built massive steel-making capacity that will now drive down global prices and lead to protectionist pressure in the U.S. This dislocation and wasted investment should make policy makers reconsider their faith in the power of monetary policy to stimulate growth, and put the emphasis back on pro-market reforms."

That was certainly good advice, but as we entered the new year, there was little evidence that it would be followed. With much fanfare, the Fed attempted to nurse interest rates upward in December 2015, getting them up to around .40 of a percentage point (40 basis points in Wall Street jargon), but even this minor change gave the stock market hysterics. The Dow Jones averages stumbled into the new year with one of the worst performances on record. Fed officials, who had promised more increases, began to reverse themselves, so it seemed likely that borrowing would continue to be cheap and saving unremunerative, with no more evidence than was shown in the preceding seven years that easy credit stimulated the economy.

Climate change was another piñata that the Journal had been pummeling for two decades, ever since Al Gore had unleashed his "Earth in the Balance" goblins from his lofty perch as vice president of the United States. As mentioned earlier, Barack Obama had remained true to the cause and to burdening American industry with ever more taxes and regulations on energy use, with the ostensible goal of lowering carbon dioxide emissions. That the scare tactics of so-called climate "scientists" had been discredited by genuine research was of little concern to the president and his supporters in the green lobby.

Holman Jenkins, author of the Business World column that we had started in 1987, was especially adept at uncovering the true motivations behind the strategies of both business leaders and politicians, not to mention religious leaders of the stature of Pope Francis. When the pope joined the crusade against carbon emissions in 2015, Holman wrote a column titled "The Pope's Solution for Warming: Pray." He noted a headline in some other publication that had credited the pope with "finding religion" on climate change.

"Maybe it would be truer to say Pope Francis has tried to annex one of the newer religions, that of global warming, to Catholic liturgy." But Holman doubted that either the ministrations of the pope or of President Obama would have much actual effect on the climate. He quoted Georgia Tech climatologist Judith Curry as saying that even if the president succeeded in reducing carbon emissions, the trivial effects would "get lost among the natural variability of climate." Thus, wrote Holman, "Mr. Obama, who has referred to the 'urgent and growing threat of changing climate,' has committed the U.S. to a program of costs without benefits."

As the Journal had broadened its coverage over the years, editorial writers had found themselves much more involved with social and ethical issues in addition to its traditional discussion of the laws of market economics and the human lawmakers who constantly try to countermand those laws, sometimes with disastrous results. And many social and ethical questions had been on the public docket for a long time as we entered the new year.

Bob Bartley had written about Roe v. Wade when the Supreme Court had first overridden state laws banning abortions in 1973. He had seen the ruling as a compromise with logic of a sort, in that it granted women the right to an abortion free of government control in the first trimester of a pregnancy. But he argued that such a vexing issue as legalized abortion could only be properly settled in the political arena, not by the courts.

Sure enough, the abortion debate raged on just as Bob had expected it would. The pro-choice faction advanced the idea that the government should not only permit abortions but, in the case of poor unwed mothers, use tax money to pay for them.

A particularly cogent editorial on the subject appeared in the Journal on November 5, 2005, observing that "The word abortion appears nowhere in the Constitution," yet that word had become the flash point of the Senate debate confirming Judge Samuel Alito for a seat on the Supreme Court. The 2005 editorial repeated once more that states already had been liberalizing abortion laws at the time Roe v. Wade took the matter out of their hands, and that by 2005 the political battles likely would have been resolved absent court intervention. It quoted Justice Antonin Scalia as saying that "by banishing the issue from the public forum that gives all participants, even the losers, the satisfaction of a fair hearing and an honest fight...the court merely prolongs and intensifies the anguish."

Journal editorials often supported Justice Scalia, who died in February 2016, because of his frequent arguments that courts should defer to state legislatures when addressing social issues outside the purview of the Constitution and limited powers it grants to the federal government. He was quoted again in the June 27, 2015, editorial that commented on Obergefell v. Hodges, in which the court again overrode state laws in finding a constitutional right to same-sex marriage. The editorial noted that "The revolution in mores about gay and lesbian participation in the institution of marriage is among the most dramatic cultural shifts in U.S. history" and that the modification of laws in 11 states to liberalize the definition of marriage had been "a declaration of social inclusion whose outcome is welcomed by ever-more Americans." It had been, as Justice Scalia had written in his dissent, "American democracy at its best." But the editorial argued yet again, as with regard to Roe v. Wade, that "the Constitution is silent about marriage and social-policy preferences, which are supposed to be settled by the people and the political branches." It asserted that by walling off the definition of marriage from political debate, the "majority may create more political polarization, not less."

The editorial also quoted the dissent of Chief Justice John Roberts: "This court is not a legislature...whether same-sex marriage is a good idea should be of no concern to us. Under the Constitution, judges have power to say what the law is, not what it should be."

By entering the lists on these complex and deeply emotive issues, the Journal had evolved from its beginnings as a market letter to a participant in the public debate in the broadest possible sense. While it could be argued that its positions on Roe and Obergefell contradicted its long-standing defense of individual freedom in that, in both cases, the court was countermanding state laws that restricted freedoms to abort a fetus and to form a same-sex bond, the Journal did not defend absolute bans on either practice. It simply argued that the Constitution and its Bill of Rights specifically defined the powers of the federal government and did so because the authors, James Madison and Thomas Jefferson, for example, sought to create a balance of power that would protect basic freedoms. In the real world, of course, state legislatures often passed laws limiting freedoms, but in no society, even a well-functioning democracy, can personal freedom be absolute and not subject to the constraints imposed by prevailing community standards. And far better to have random abuses at the state level than to suffer trespasses national in scope conceived in Washington.

Elsewhere as 2016 began, Russian president Vladimir Putin, a child of the Cold War era Soviet secret police, was still testing the United States to see how far he could go in thwarting U.S. policies and mostly getting away with it in places like Ukraine and the Middle East. The Middle East and Africa were again slaughter houses. Sunnis and Shia Muslims were killing each other in Syria and Iraq, with Iran and Russia helping out Syrian president Bashar Assad with his barbarism on the Shia side and Sunnis doing much of their handiwork under the banner of Islamic State, which had seized control of large swaths of Syria and Iraq. That's a highly oversimplified description of the mayhem, which to be complete, would have to include Al Qaeda, the Afghan Taliban and various other murderous groups, including those in North and sub-Saharan Africa.

Russia's occupation of eastern Ukraine seemed to be a fait accompli. China was in the process of taking control of the South China Sea, much to the consternation of the Philippines, Vietnam and the other nations bordering that sea. And North Korea was testing long-range missiles capable of delivering its nuclear weapons as far into the North American continent as Chicago.

Domestically, as mentioned earlier, Americans were turning to radical "nonestablishment" candidates like Donald Trump and Bernie Sanders. These protest votes might have been cathartic for those casting them, but they seemed at the time to be a reckless way to select a president who would be capable of leading the country out of its deep problems with mounting debt, overly intrusive government, distorted monetary policy and threats from abroad.

In short, the Journal's editorialists and contributors of articles and letters had a lot of issues to discuss. The Journal, after 126 years of supplying its readers with news of events and ideas, was a favored venue for conducting this debate. It had come a long way from its small beginnings dispatching flimsies with news of business and finance from the basement of a soda fountain and candy store a few doors down Broad Street from that fabled New York hub of international finance, the New York Stock Exchange at Broad and Wall.

CHAPTER 25

The Trump Shock

As the party primaries got under way in 2016, the initial trepidation about Trump among some members of the Journal editorial page staff was soon excited further. Trump lost the Iowa caucus to Ted Cruz, a Texas senator whose maverick populist positions also had raised doubts among Journal editors. But then the peripatetic Trump, hopping from state to state in his private jet and attracting large crowds at his rallies, won a string of primary victories. He won in New Hampshire, South Carolina, Nevada and Alabama, before losing again to Cruz in Alaska. He followed up by winning in 16 more states by the end of March, and it was clear that he was touching a responsive chord among Republican voters.

Trump continued his boorish behavior, sometimes insulting his fellow candidates by, for example, calling former Florida governor Jeb Bush a "low-energy" candidate. With his string of victories, he went into the Republican Convention in July with enough votes to win the nomination but still widely unpopular, even among Republicans, in the opinion polls. Some Republican diehards tried to sell the idea that the delegates from states Trump had won were not really committed and could vote their consciences. That idea, which could have split the party, got little purchase.

In response to the nomination, Journal columnist Bret Stephens became more vocal in his opposition to Trump. The Trump candidacy seemed to be particularly troubling to Jewish intellectuals. William Kristol, editor of the neoconservative Weekly Standard magazine and son of onetime Journal luminary Irving Kristol, was strongly anti-Trump. So were Journal editorial page alumni David Brooks, a conservative columnist for the New York Times, and Max Boot, who had made himself a renowned author of books and articles on military strategy from his perch at the New York Council on Foreign Relations. Pulitzer Prize winner Dorothy Rabinowitz on the Journal editorial board shared their views. These bright and talented writers seemed to see in Trump's populist screeds the rantings of a demagogue. But as a Jewish intellectual with a different view, New York Sun editor Seth Lipsky pointed out to me in a conversation, it would be hard to attribute anti-Semitic views to a candidate whose son-in-law and close adviser, Jared Kushner, is a Jew.

Bret, nonetheless, would eventually renounce his allegiance to the Republican Party and threaten to vote for Hillary Clinton. Other editorial page staffers took a different view. Columnist William McGurn, a onetime speech writer for George W. Bush, and assistant editor James Freeman argued the case that whatever one might think about Trump, it was important for the Republicans to do well in the coming election to prevent another Progressive blowout like the one that gave us ObamaCare and Dodd-Frank in 2010. Holding onto the Senate to stall any attempts by Hillary to pack the Supreme Court with Progressive appointees was of prime importance.

While Bret was the most ardent critic of Trump, the staff was united in its oppositions to Trump's positions on some issues, especially his seeming antipathy toward trade and immigration and his flamboyant promise to build a "wall" separating the United States from Mexico. Americas columnist Mary Anastasia O'Grady was particularly caustic in her comments on Trump's threat to dump the North American Free Trade Agreement (NAFTA). She wrote that "Mr. Trump is so reckless on trade that he makes Hillary Clinton and the Democrats, who wrote the book on Big Labor protectionism, seem sane." Offering an exhaustive account of NAFTA's benefits, particularly the free access of U.S. farm products to the Mexican market, she concluded with, "Mr. Trump's outlandishness is supposed to be one of his strengths. But when it comes to trade, he is not only politically incorrect. He is factually incorrect."

A Journal postnomination editorial argued that the large ego of the newly nominated Trump itself endangered his chances: "Democrats are confident that Hillary will win if they can make the election about Donald Trump, and Mr. Trump seems happy to oblige." The editorial was perceptive in its view that the "public desire for change is nonetheless real and growing, and Democrats know that Mrs. Clinton is the least convincing 'change maker' in American politics." But Trump's various gaffes, such as his seeming defense of Russian aggression in Ukraine and his failure to exploit Hillary's mishandling of classified material as secretary of state, were nothing short of political malpractice. "She and Democrats must be amazed that they've drawn an opponent who so easily plays into their hands."

An early mauling by Hillary's friends in the press was a foretaste of what was to come. A tendentious New York Times opinion piece on August 7 written by Neil Barsky, a onetime Wall Street reporter, dealt not with the current state of Trump's business but with the financial difficulties he had had 16 years previous. The headline: "Trump, the Bad, Bad Businessman." Times editors were obviously bent on dismantling the candidate's reputation, built partly with TV shows like "The Apprentice," as a shrewd and successful tycoon.

Meanwhile, Journal columnists were carrying on their normal business of commenting on the foibles of Obama's minions. Washington columnist Kim Strassel on August 5 brought up the long-standing issue of how it violates due process and fairness for government agencies to act as their own prosecutors, judges and juries, a practice encouraged by the Obama administration. The victim in this case was Lynn Tilton, the founder and CEO of a financial firm called Patriarch Partners and a vocal critic of how the Obama administration handled the aftermath of the 2008 mortgage bond crisis. It may only have been a coincidence, but after her attack, the SEC brought charges of investor fraud against her. Instead of filing in court, the agency brought the case before one of its own "administrative law judges," who, as Kim pointed out, have a conviction rate of 90% versus 69% for cases tried in court. Ms. Tilton sued for a court trial without success. Wrote Kim: "The Tilton ordeal shows another Obama agency that—like the EPA and the IRS—seems to think it gets to operate outside the rules of democracy."

Indeed, it seemed that the widespread political discontent in America, as reflected in the nomination of Donald Trump and the near defeat of Hillary Clinton by left-wing maverick Bernie Sanders, might well be related to the Obama habit of thumbing his nose at constitutional norms, for example, bypassing Senate advise and consent or making laws through the issuance of executive orders. Steady editorial page criticisms of this form of executive rule might well have been finding purchase with voters.

As the presidential campaigns wore on, the two staff writers who inhabit the Journal's Tuesday columns page moved into direct opposition, although without acknowledging that they were at odds with each other. Bret pursued his attacks on Donald Trump, dismaying for his apostasy the many readers who regarded the Journal as what Truman had called the "Republican Bible." William McGurn defended Trump.

A Stephens column on September 13 titled "Never Trump for Dummies" argued his position in a question and answer format: "Q: How can you call yourself a conservative columnist when you're rooting for Hillary Clinton in this election? A: Because Donald Trump is anti-conservative, un-American, immoral and dangerous."

Bret went on to write that Trump was unfit as a person to be president, arguing that "Mr. Trump's nativist brand of politics is much further removed from conservatism than Mrs. Clinton's mainstream liberalism." He defined conservatism as "a principled commitment to limited government, free markets, constitutional rights, equal opportunity, personal responsibility, e pluribus unum and Pax Americana." He cited Trump's opposition to birthright citizenship as an affront to the 14th Amendment, his threats to sue the press as an assault on press freedom and his claim that federal district judge Gonzalo Curiel's Mexican heritage affected his impartiality as "an assault on the American creed."

On October 18, McGurn wrote a column under the headline "The Cheap Moralizing of Never Trump," counterattacking Hillary Clinton's description of half of Trump's followers as irredeemable "deplorables" who were racist, sexist and homophobic. McGurn pointedly remarked that this was an old argument among Democrats, but it was now being heard from the right as well.

"Which puts conservative Never Trumpers in a curious position vis-à-vis government of, by and for the people: Are the tens of millions of people who will pull the lever for Trump in November evil, too, or just invincibly stupid?" McGurn asserted that the argument that Trump voters are morally corrupt isn't really an argument at all but an attempt to close off all argument by declaring the GOP candidate repellent.

Wrote McGurn: "In the end, the strongest argument for a Trump vote has always been this: The alternative is a President who lies, whose public life has always been a series of scandals from cattle futures to the destruction of documents under subpoena, who would be a third term for disastrous Obama policies at home and abroad..."

This debate between two members of the Journal editorial board was far more incisive and to the point than any of the three staged televised "debates" by the two candidates, which mostly degenerated into mud-ball fights. It was informative to Journal readers as they pondered the alternatives in this remarkable election year, which pitted a boorish TV celebrity against a seasoned and well-financed career politician loaded with extra baggage. It no doubt made Paul glad that the Journal practice of never endorsing a politician was alive and well.

An editorial on August 31 reflected what could be loosely described as an editorial board consensus. It was titled "Neither for President" and cited a Monmouth University survey showing that 35% of those sampled had a "favorable" opinion of neither candidate, a percentage exceeding the 33% with a "favorable" opinion of Clinton and 24% of Trump. The editorial concluded: "If 'neither' could make it onto the November ballot, maybe we would reconsider our longstanding editorial policy of not endorsing candidates."

That, of course, was just a short, tertiary editorial to add some mirth to all the "sturm und drang" of this disturbing election year choice between a candidate with serious legal problems, Hillary, and a bumptious amateur who seemed to have only a shallow understanding of the nation's problems, particularly those having to do with foreign policy. As the election neared, the Journal resumed a level of seriousness befitting the selection of the person who would inherit the expansive powers that accrue to a modern American president.

The columnists hardened their positions. Bret Stephens wrote a column titled "My Former Republican Party" in which he declared: "I don't see the point of belonging to a party on the increasingly dubious assumption that it's slightly less bad than the opposition."

Three days later, on October 28, Kim Strassel's Potomac Watch column carried the headline "Grifters-in-Chief." She wrote that the electorate can be certain of one thing—that a Clinton presidency would be built, from the ground up, "on self-dealing, crony favors and an utter disregard for the law." She cited a WikiLeaks discovery of a memo by "long-time Clinton errand boy" Douglas Band bragging about his role in bringing about a sharp upswing in donations to the Clinton Foundation after Hillary became secretary of state in 2009. It made clear, Kim wrote, that the Clintons do not draw any lines between their "charitable" work, their political activity, their government jobs or (and most important) their personal enrichment. Kim concluded: "This is how the Clintons operate. They don't change. Anyone who pulls the lever for Mrs. Clinton takes responsibility for setting up the nation for all the blatant corruption that will follow."

On November 2, Holman Jenkins followed up with a column titled "Hillary Becomes the Unsafe Hand" about Secretary of State Hillary's exposing her correspondence on a private email server to hackers as part of a long line of gaffes dating back to the missing billing records when she practiced law in Little Rock. Wrote Holman: "Mrs. Clinton is a screw-up." The Clinton campaign had tried to sell the idea that she was the "safe-hands candidate" more deserving of trust than the mercurial Donald Trump. But Holman argued that an outsider like Trump would at least dislodge the political elite. If Clinton won, "hers will be an embattled and investigated presidency from day one. Moderates will flee. Republicans will find it hard to cooperate with her." She would be forced back on the hard left of her party, "people who are already drawing up 'blacklists' of potential appointees suspected of sympathy with the private sector." In short, if Hillary ascended to the Oval Office, all her unseemly trappings would come with her, diminishing the office of the presidency.

In the days before the election, it became Paul Gigot's job to shape the Journal's institutional position on the two candidates. A lead editorial about Hillary came first on the preelection Friday. It began: "Americans go to the polls next week facing what millions believe is the worst presidential choice in their lifetimes." Both Clinton and Trump were described as "deeply flawed." It would be the purpose of consecutive editorials "to summarize the risks—and the fainter hopes" that each candidate would bring to the presidency.

Hillary would want "higher taxes, more spending on entitlements that are already unaffordable, more subsidies and price controls in ObamaCare, more regulations on businesses of all kinds, more limits on political speech, more enforcement of liberal values on schools and churches." But more to the point, it argued that "the Clinton blending of public office with private gain erodes confidence in honest government."

The editorial concluded that the case for Mrs. Clinton is that "she is a familiar member of the elite and thus less likely to jump into the unknown, particularly on foreign policy. The case against her is everything else we know about her political history."

The next day's editorial was titled "The Gamble of Trump" and asserted that a broken Washington needs to be shaken up and refocused on the public good, and who better to do it than a political outsider. But, alas, the would-be reformer had arrived "as a flawed personality who has few convictions and knows very little about the world." In economic policy, there would be a conflict between his proffered "pro-growth domestic reforms and his anti-growth trade policy."

But the editorial posited that the biggest gamble would be on foreign and security policy. "The good news is that Mr. Trump wants to rebuild U.S. defenses that have eroded on Mr. Obama's watch. He would be more candid about, and more aggressive against the Islamist terror threat." But "the irony is that Mr. Trump shares Mr. Obama's desire to have America retreat from world leadership."

The ending summed up both editorials with the thought that "the choice comes down to the very high but predictable costs of four more years of brute Progressive government under Hillary Clinton, versus a gamble on the political unknown of Donald Trump."

On the morning of November 10, readers of The Wall Street Journal were greeted with a banner headline proclaiming "A New Political Order." Although somewhat melodramatic, it hardly seemed like an exaggeration. The previous morning, Hillary Clinton had sadly conceded that she had been defeated by the upstart tycoon and TV personality, Donald Trump. The voters had sent a message to Washington that they wanted a change from the increasingly interventionist and paternalistic policies they had experienced in the preceding decade, dating back to when the Progressives had seized control of the Senate in 2006.

Gigot's editorial called the unlikely Trump victory "a political earthquake of a kind that rarely disturbs American politics." Indeed, the editorial harked back to Andrew Jackson's victory 188 years earlier as the last time a winner had so defied the existing order. "The political and media establishments are bewildered, and no doubt many voters are too."

One exception seemed to be the stock market; the Dow Jones Industrials gained 256.95 on the results, beginning what would be a steady rise to record levels. Paul attributed this to the market's likely belief that Trump would lift the government's restraints on the private economy. He wrote that Trump could succeed if he prioritizes economic growth but held that this would require him to govern differently from how he campaigned, no doubt alluding to the candidate's antitrade rants. "The President-elect is about to learn, and fast, that the office he will soon hold is the ultimate art of the deal," a reference to Trump's popular book.

Journal opinion moved from skepticism to a more favorable opinion of Trump as he began to roll out his cabinet nominees. Most proved to be supporters of causes that the Journal itself had supported over the years. Betsy DeVos, his pick for secretary of education, had fought against the teachers' unions to give parents more choice in where their children would be schooled. The Journal had long argued for this freedom, particularly for inner-city parents, so that they could take their children out of failing public schools and put them in publicly funded but more independent charter schools. While education is a state and local function, the federal government has increasingly influenced policy at lower levels through grants and mandates. Since the Republicans were now in control of over 30 state governments, the opportunities for school reform seemed bright.

As for ObamaCare, Trump signaled that it was up for reform by selecting Georgia Congressman Tom Price to be his secretary of Health and Human Services. Dr. Price had been an orthopedic surgeon and an assistant professor of medicine at Emory University before entering politics. In Congress he had authored ObamaCare reform legislation that would put more power in the hands of patients, introduce more competition and lessen bureaucracy in the provision of health insurance. The chances of his ideas becoming law are markedly improved with his cabinet role and the support of both Trump and House Republican Speaker Paul Ryan.

The selection of Ben Carson, also a former surgeon, for secretary of Housing and Urban Development (HUD) suggested that Trump bore no grudges against his opponents in the Republican primary. It also offered the Journal hope for the realization of one of its long-term objectives, the curbing of the market power of mortgage giants Fannie Mae and Freddie Mac. When the two went broke during the 2008 mortgage crisis, they had been placed under the control (conservatorship) of a HUD division, and there they remained in 2016. What that meant in practice was that American taxpayers were backing something like half of all the $11 trillion in home mortgages outstanding in America. Fannie and Freddie in 2016 were still doing business as usual, piling up still more taxpayer obligations.

Journal editors were less enthusiastic about Wilbur Ross, the selection to head the Commerce Department, fearing that he might share Trump's worst instincts on trade and foreign investment. Ross, who had made billions buying up and reorganizing sick companies, was an early supporter of Trump's promise to renegotiate trade deals. On the weekly Fox TV "Journal Editorial Report," columnist Mary O'Grady, a critic of Trump's claim that the North American Free Trade Agreement was a bad deal, quipped that Trump could have done worse when he appointed Goldman Sachs alumnus Steven Mnuchin to be his Treasury secretary, but with Ross "he couldn't have done worse." Journal editors feared that Ross would be the kind of secretary who would try to resurrect industrial policy, the government attempts to pick winners that has a notorious record of generating crony capitalism, protectionism and failure.

In his Wonder Land column on November 10, Dan Henninger, a

onetime Trump critic, challenged the idea that Trump had split the Republican Party. "Set aside the issues of trade and immigration, and the Trump agenda overlaps with most of his primary opponents and the congressional majority..." He urged Trump to further discredit the "split" theory by sitting down with Speaker Ryan and Senate majority leader Mitch McConnell to work out a "reform agenda on taxes, health care, energy and financial regulation."

And indeed, the once truculent Donald Trump seemed to be intent on making friends with everyone after his election. As mentioned before, he selected one of his primary adversaries to lead HUD. His choice for Transportation secretary, who would have important responsibilities in trying to end Obama's war against the internal combustion engine and reform the air traffic control system, was none other than former Labor secretary Elaine Chao, the wife of Senate leader McConnell.

And so, as Donald Trump organized a reform cabinet in preparation for his inauguration as the 45th U.S. president in 2017, it was with good wishes from several Journal opinion writers who had been dubious about this candidacy. Much of what they had supported in their writings during their years of broad opposition to the policies of the Obama administration—school choice, health insurance reform, clipping the wings of the regulatory agencies, tax reform, renewed respect for private property, a Supreme Court more respectful of the Constitution and the liberalizing of government interference with the financial sector—now seemed within the realm of possibility.

The voting public, in a strange and unexpected way, had opted for many changes that were consistent with the Journal's advocacy, for over a century of free people, free markets. The voters had tired of the excessive interference by government with their freedom to trade their goods, services and labor in ways that befitted their needs. They had come to recognize excessive governance stifles opportunities for economic advancement. A Republican Party now in full control of the federal government and most state houses had staked a claim on fulfilling their hopes. Whether it would succeed was yet to be learned.

CHAPTER 26

Dow's Legacy

The marvelous historical archive of major newspapers operated by ProQuest LLC in Ann Arbor, Michigan, at last count listed well over 12 million entries for The Wall Street Journal since its founding in 1889. Those entries range from 2,000-word articles to simple masthead data. The number increases, of course, with each new issue. The archive is easily searchable, and much of the original material in this book derives from reading computer printouts of the actual pages preserved by ProQuest.

I've only skimmed the highlights of Journal commentary as world history unfolded. But I've attempted to provide a glimpse of what Journal editors and writers had to say as major events stirred them into quick action and forced them to offer the best interpretations they could in the heat of breaking news. Barney Kilgore once said that newspaper articles are the first draft of history, and the writers of those first drafts did so under sometimes severe deadline pressures, depending upon how close to what editors call "drop-dead lock-up" the events occurred.

But on the whole, the Journal record for analyzing news developments and providing informed commentary has been good enough to attract a very large following. Going into 2017, the Journal was still adding to its more than 2.5 million print and online subscribers worldwide. Dow Jones CEO William Lewis described the operations of the modern Journal in an in-house newsletter praising employees for their response to a big East Coast snowstorm on January 30, 2016: "Delivering 1.6 million Wall Street Journal print editions every day is a global task, requiring logistical expertise, tenacity and a decent sense of humor. The papers come from 35 printing plants, 18 plane flights, 538 trucks and thousands of individual carriers."

The Dow Jones operatives producing the online WSJ.com that Gordon Crovitz had pioneered were constantly improving the online formats, particularly to make access to news easy for subscribers using mobile devices such as smartphones and iPads. They had recognized that many people now get most of their news and information by swiping their smartphone screens and opening up an app such as WSJ. A smartphone has a more restricted viewing space than a print newspaper, but on the other hand, electronic delivery is more flexible in being able to deliver up-to-the-minute news, comments on articles and access to earlier columns and features offered only online.

The opinion pages, which still attract a remarkably high proportion of Journal readers, have adapted to cyberspace as well. James Taranto had firmly established the Bartley-invented Best-of-the-Web column as a popular online feature and as 2016 ended moved up to editorial page features editor, replacing Melanie Kirkpatrick, who had returned from retirement temporarily to fill a gap created when Mark Lasswell left to write a book. Mary Kissel was doing WSJ.Com videos interviewing interesting visitors to the Journal in New York. Bret Stephens and others were doing audio podcasts. On "The Journal Editorial Report," a weekend public affairs program on Fox cable news, Paul Gigot was still gathering together several staff writers and usually a guest to discuss the issues of the day. It has about 1.5 million viewers.

Whereas a Leisure & Arts page was an innovation not many years ago, under the Murdoch regime, the Journal now has a full Saturday Review section devoted to books, theater and other cultural subjects, along with other arts coverage on weekdays. All these offerings have made opinion writing as well as news pretty much a 24-hour-a-day business, with pressures to stay on top of the news greater than ever before.

As the year 2017 dawned, Journal columnists were offering readers a broad range of discussion. Mary O'Grady's Americas columns illuminating the often tempestuous ways of Latin governance were often translated into Spanish and Portuguese in Latin American newspapers. William McGurn, who had left the Journal to write speeches for George W. Bush and had done a stint as editorial page editor of the New York Post, was back writing a weekly column on domestic policy. Holman Jenkins was delving into the intricacies of business and government strategies. William Galston of Brookings Institution was providing readers with an alternative point of view more aligned with the Democratic Party.

Dan Henninger's Wonder Land column leaned heavily toward cultural trends, and Karl Rove, the big-league political strategist for George W. Bush and others, monitored political trends. Kim Strassel, writing from Washington, provided insights into the various shenanigans that go on in the nation's capital.

Alas, Bret Stephen's rebellion against the Republican Party had attracted the attention of Arthur "Pinch" Sulzberger III, CEO of the New York Times, whose sympathies lie with the Democrats. To liven up his sometimes tired-sounding and predictable stable of columnists, Pinch made Bret a generous offer, inviting him to bring his talents to the Times. Bret accepted. It was a loss to the Journal of a gifted writer who apparently was no longer comfortable with the Journal's traditions.

On the op-ed page, Peggy Noonan, also a former presidential speech writer for Ronald Reagan, offered readers her special conversational style in discussing events of the day. Jason Riley, a former editorial page staffer who had moved to the Manhattan Institute, provided a weekly column that was notably out of step with African American demands for affirmative action. Jason's book, "Please Stop Helping Us," had argued that affirmative action often did his fellow African Americans more harm than good.

As 2017 wore on, the editorial page view of President Trump was more accepting than it had been during his campaign, partly because of his many excellent choices of cabinet officers and agency heads. It gave support to his efforts to eliminate wasteful and coercive federal regulation and to reform the tax code and ObamaCare. But it continued to attack Trump's protectionist initiatives and nativist tendencies and the absolutism of the troublesome "freedom caucus" Republicans in the House. In other words, the Journal stuck to its traditional positions.

Over the course of time, Journal writers have often been surprised by unexpected developments. But, of course, no reporter can ever know the full story of events he is covering on the fly. Even historians, years later, often remain puzzled as evidenced by the continuing mystery, for example, of who might have encouraged Lee Harvey Oswald to assassinate JFK. But on the whole, the Journal commentary record looks good. If that sounds self-serving from someone who was for many years one of the opinion writers and editors, so be it. I was just one of many and by no means the most talented.

What is truly remarkable to me, however, is how consistent the Journal's commentary has been for all those years going back to the thoughtful and upright Charles Dow. "Free people, free markets" has served as an inspiring banner to both writers and readers. It has been frequently under fire, usually not directly, but most often through arguments favoring expanded state powers, and it is a bit battle worn in this modern era. There are no guarantees in history; entire civilizations have been destroyed by brutal tyrannies. But those of us who have marched under the Journal editorial page banner hope it can be kept flying for another 100 years.

OTHER WRITINGS

George Melloan is author of three other books, the most recent being "When the New Deal Came to Town: A Snapshot of a Place and Time with Lessons for Today" (Simon & Schuster, 2016). This book details how the U.S. government, first under the Hoover administration and a Republican Congress and then under Franklin D. Roosevelt and a Democratic Congress, attempted to micromanage an economic recovery after the 1929 crash. The efforts of both failed and the U.S. suffered a decade of hard times.

His book "The Great Money Binge: Spending Our Way to Socialism" (Simon & Schuster, 2009) explained the causes of the great credit bubble of the early 2000s and the subsequent 2008 market crash. The primary causes were an easy credit policy conducted by the Federal Reserve Board, combined with government policies to promote home ownership, including pressure on banks to write high-risk mortgages, large numbers of which would later turn sour. That cast doubt on the quality of mortgage-backed securities broadly circulated among banks and investors internationally.

Mr. Melloan and his wife, Jody, co-wrote "The Carter Economy" (John Wiley & Sons, 1978), an account of the economic policies adopted by Jimmy Carter in the first year of his administration. The book correctly predicted that President Carter would run into trouble because of his insistence on preserving the price controls first applied by the Nixon administration, and his inattention to monetary policy, the combination of which would lead to ruinous inflation of 14% two years later.